Shugo Chara Chan!

Original Concept: **PEACH-PIT**

CONTENTS

Shugo Chara Chan!
Manga by Naphthalene Mizushima

+ + + + + + + + + + + + + + +

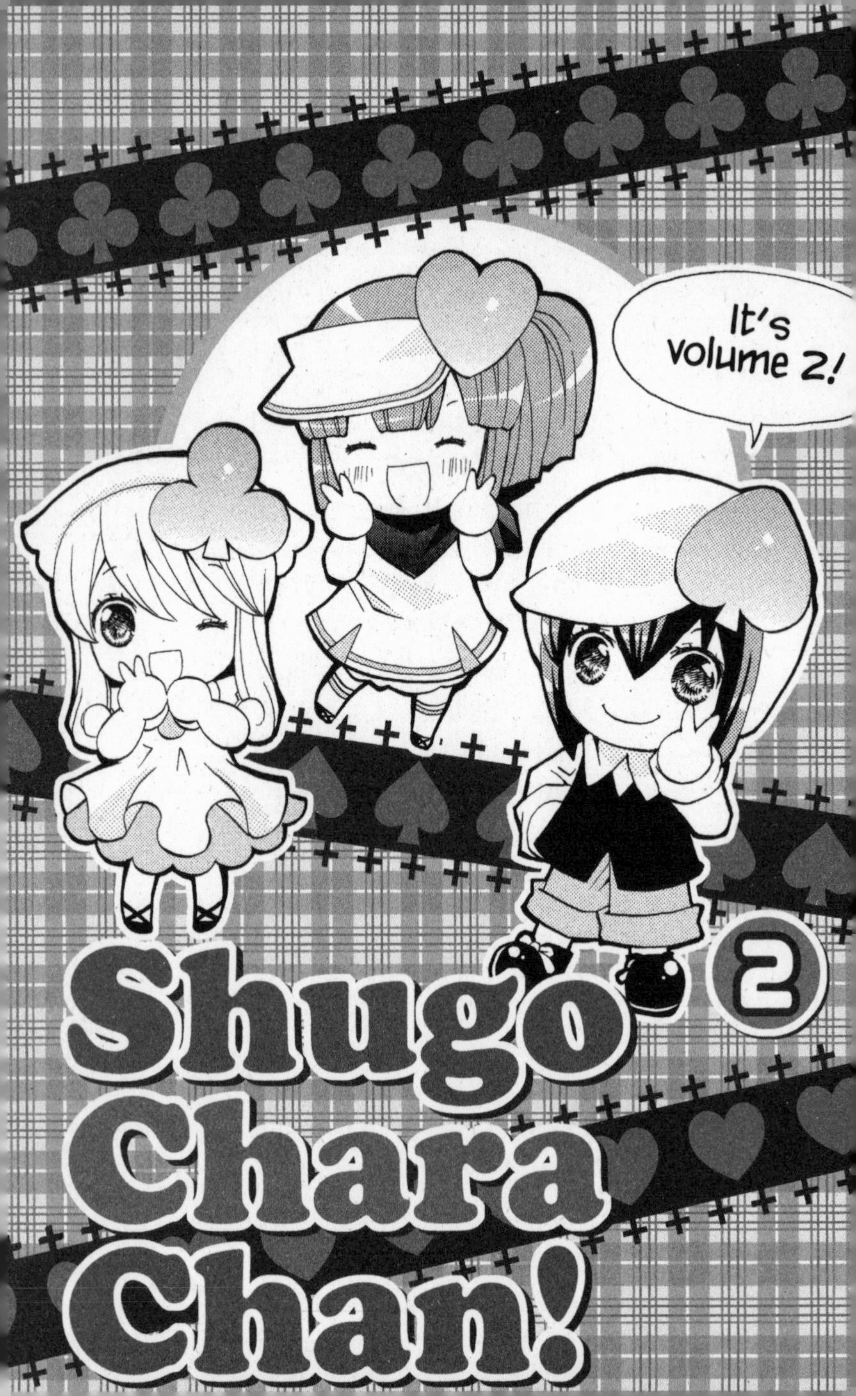
It's volume 2!
Shugo Chara Chan!
2

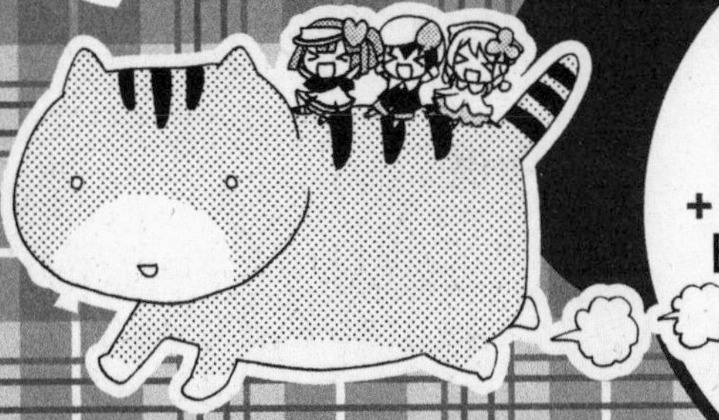

Shugo Chara Chan! Kids☆

Manga by Kinomin

Shugo Chara Chan! Festival

Manga by Naphthalene Mizushima

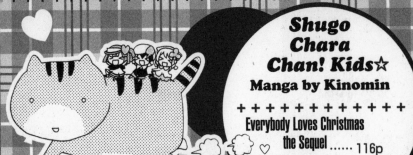

Guardian Characters are who you want to be, born from the Heart's Egg of kids. Ran, Miki, and Su are the Guardian Characters of Amu, the cool and awesome girl in grade school. There's something fun going on everyday for these tiny, upbeat girls. Come take a peek!

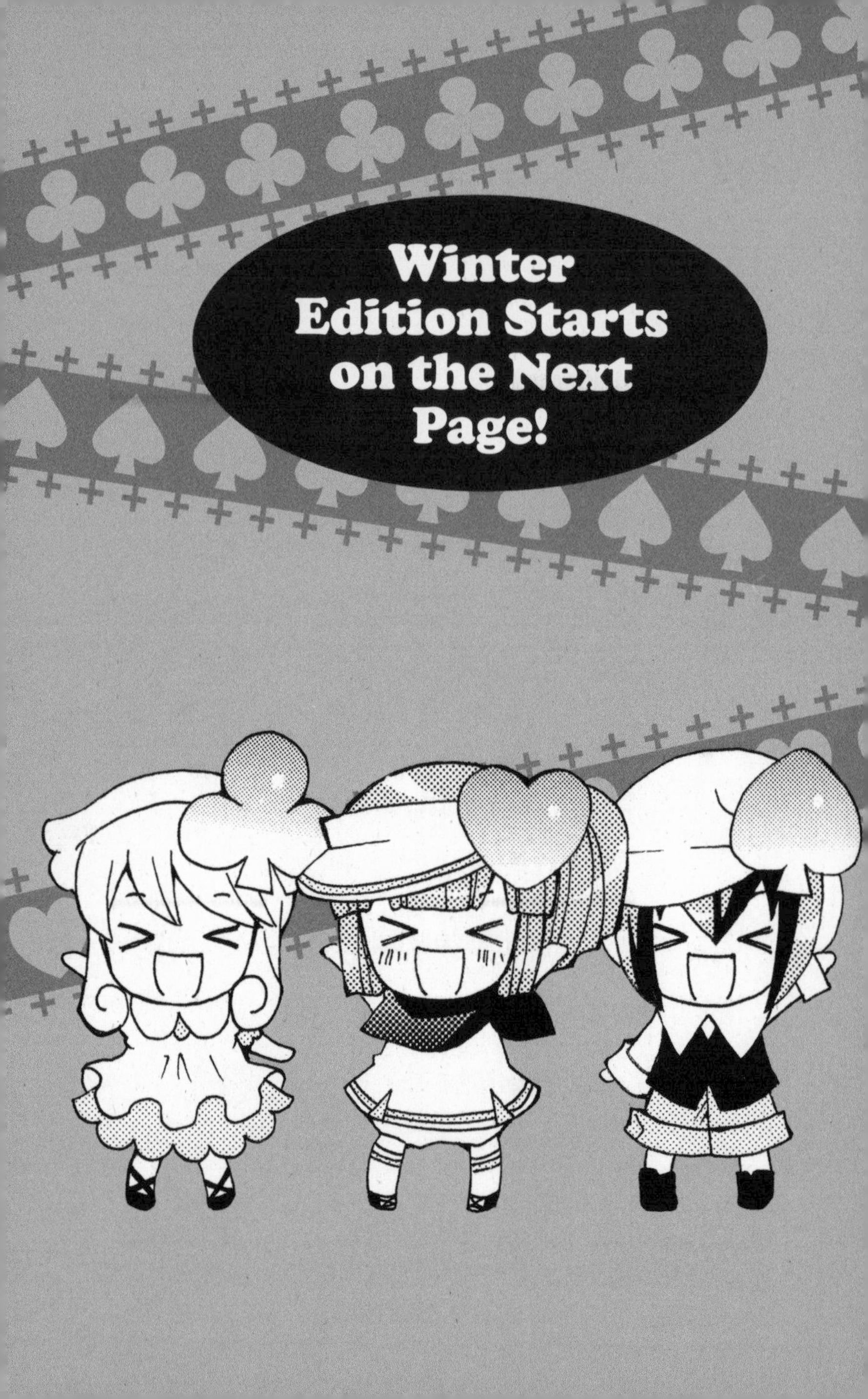
Winter Edition Starts on the Next Page!

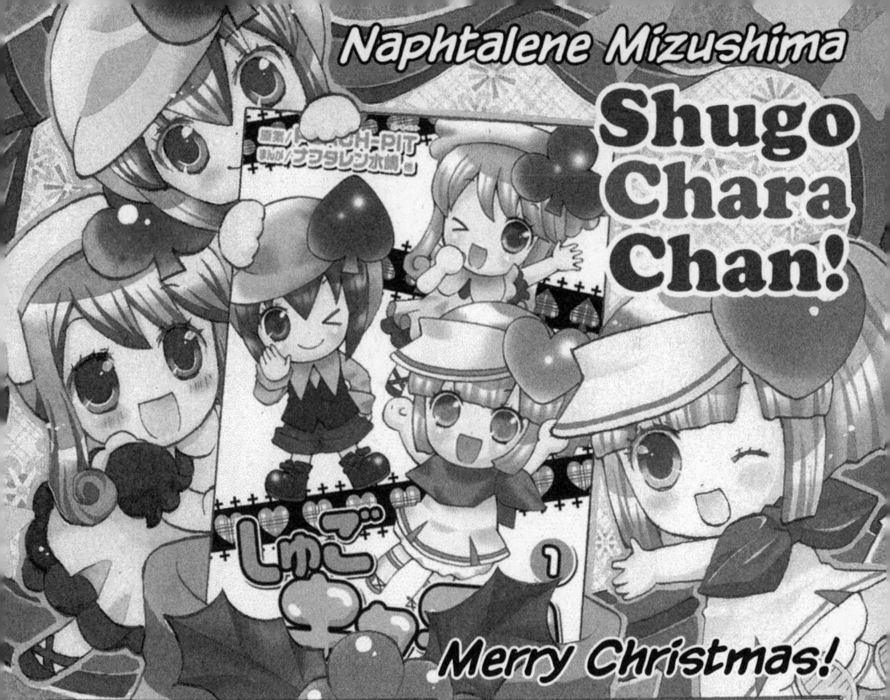

Naphtalene Mizushima
Shugo Chara Chan!
Merry Christmas!

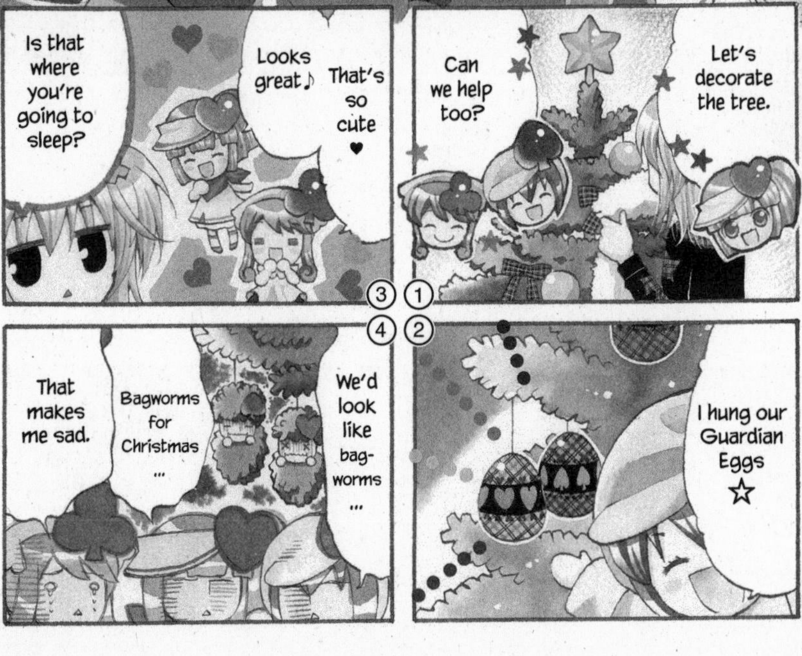

Let's decorate the tree.
Can we help too?
I hung our Guardian Eggs ☆
Looks great♪
That's so cute ♥
Is that where you're going to sleep?
We'd look like bag-worms ...
Bagworms for Christmas ...
That makes me sad.

Making it Work

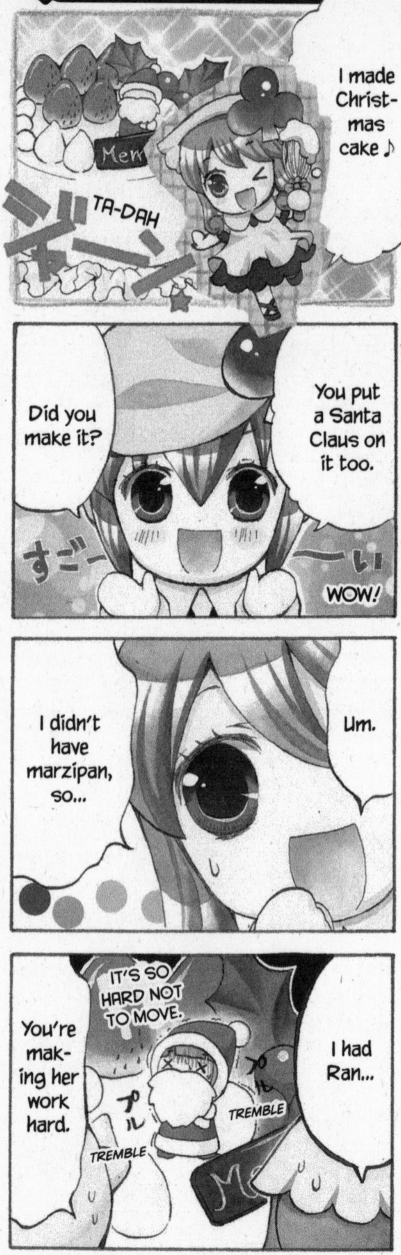
I made Christmas cake ♪
TA-DAH
You put a Santa Claus on it too.
Did you make it?
WOW!
Um.
I didn't have marzipan, so...
I had Ran...
IT'S SO HARD NOT TO MOVE.
You're making her work hard.
TREMBLE
TREMBLE

Teasing

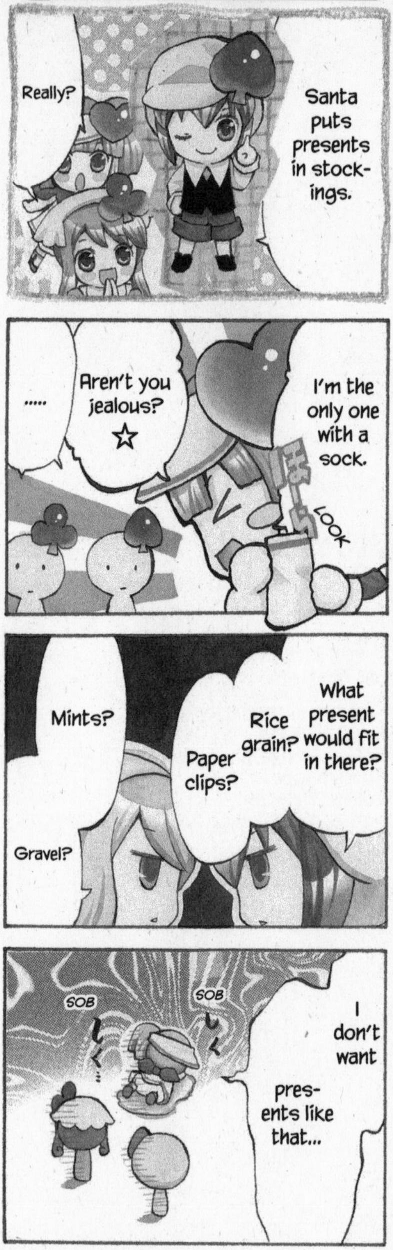
Santa puts presents in stockings.
Really?
I'm the only one with a sock.
LOOK
Aren't you jealous? ☆
.....
What present would fit in there?
Rice grain?
Paper clips?
Mints?
Gravel?
I don't want presents like that...
SOB
SOB

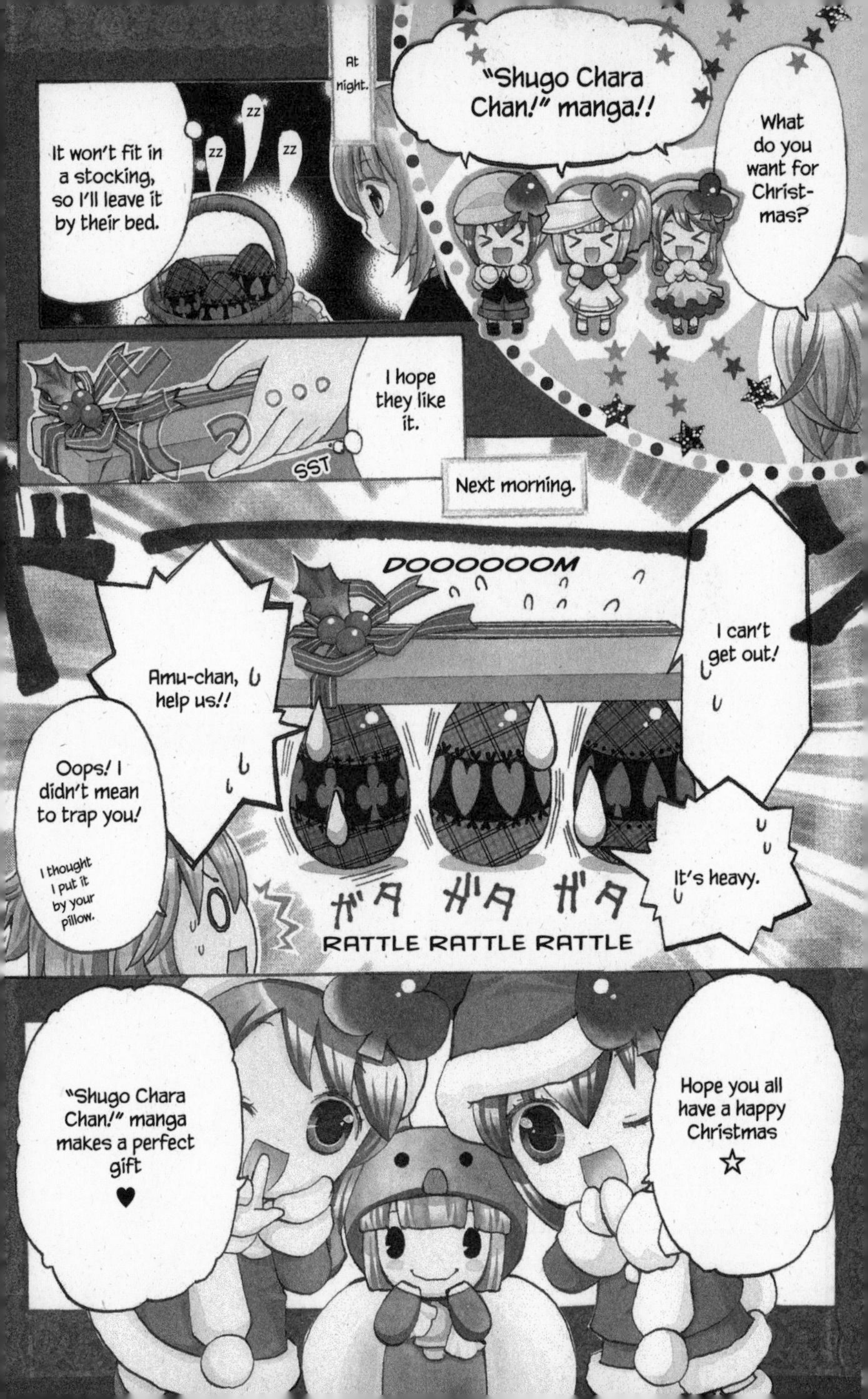
What do you want for Christmas?
"Shugo Chara Chan!" manga!!
At night.
ZZ ZZ ZZ
It won't fit in a stocking, so I'll leave it by their bed.
I hope they like it.
SST
Next morning.
I can't get out!
DOOOOOOM
Amu-chan, help us!!
It's heavy.
ガタ ガタ ガタ
RATTLE RATTLE RATTLE
Oops! I didn't mean to trap you!
I thought I put it by your pillow.
Hope you all have a happy Christmas ☆
"Shugo Chara Chan!" manga makes a perfect gift ♥

Shugo Chara Chan!

ONE-PANEL MANGA ☆

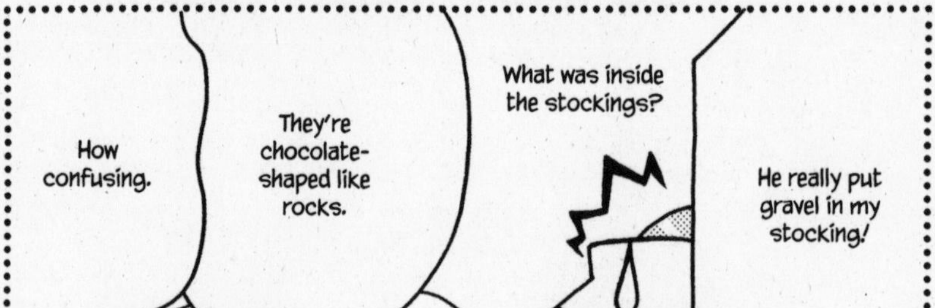

He really put gravel in my stocking!
What was inside the stockings?
They're chocolate-shaped like rocks.
How confusing.
They really sell chocolates like these.

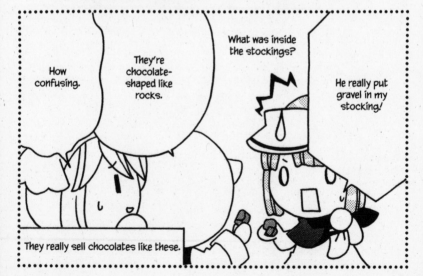

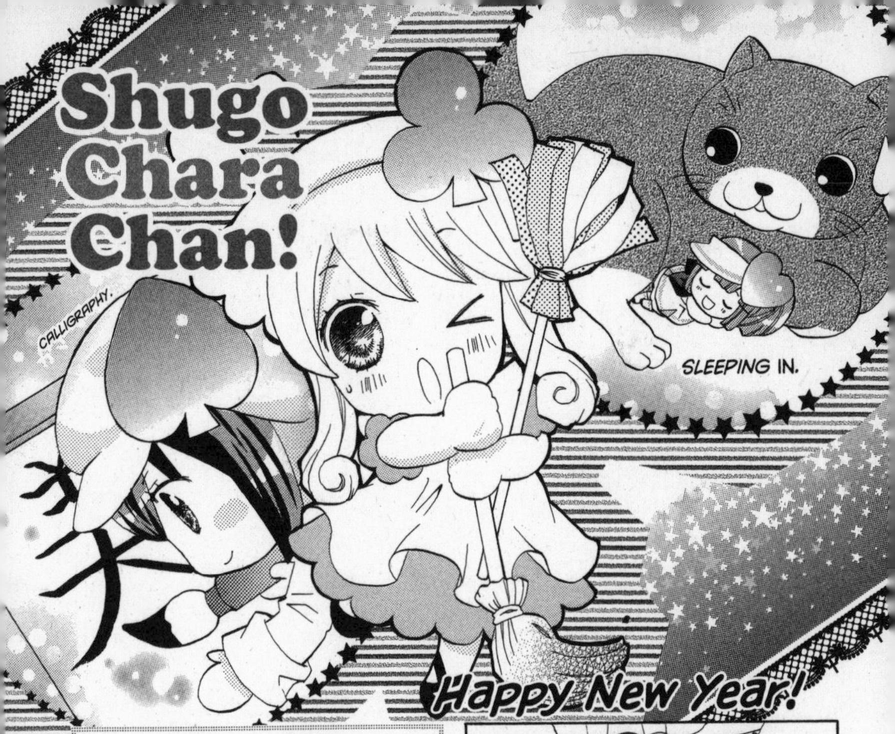
Shugo Chara Chan!
SLEEPING IN.
CALLIGRAPHY.
Happy New Year!

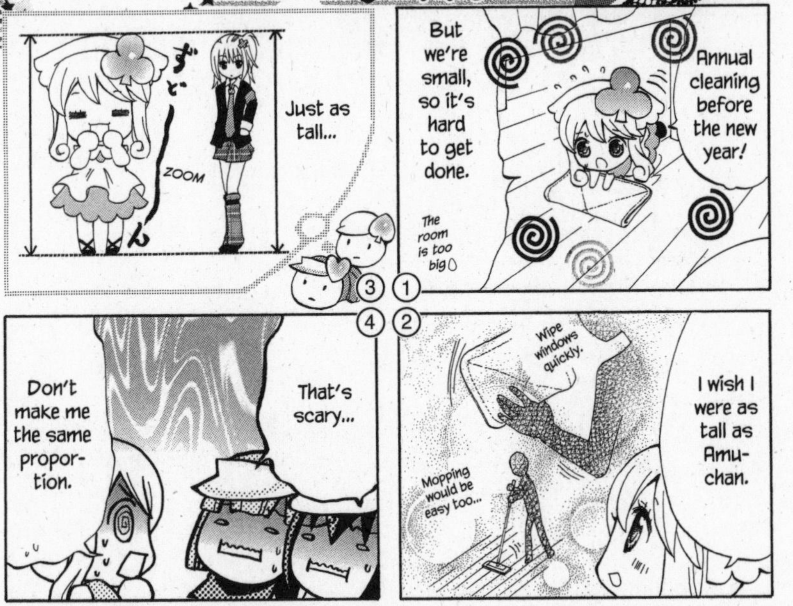
1
Annual cleaning before the new year!
But we're small, so it's hard to get done.
The room is too big
2
I wish I were as tall as Amu-chan.
Wipe windows quickly.
Mopping would be easy too...
3
Just as tall...
ずど
ZOOM
ん
4
That's scary...
Don't make me the same proportion.

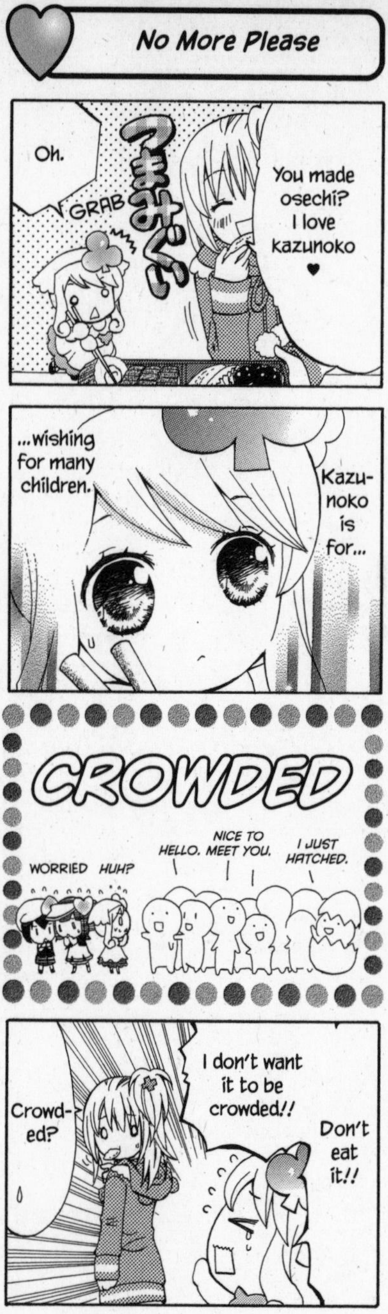
No More Please
You made osechi? I love kazunoko ♥
Oh.
GRAB
つまみぐい
Kazu-noko is for...
...wishing for many children.
CROWDED
I JUST HATCHED.
NICE TO MEET YOU.
HELLO.
HUH?
WORRIED
Don't eat it!!
I don't want it to be crowded!!
Crowd-ed?

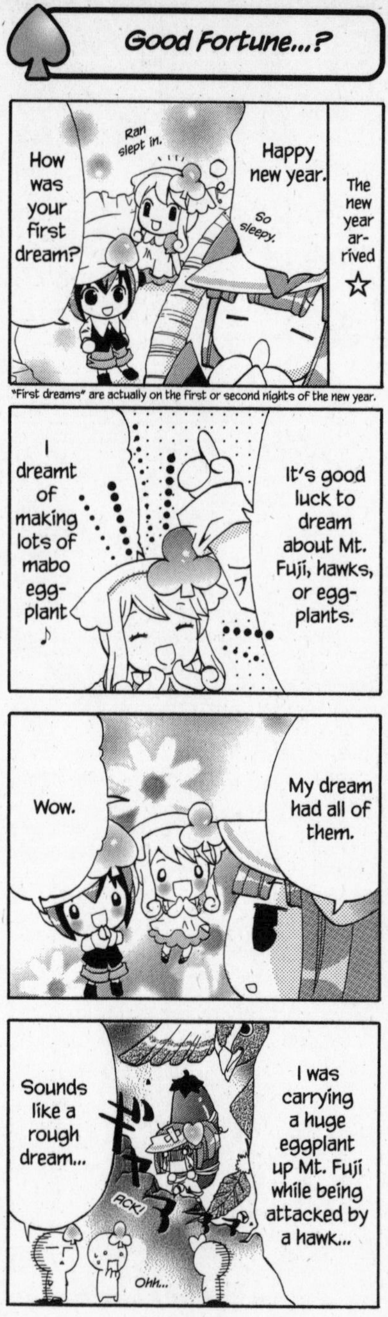
Good Fortune...?
The new year arrived ☆
Happy new year.
So sleepy.
Ran slept in.
How was your first dream?
"First dreams" are actually on the first or second nights of the new year.
It's good luck to dream about Mt. Fuji, hawks, or egg-plants.
I dreamt of making lots of mabo egg-plant ♪
My dream had all of them.
Wow.
I was carrying a huge eggplant up Mt. Fuji while being attacked by a hawk...
Sounds like a rough dream...
ACK!
Ohh...

Double Mochi!

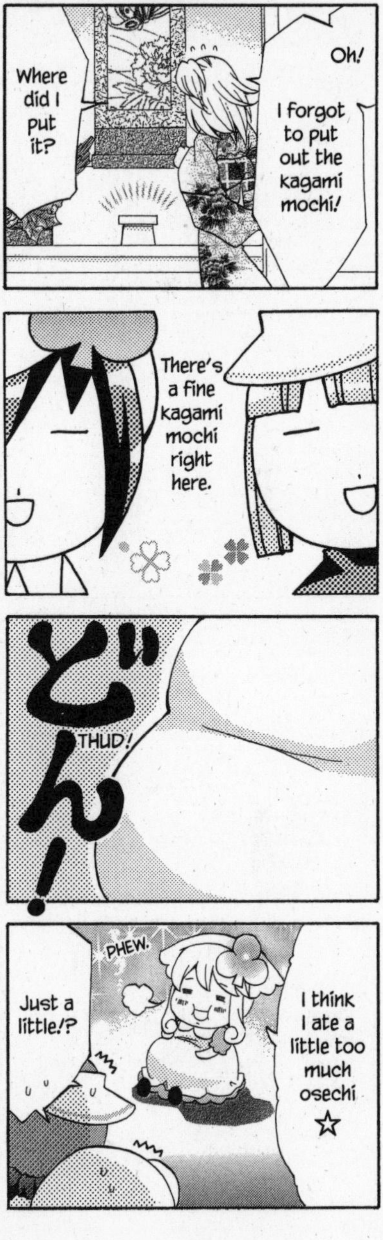
Oh!
I forgot to put out the kagami mochi!
Where did I put it?
There's a fine kagami mochi right here.
どん!
THUD!
I think I ate a little too much osechi ☆
PHEW.
Just a little!?

Of Course

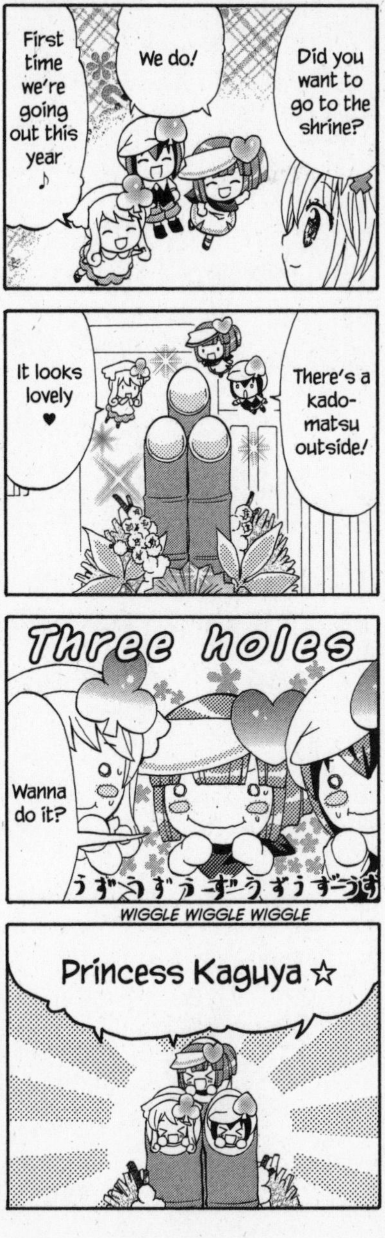
Did you want to go to the shrine?
We do!
First time we're going out this year ♪
There's a kado-matsu outside!
It looks lovely ♥
Three holes
Wanna do it?
WIGGLE WIGGLE WIGGLE
Princess Kaguya ☆

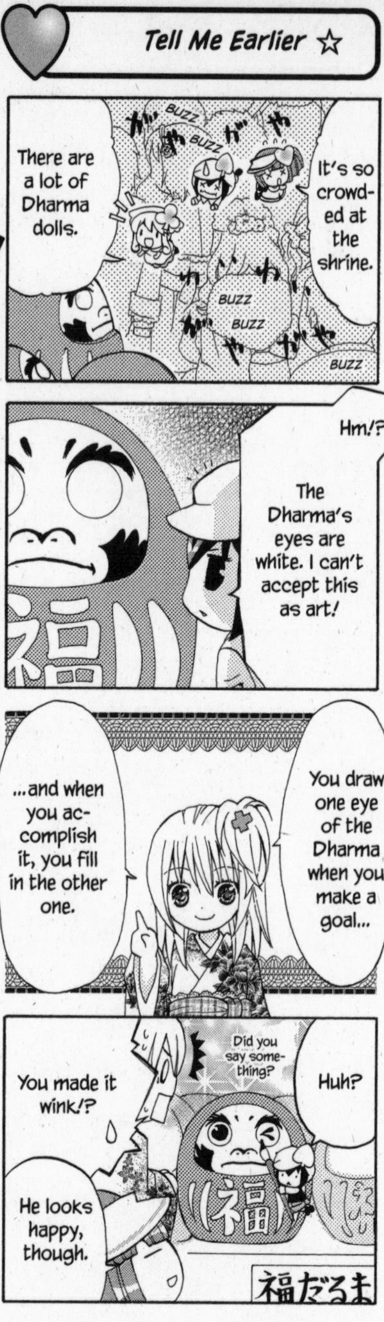
Tell Me Earlier ☆
It's so crowded at the shrine.
There are a lot of Dharma dolls.
BUZZ BUZZ
BUZZ BUZZ
BUZZ
Hm!?
The Dharma's eyes are white. I can't accept this as art!
You draw one eye of the Dharma when you make a goal...
...and when you accomplish it, you fill in the other one.
Huh?
Did you say something?
You made it wink!?
He looks happy, though.
福だるま

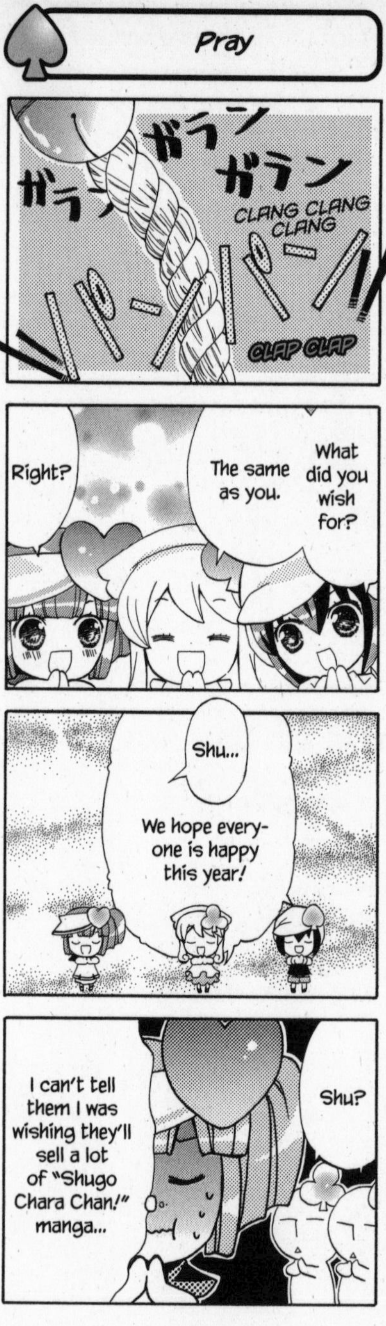
Pray
ガラン ガラン ガラン
CLANG CLANG CLANG
パーン パーン
CLAP CLAP
What did you wish for?
The same as you.
Right?
Shu...
We hope everyone is happy this year!
Shu?
I can't tell them I was wishing they'll sell a lot of "Shugo Chara Chan!" manga...

Shugo Chara Chan!

ONE-PANEL MANGA ☆

BIG (ANNUAL) CLEANING... WHAT ABOUT REGULAR CLEANING?

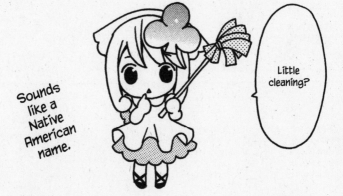

Little cleaning?
Sounds like a Native American name.

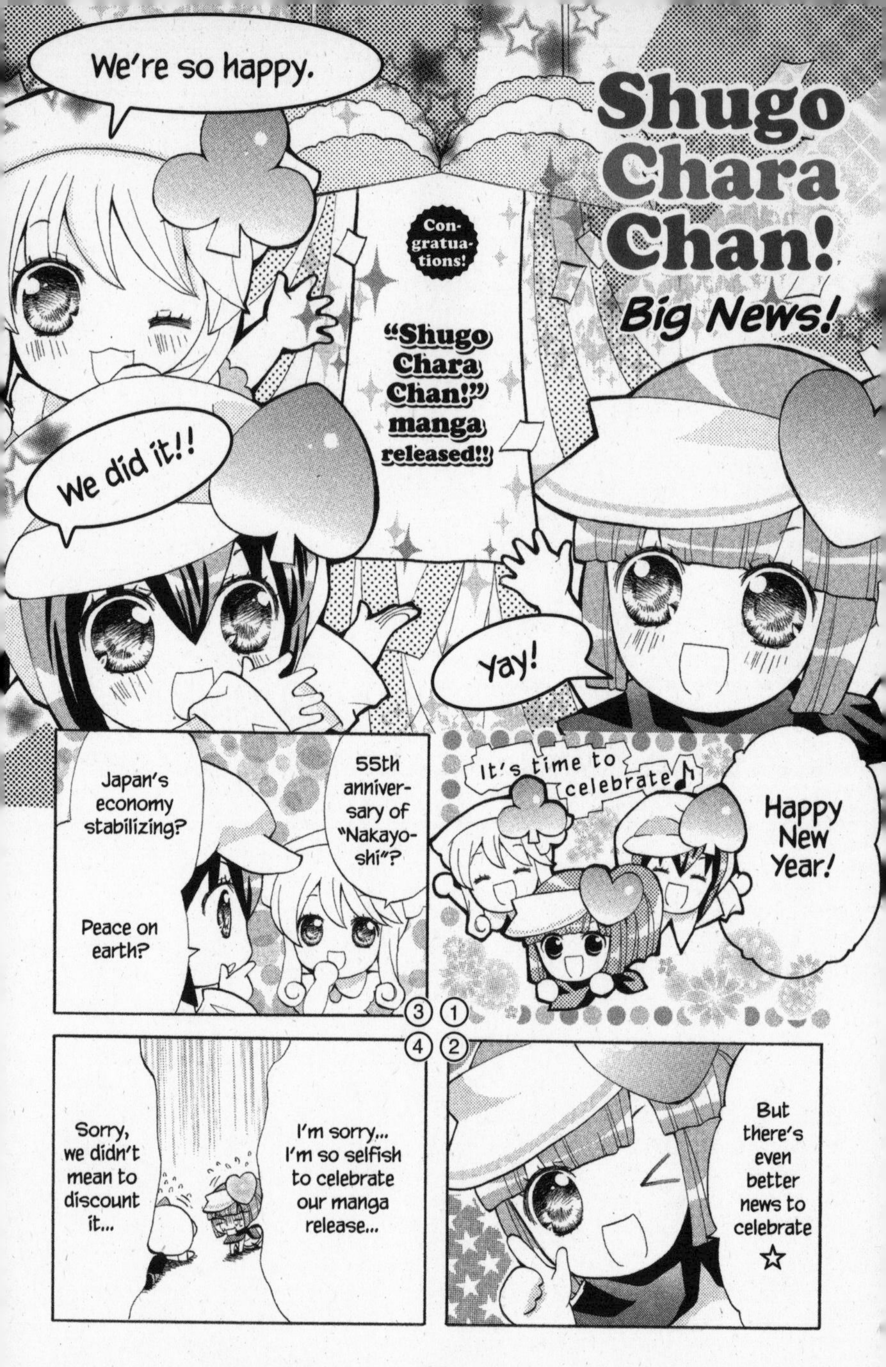
Shugo Chara Chan!
Big News!
Congratulations!
"Shugo Chara Chan!" manga released!!
We're so happy.
Yay!
We did it!!
Happy New Year!
It's time to celebrate♪
But there's even better news to celebrate ☆
55th anniversary of "Nakayoshi"?
Japan's economy stabilizing?
Peace on earth?
I'm sorry... I'm so selfish to celebrate our manga release...
Sorry, we didn't mean to discount it...

Bad Guardian

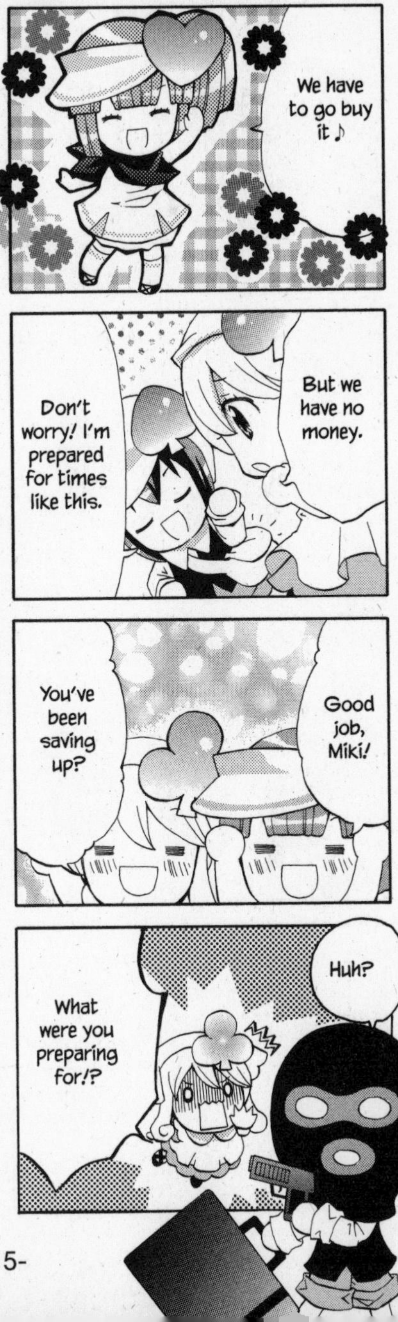
We have to go buy it ♪
But we have no money.
Don't worry! I'm prepared for times like this.
Good job, Miki!
You've been saving up?
Huh?
What were you preparing for!?

Like Air

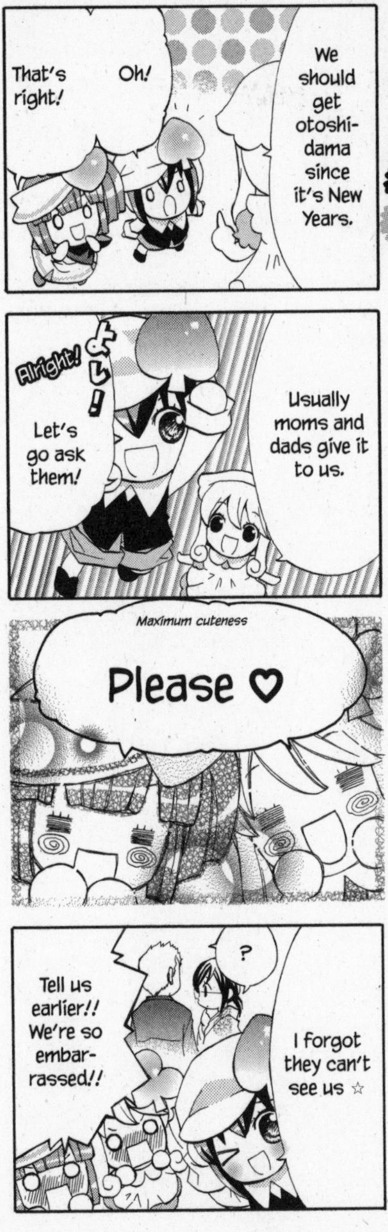
We should get otoshi-dama since it's New Years.
Oh!
That's right!
Usually moms and dads give it to us.
Alright! よし!
Let's go ask them!
Maximum cuteness
Please ♡
?
I forgot they can't see us ☆
Tell us earlier!! We're so embarrassed!!

Like Air Again

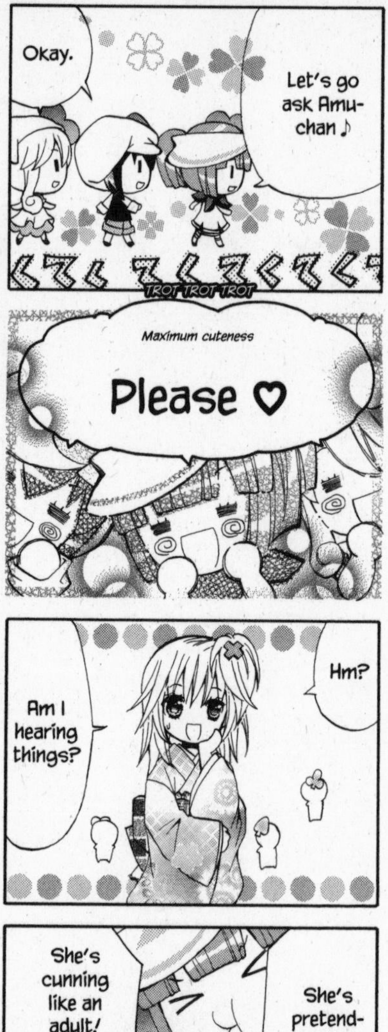
Let's go ask Amu-chan ♪
Okay.
TROT TROT TROT
Maximum cuteness
Please ♡
Hm?
Am I hearing things?
She's pretending not to hear or see us!?
She's cunning like an adult!
Even though she's a kid.
BOO!

We Mean It

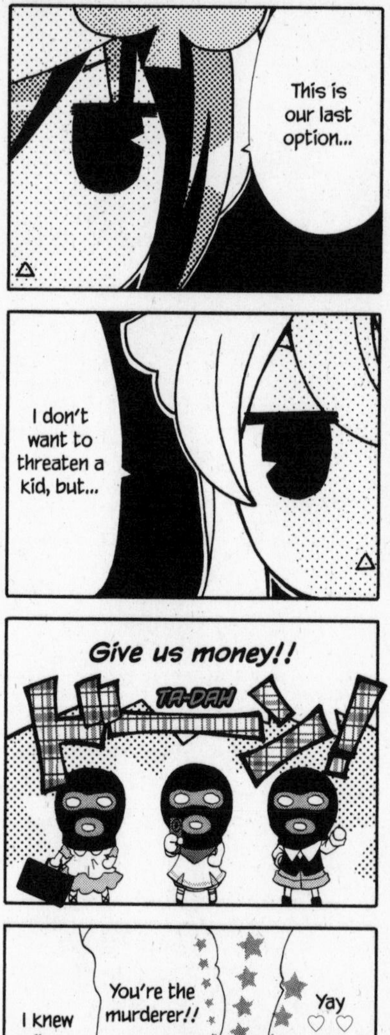
This is our last option...
I don't want to threaten a kid, but...
Give us money!!
TA-DAH
Yay ♡♡ We're playing cops and robbers ♡
You're the murderer!!
I knew it...
SQUEEZE

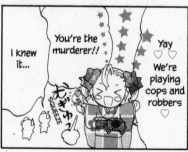

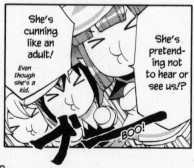

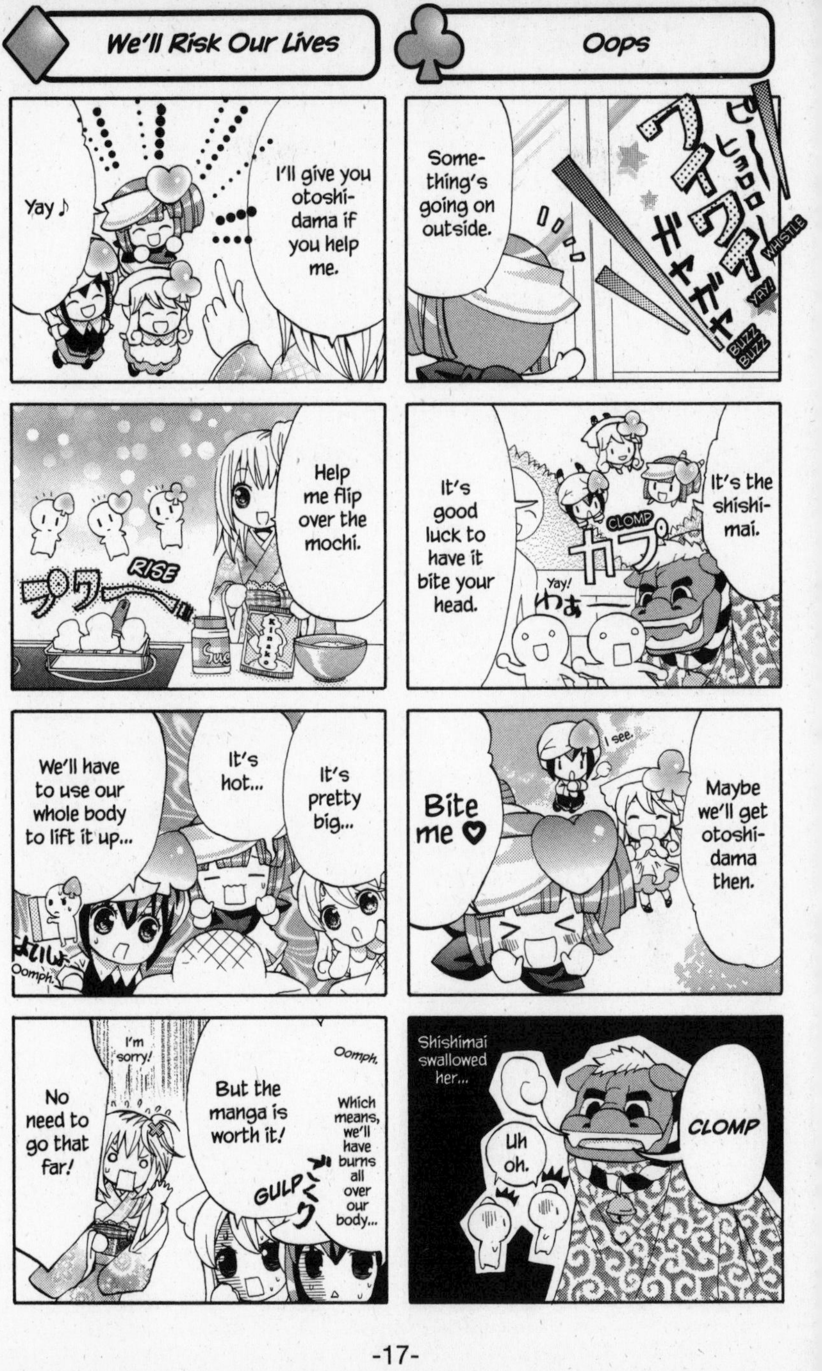
Oops
ピーヒョロロ~
WHISTLE
ワイワイ
YAY!
ガヤガヤ
BUZZ BUZZ
Something's going on outside.
It's the shishi-mai.
カプ
CLOMP
It's good luck to have it bite your head.
わぁーー
Yay!
Maybe we'll get otoshi-dama then.
I see.
Bite me ♡
CLOMP
Uh oh.
Shishimai swallowed her...
We'll Risk Our Lives
I'll give you otoshi-dama if you help me.
Yay♪
Help me flip over the mochi.
Kinako
Sug
RISE
It's pretty big...
It's hot...
We'll have to use our whole body to lift it up...
Oomph.
Which means, we'll have burns all over our body...
Oomph.
GULP
But the manga is worth it!
I'm sorry!
No need to go that far!

Klutz

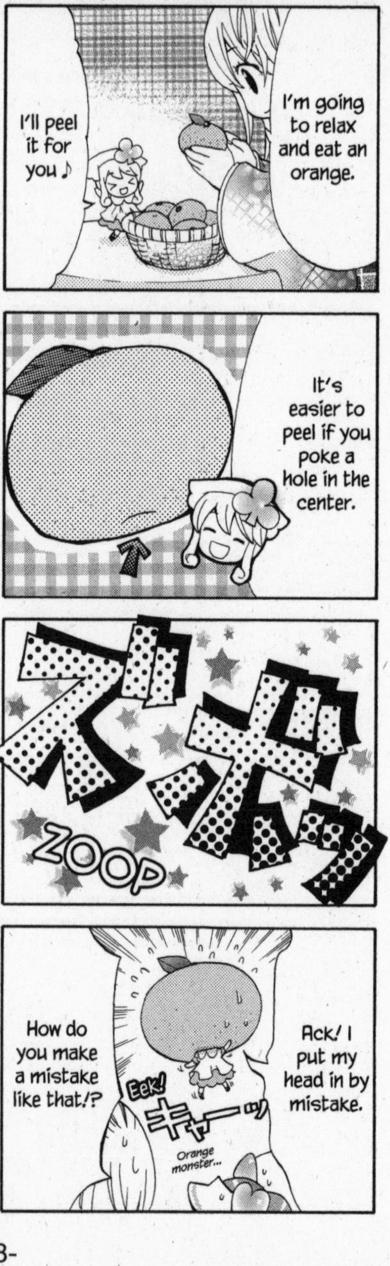
I'm going to relax and eat an orange.
I'll peel it for you ♪
It's easier to peel if you poke a hole in the center.
ZOOP
Ack! I put my head in by mistake.
Eek!
How do you make a mistake like that!?
Orange monster...

Try Your Best ☆

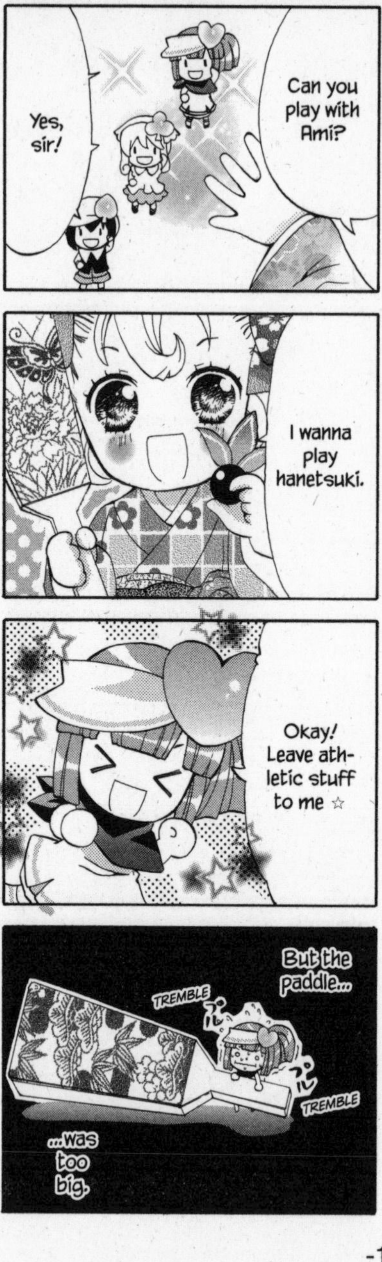
Can you play with Ami?
Yes, sir!
I wanna play hanetsuki.
Okay! Leave ath-letic stuff to me ☆
But the paddle...
TREMBLE
TREMBLE
...was too big.

I Love Sports!

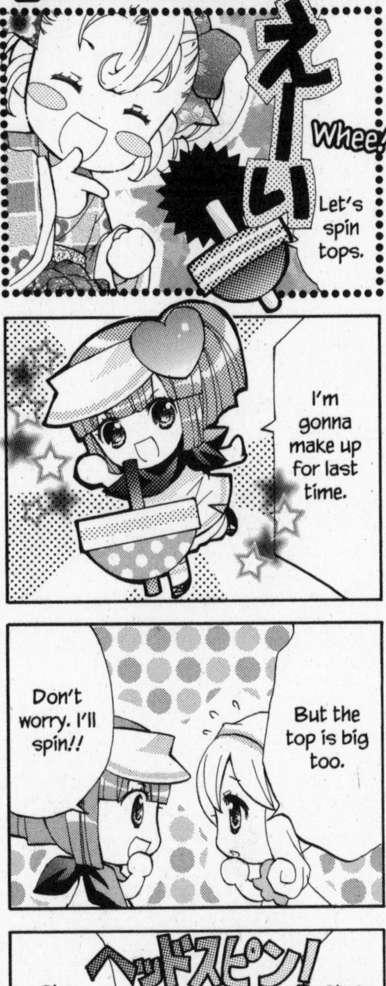
えい
Whee!
Let's spin tops.
I'm gonna make up for last time.
But the top is big too.
Don't worry. I'll spin!!
ヘッドスピン!
Head spinning!
She's spin-ning her-self!?
くる SPIN
くる SPIN
くる SPIN
くる SPIN
くる くる
SPIN SPIN
She looks cool, though.

Of Course This Would Happen...

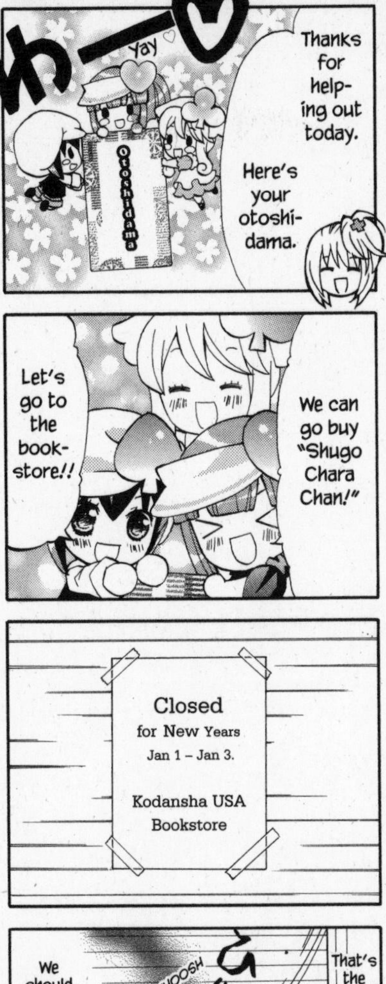
わー♡
Yay
Thanks for help-ing out today.
Here's your otoshi-dama.
Otoshidama
We can go buy "Shugo Chara Chan!"
Let's go to the book-store!!
Closed
for New Years
Jan 1 – Jan 3.
Kodansha USA Bookstore
That's the punch line?
WHOOSH
We should have known...

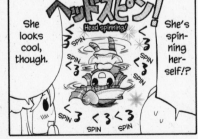

Shugo Chara Chan!

ONE-PANEL MANGA ☆

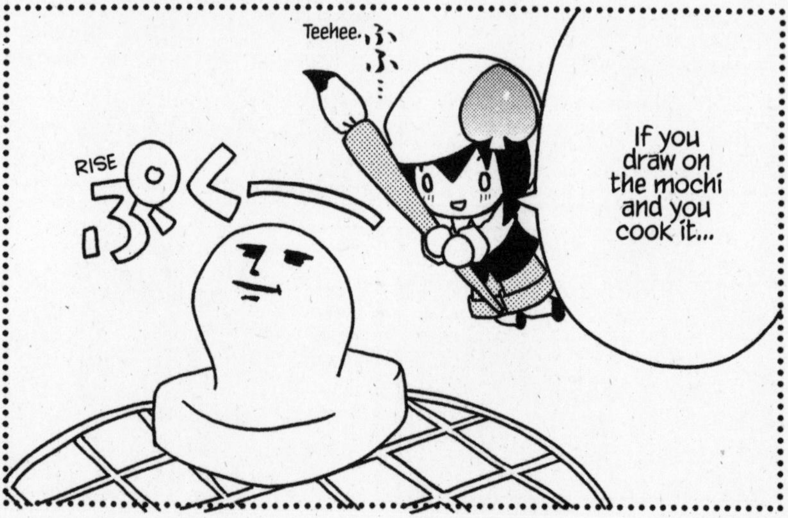
If you draw on the mochi and you cook it...
Teehee. ふふ…
RISE ぷくー

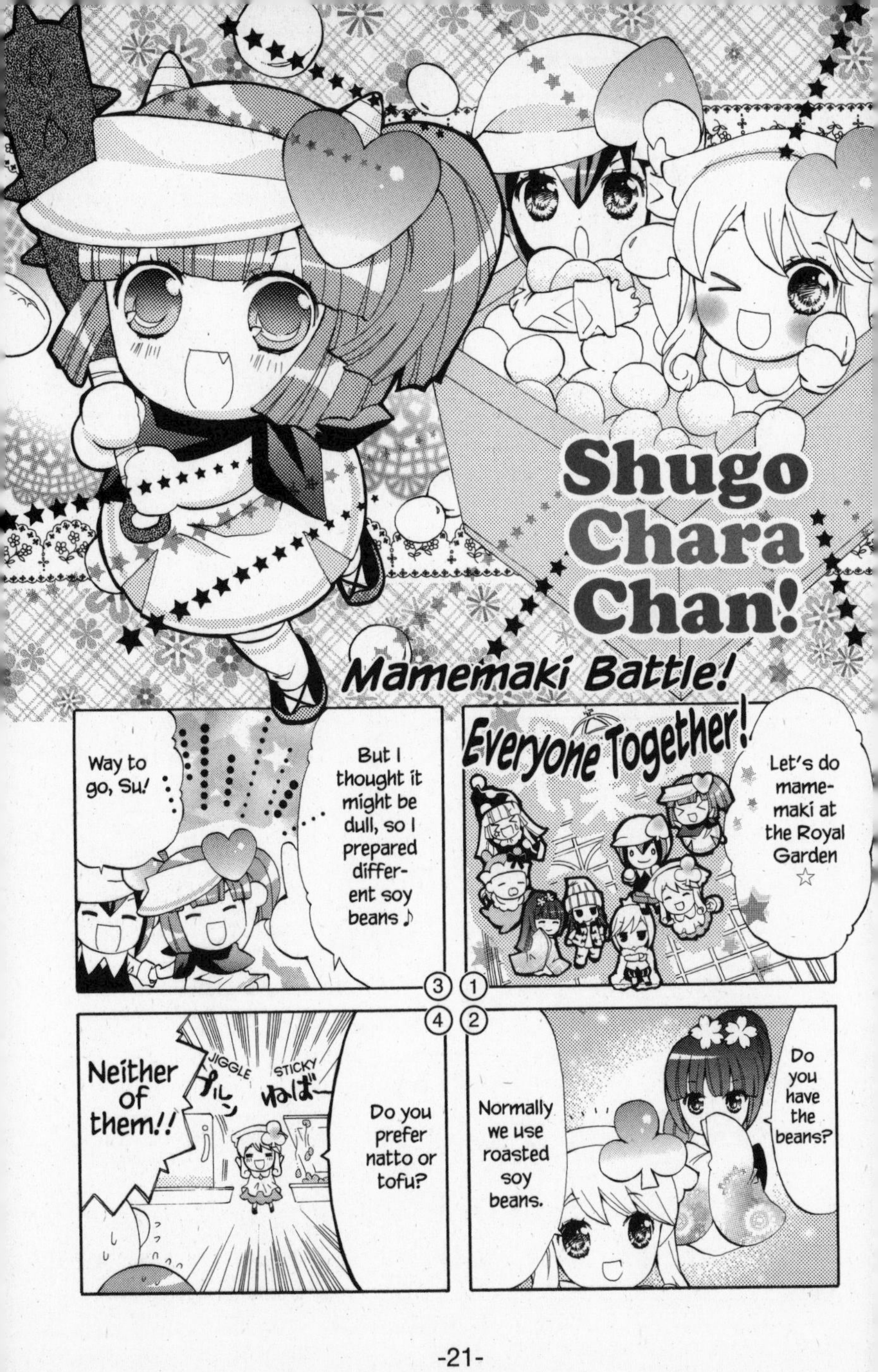
Shugo Chara Chan!
Mamemaki Battle!
Everyone Together!
Let's do mame-maki at the Royal Garden ☆
Do you have the beans?
Normally we use roasted soy beans.
But I thought it might be dull, so I prepared differ-ent soy beans ♪
Way to go, Su!
Do you prefer natto or tofu?
JIGGLE
プルン
STICKY
ねばー
Neither of them!!

Because We're Girls ♡

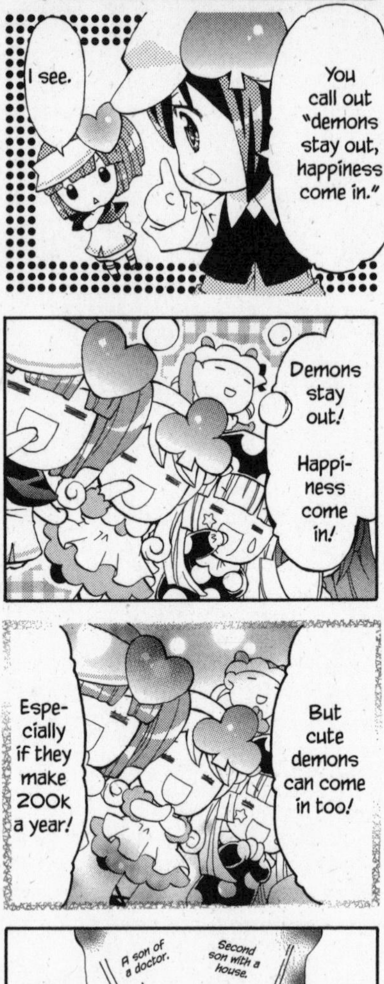
You call out "demons stay out, happiness come in."
I see.
Demons stay out! Happiness come in!
But cute demons can come in too!
Especially if they make 200k a year!
Women are scary...
Second son with a house.
A son of a doctor.
Yeah...

Bon Appetite

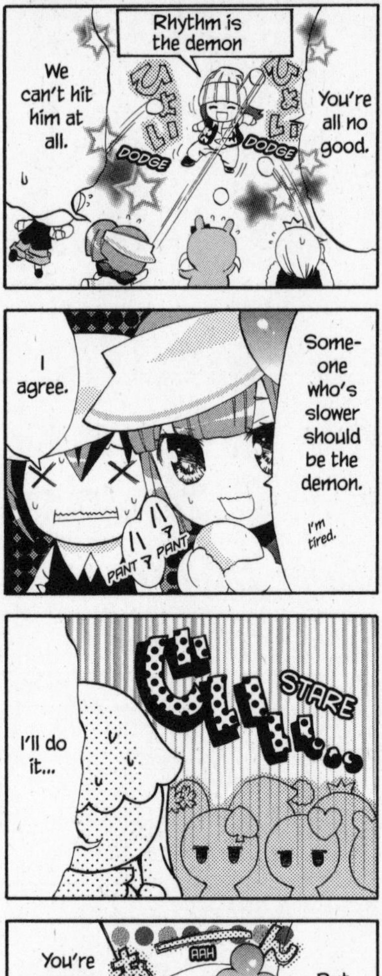
Rhythm is the demon
You're all no good.
DODGE
DODGE
We can't hit him at all.
Some-one who's slower should be the demon.
I'm tired.
I agree.
PANT PANT
STARE
I'll do it...
AAH
But make sure you aim for my mouth, okay?
You're gonna eat them all!?
You look happy to be the demon.

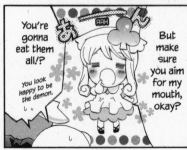

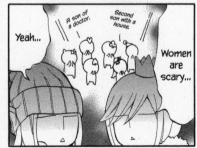

New Sport

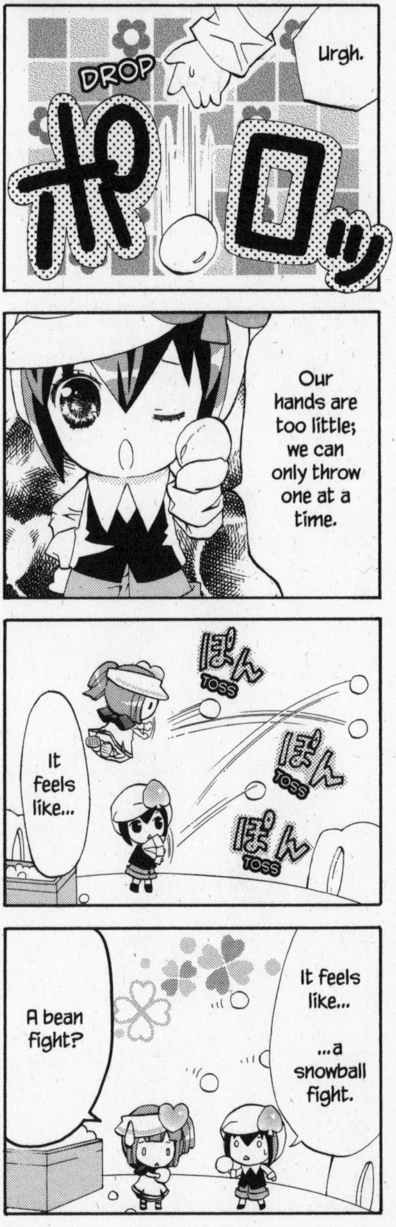
Urgh.
DROP
ポロッ
Our hands are too little; we can only throw one at a time.
ぽん
TOSS
ぽん
TOSS
ぽん
TOSS
It feels like...
It feels like...
...a snowball fight.
A bean fight?

Cute Together

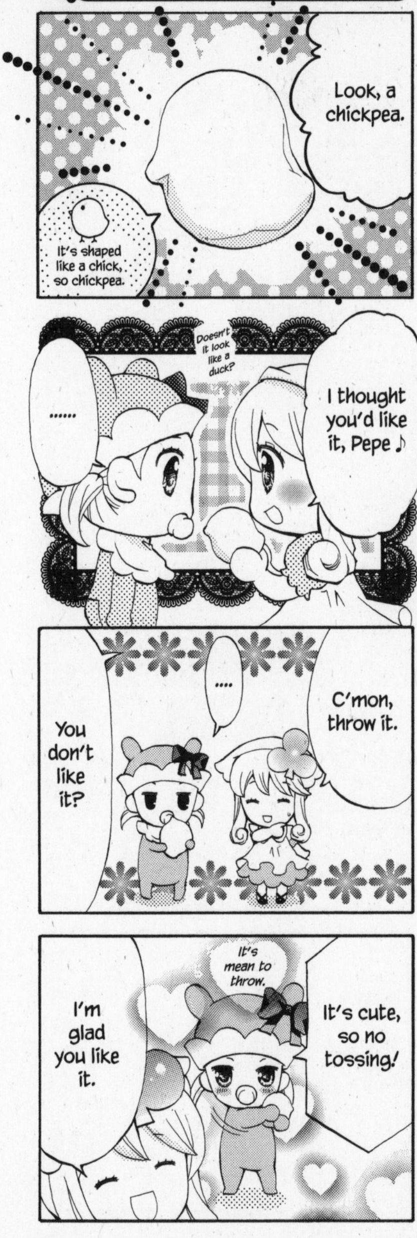
Look, a chickpea.
It's shaped like a chick, so chickpea.
I thought you'd like it, Pepe♪
Doesn't it look like a duck?
......
C'mon, throw it.
....
You don't like it?
It's cute, so no tossing!
It's mean to throw.
I'm glad you like it.

Love to Play

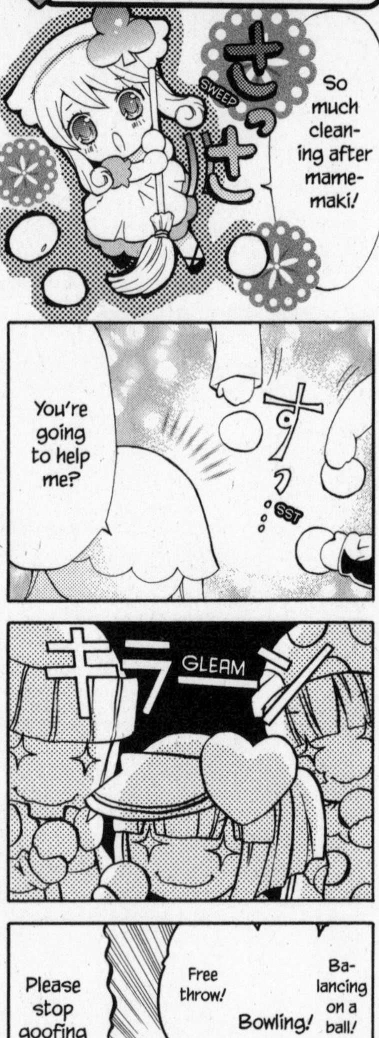

さっさ
SWEEP
So much clean-ing after mame-maki!
You're going to help me?
すっ
SST
キラーン
GLEAM
Ba-lancing on a ball!
Bowling!
Free throw!
Please stop goofing off!!

Wrap Up with This

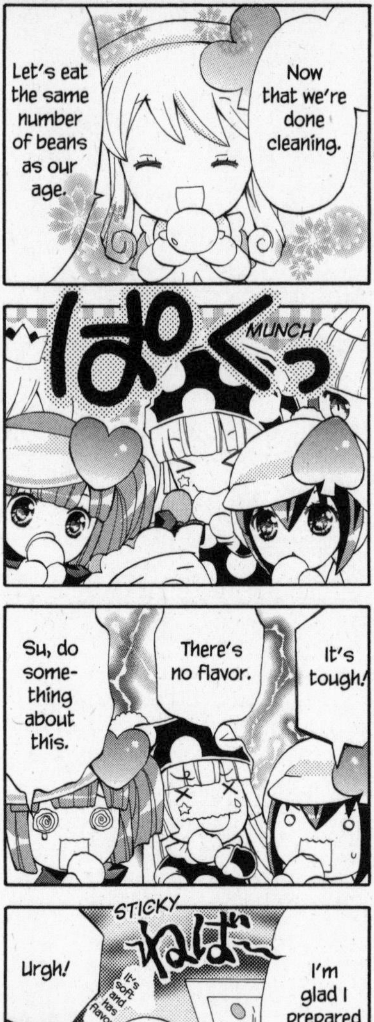

Now that we're done cleaning.
Let's eat the same number of beans as our age.
ぱくっ
MUNCH
It's tough!
There's no flavor.
Su, do some-thing about this.
I'm glad I prepared this ☆
STICKY
It's soft and has flavor.
Urgh!

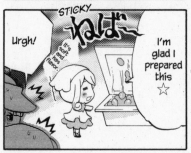

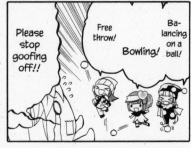

Shugo Chara Chan!

ONE-PANEL MANGA ☆

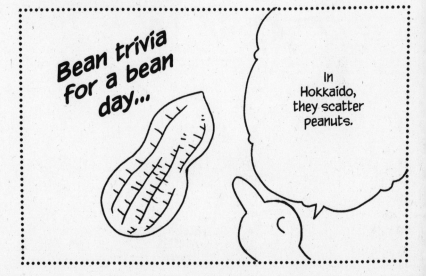

In Hokkaido, they scatter peanuts.
Bean trivia for a bean day...

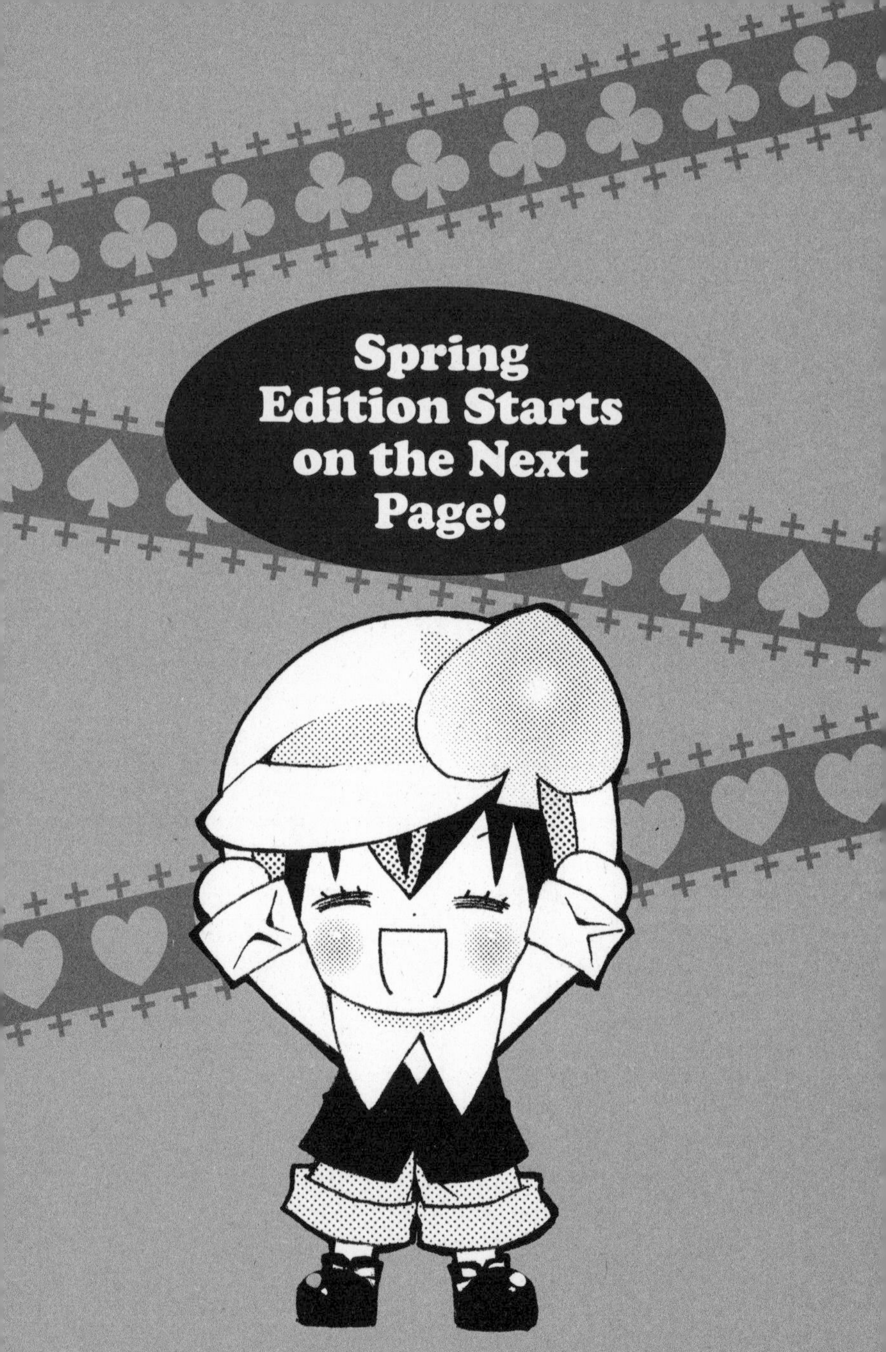
Spring Edition Starts on the Next Page!

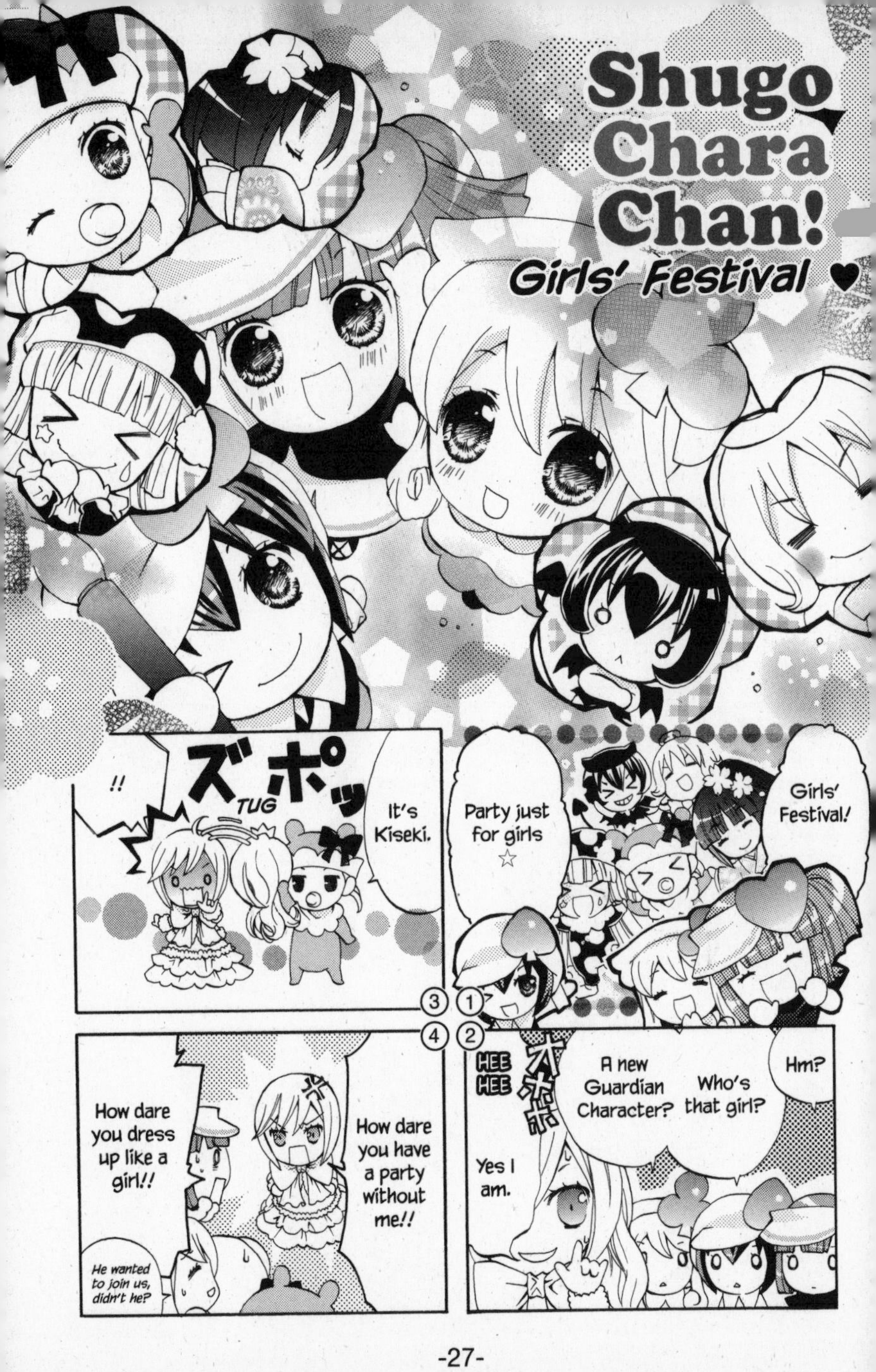
Shugo Chara Chan!
Girls' Festival ♥
Girls' Festival!
Party just for girls ☆
Hm?
Who's that girl?
A new Guardian Character?
HEE HEE
オホホ
Yes I am.
It's Kiseki.
ズポッ
TUG
!!
How dare you have a party without me!!
How dare you dress up like a girl!!
He wanted to join us, didn't he?

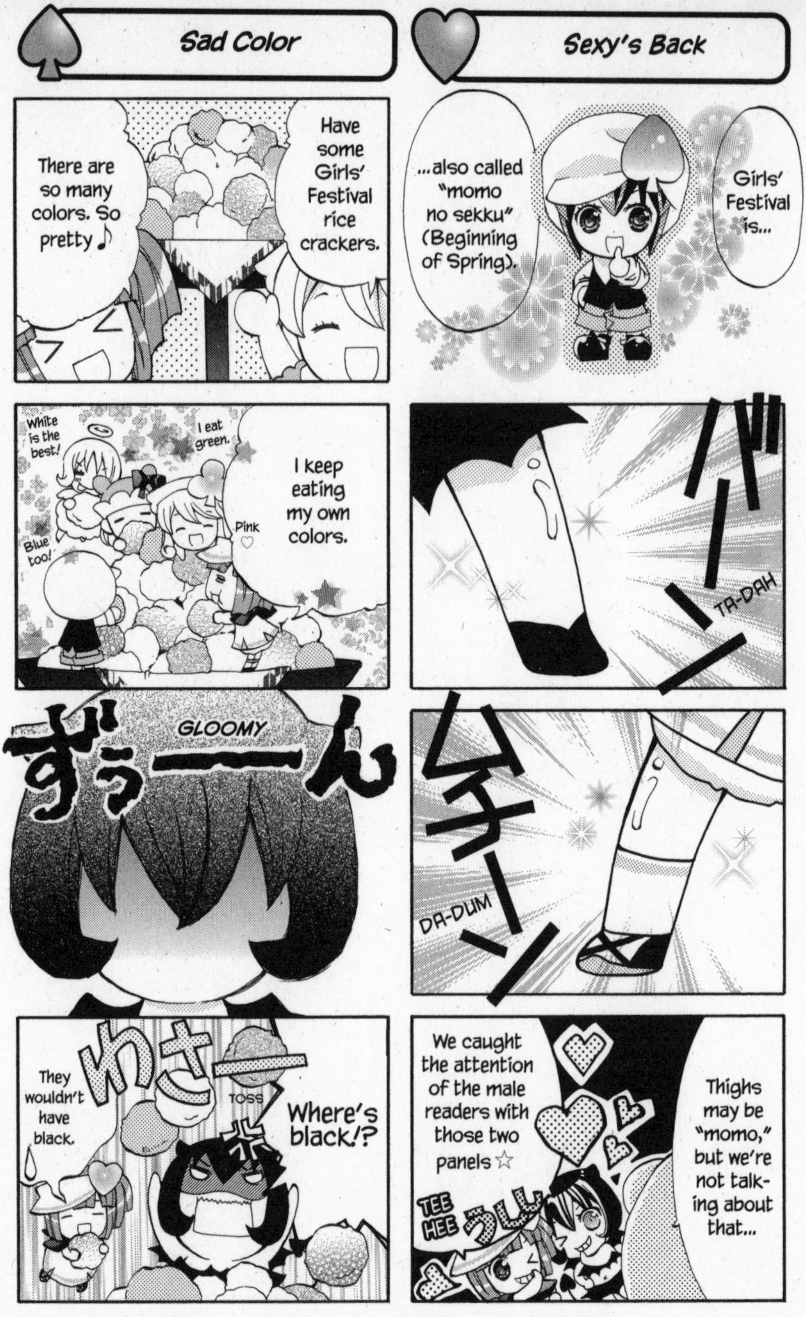
Sexy's Back
Girls' Festival is...
...also called "momo no sekku" (Beginning of Spring).
TA-DAH
DA-DUM
Thighs may be "momo," but we're not talking about that...
We caught the attention of the male readers with those two panels ☆
TEE HEE
Sad Color
Have some Girls' Festival rice crackers.
There are so many colors. So pretty ♪
I keep eating my own colors.
Pink ♡
I eat green.
White is the best!
Blue too!
GLOOMY
Where's black!?
TOSS
They wouldn't have black.

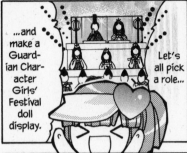

Scary

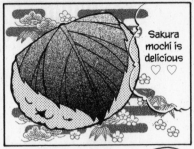

Sakura mochi is delicious ♡ ♡
Are they called sakura mochi because they're pink?
MUNCH MUNCH
もぐもぐ
It's because it's wrapped with cherry blossom leaves.
I see.
So they use a part of the cherry blossom tree.
Does that mean uguisu mochi...
...contains a part of a mockingbird?
Gulp
ごくり

Note: uguisu mochi is named that because of its shape!

Oh Yeah

Let's all pick a role...
...and make a Guardian Character Girls' Festival doll display.
Sounds fun ♪
I want to be the hina princess.
Me too!
I will do it.
I want to too.
バチ SPARK
バチ SPARK
Whaaat!?
バチ SPARK
The princess is popular, but if you take out the honorifics...
She's just a "hina" (chick).
You're okay with that?
Cheep.
ぴよっ
Chick, huh?
I guess you're right.
う〜ん。。。
Hmm...

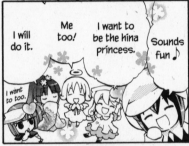

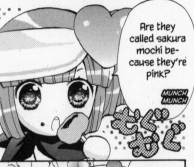

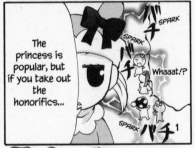

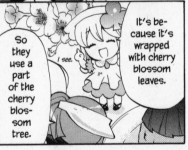

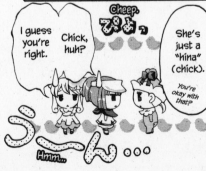

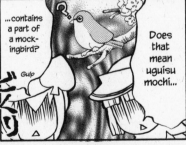

Girls' Battle

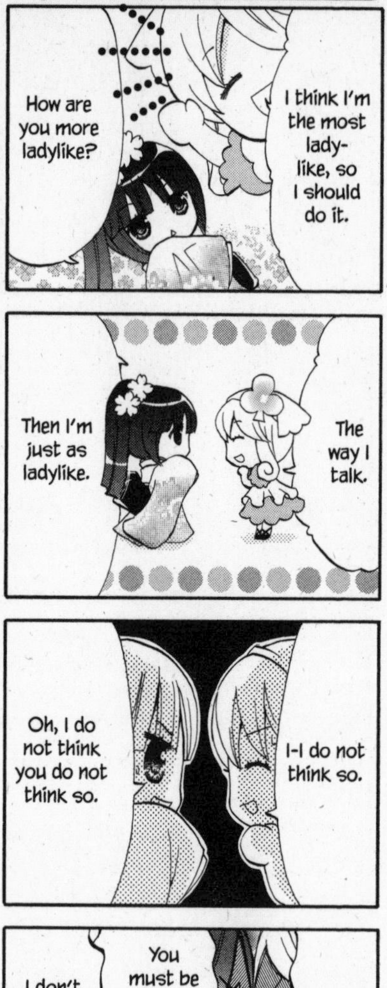

I think I'm the most lady-like, so I should do it.
How are you more ladylike?
The way I talk.
Then I'm just as ladylike.
I-I do not think so.
Oh, I do not think you do not think so.
I do think that I do not think so.
You must be mis-taken. I do think I do not think you do not think so.
I don't know what's going on.

You Sure?

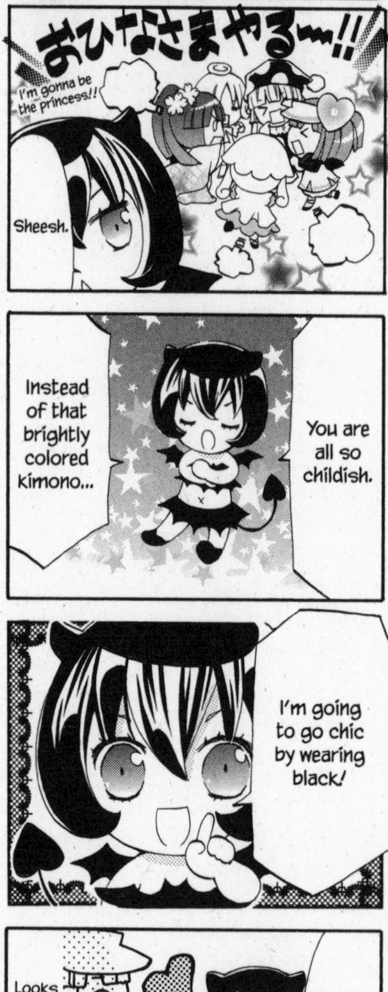

おひなさまやる〜〜!!
I'm gonna be the princess!!
Sheesh.
You are all so childish.
Instead of that brightly colored kimono...
I'm going to go chic by wearing black!
See ♪
Looks like funeral kimono ...

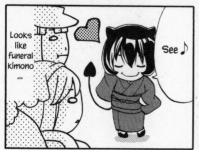

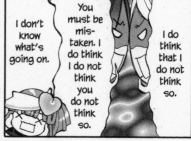

No, It's Still Bad

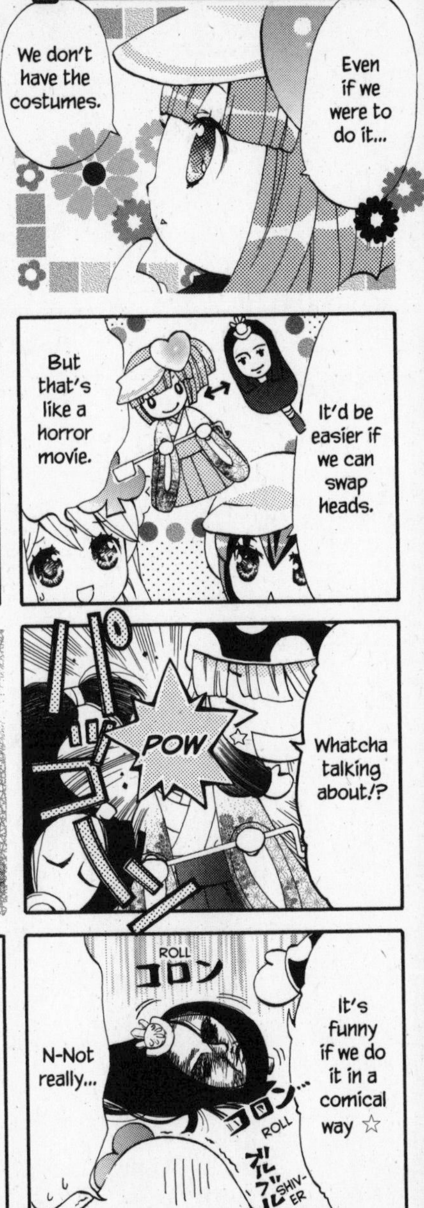

Even if we were to do it...
We don't have the costumes.
It'd be easier if we can swap heads.
But that's like a horror movie.
Whatcha talking about!?
POW
It's funny if we do it in a comical way ☆
ROLL
コロン
N-Not really...
コロン…
ROLL
SHIVER

White Drink

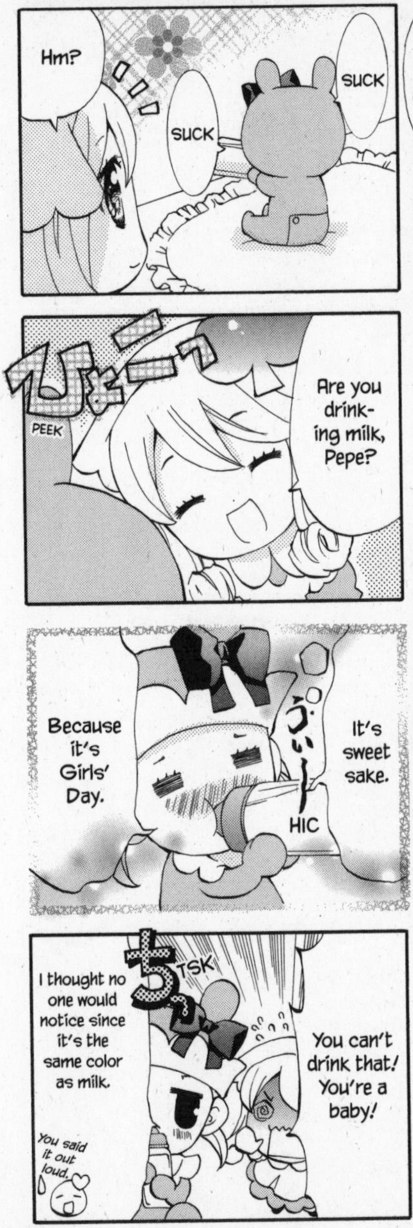

SUCK
SUCK
Hm?
Are you drinking milk, Pepe?
PEEK
It's sweet sake.
Because it's Girls' Day.
HIC
You can't drink that! You're a baby!
TSK
I thought no one would notice since it's the same color as milk.
You said it out loud.

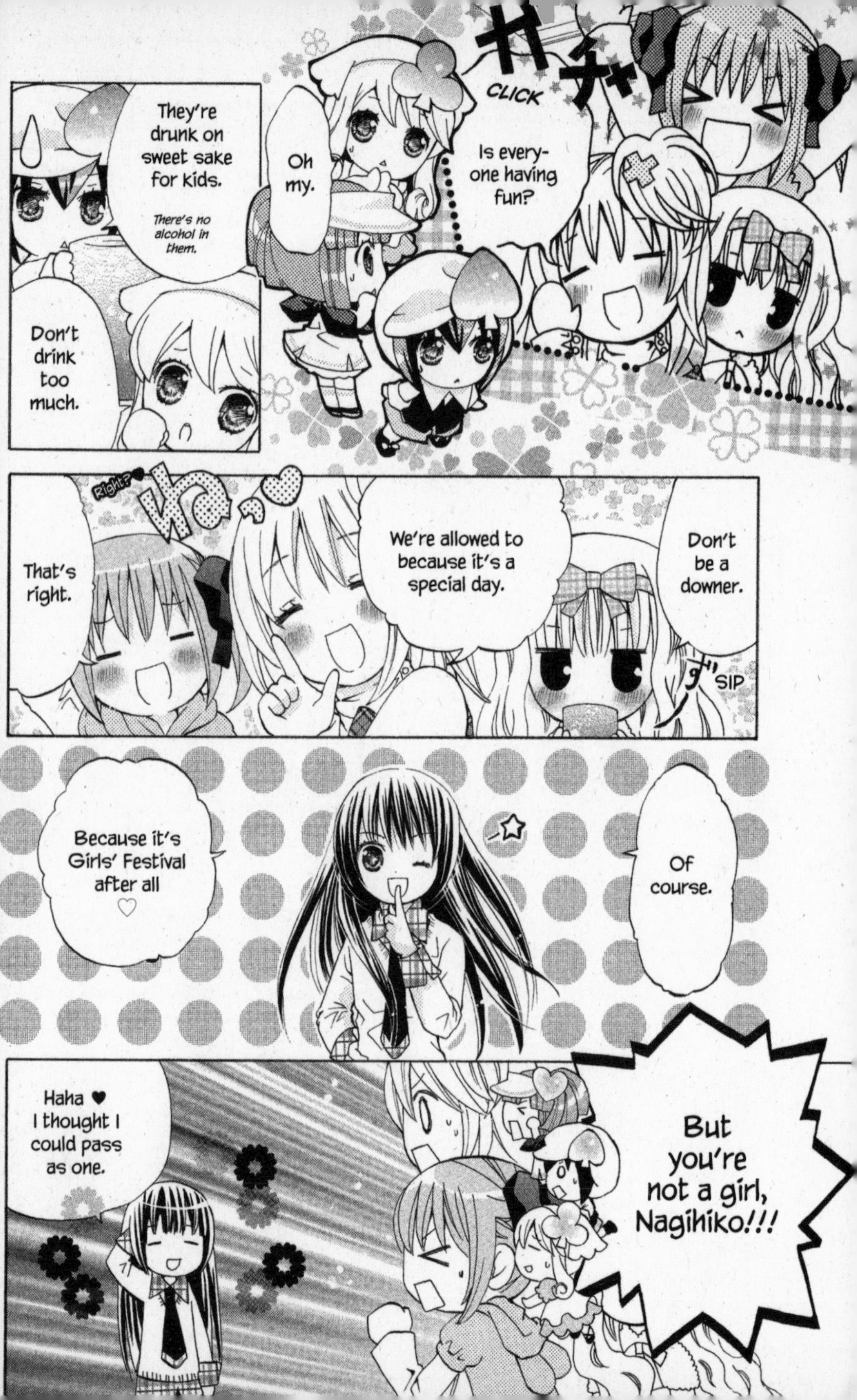
CLICK
Is every-one having fun?
Oh my.
They're drunk on sweet sake for kids.
There's no alcohol in them.
Don't drink too much.
Don't be a downer.
SIP
We're allowed to because it's a special day.
Right?♥
That's right.
Of course.
Because it's Girls' Festival after all ♡
But you're not a girl, Nagihiko!!!
Haha ♥ I thought I could pass as one.

Shugo Chara Chan!

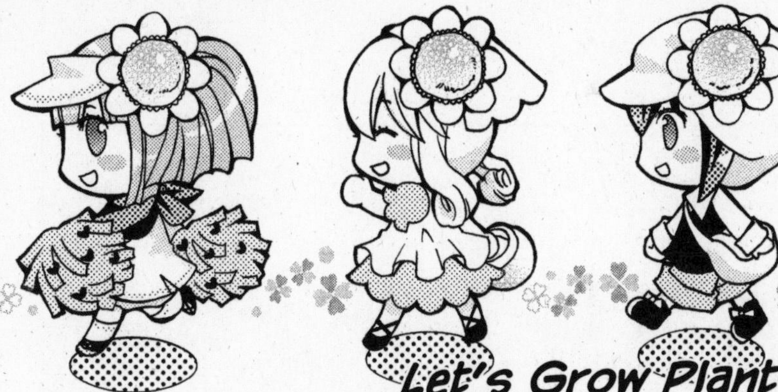

Let's Grow Plants!

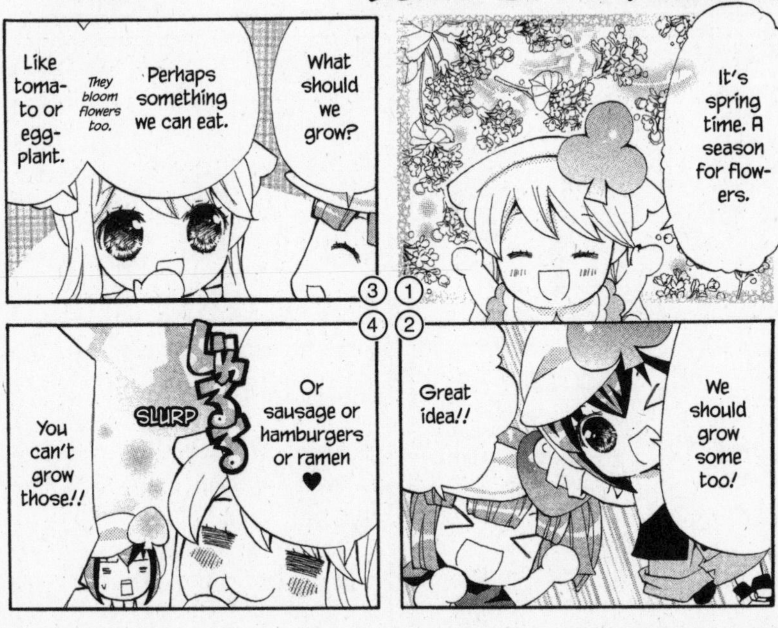

It's spring time. A season for flow-ers.
We should grow some too!
Great idea!!
What should we grow?
Perhaps something we can eat.
They bloom flowers too.
Like toma-to or egg-plant.
Or sausage or hamburgers or ramen ♥
SLURP
You can't grow those!!

Isn't it a Seed?

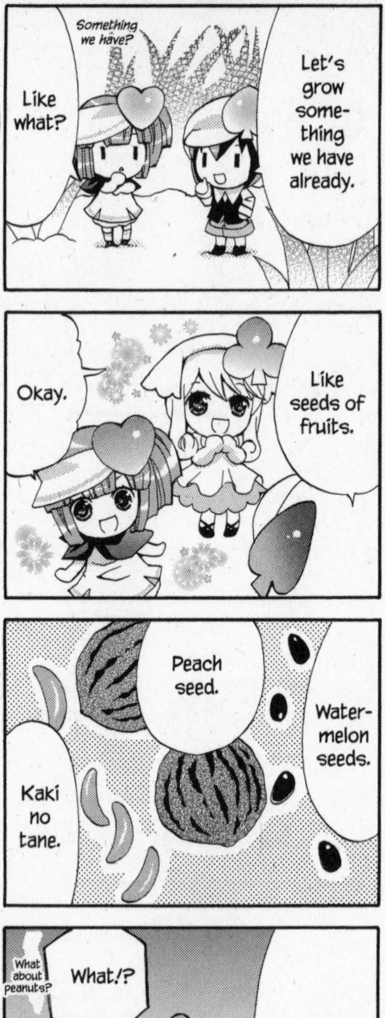

Let's grow some-thing we have already.
Like what?
Something we have?
Like seeds of fruits.
Okay.
Water-melon seeds.
Peach seed.
Kaki no tane.
I don't think kaki no tane is a seed.
What!?
What about peanuts?

Just One Bite

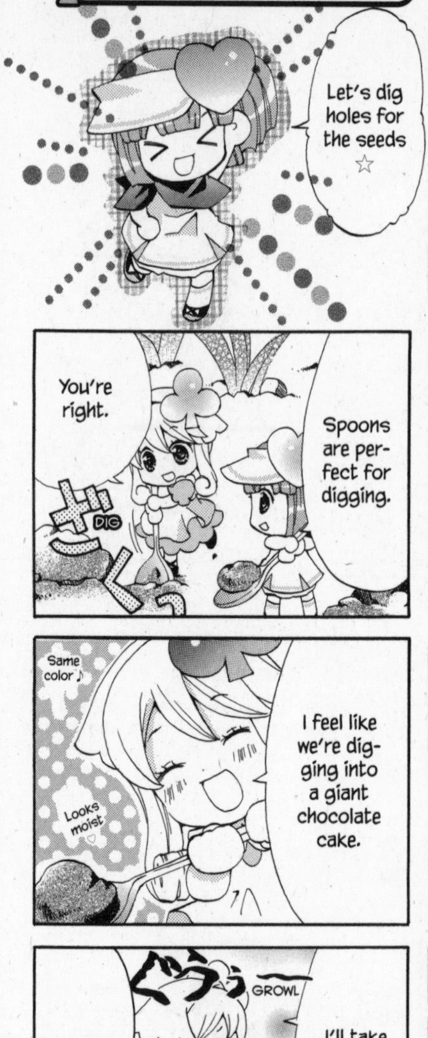

Let's dig holes for the seeds ☆
Spoons are per-fect for digging.
You're right.
DIG
I feel like we're dig-ging into a giant chocolate cake.
Same color ♪
Looks moist ♡
I'll take a little bite.
GROWL
No!!
GROWL

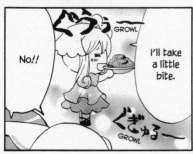

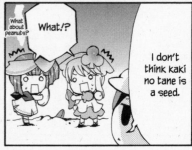

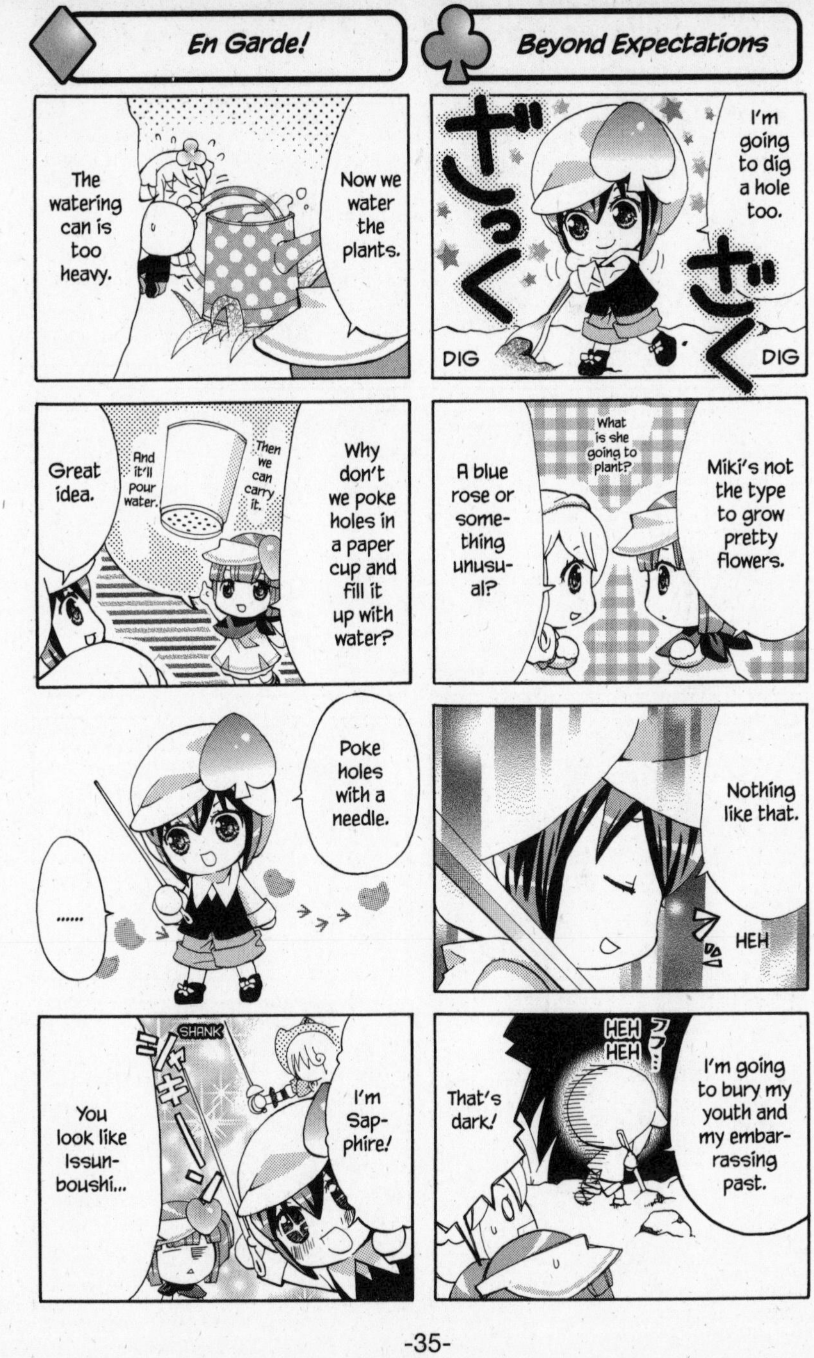
Beyond Expectations
I'm going to dig a hole too.
ざっく
ざっく
DIG
DIG
Miki's not the type to grow pretty flowers.
What is she going to plant?
A blue rose or something unusual?
Nothing like that.
HEH
I'm going to bury my youth and my embarrassing past.
HEH HEH
フフ…
That's dark!
En Garde!
Now we water the plants.
The watering can is too heavy.
Why don't we poke holes in a paper cup and fill it up with water?
Then we can carry it.
And it'll pour water.
Great idea.
Poke holes with a needle.
......
I'm Sapphire!
SHANK
You look like Issun-boushi...

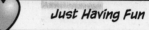

Just Having Fun

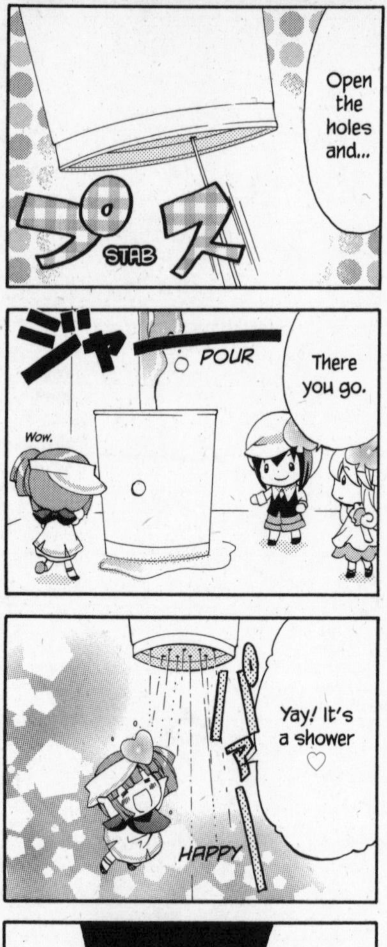

Open the holes and...
プス
STAB
There you go.
ジャー
POUR
Wow.
Yay! It's a shower ♡
HAPPY
You can shower in warm water at home. Why are you appealing to the masses like that?
Even the masses don't take showers with a paper cup.

You're All Wrong

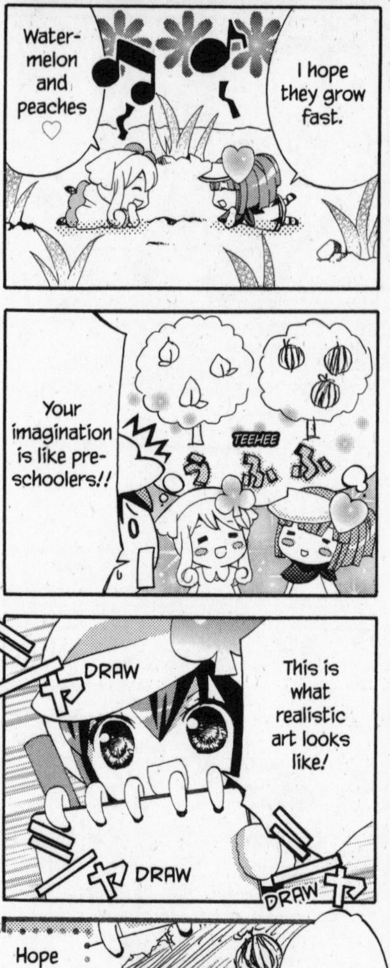

I hope they grow fast.
Water-melon and peaches ♡
Your imagination is like pre-schoolers!!
うふふ
TEEHEE
This is what realistic art looks like!
DRAW
DRAW
DRAW
Miki, you're so good!
Hehe.

Note: Watermelon does not grow on trees!

Hope the plants grow fast, so you get to see what they really look like ♡

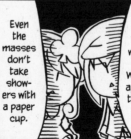

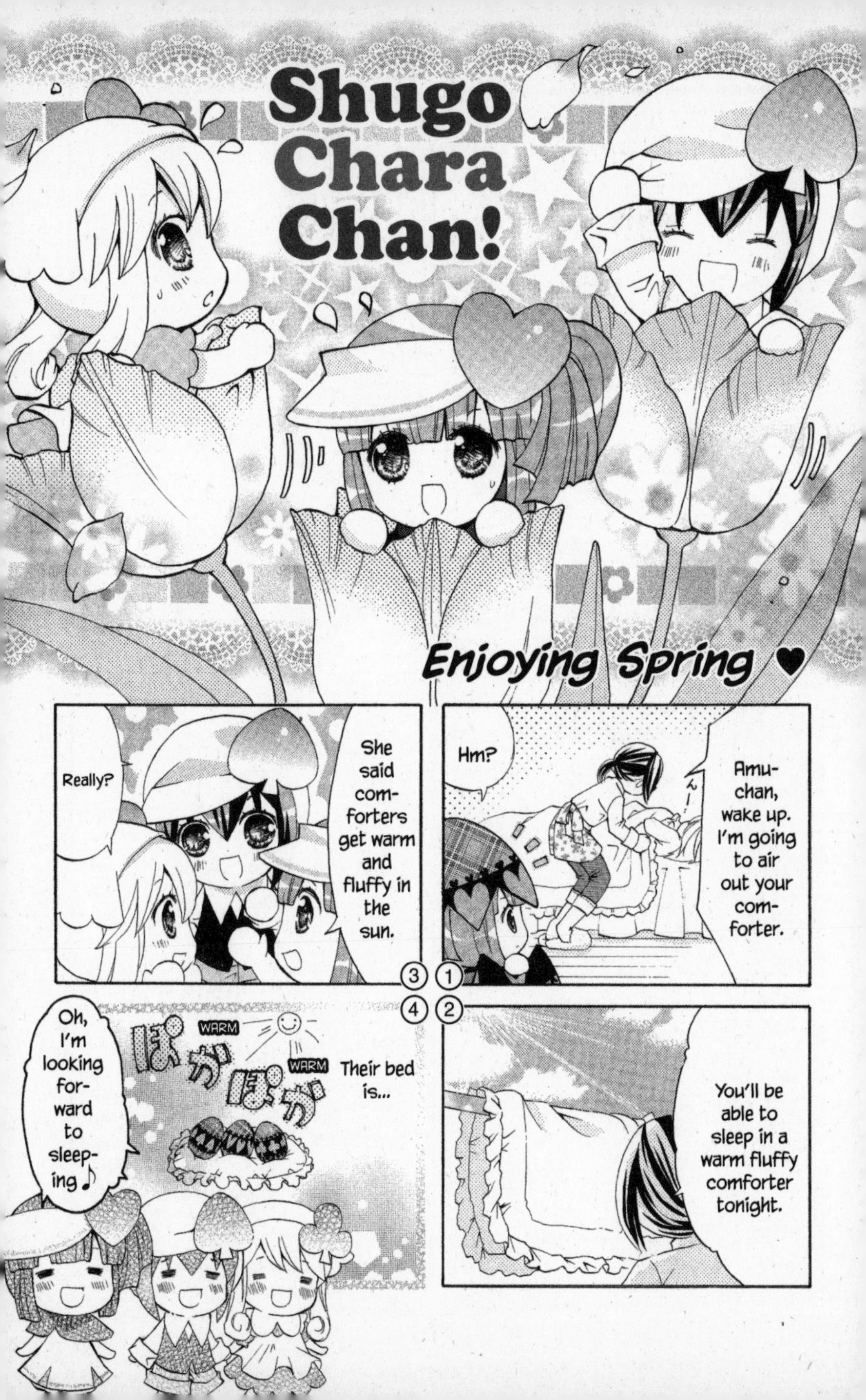
Shugo Chara Chan!
Enjoying Spring ♥
Amu-chan, wake up. I'm going to air out your comforter.
Hm?
You'll be able to sleep in a warm fluffy comforter tonight.
She said com-forters get warm and fluffy in the sun.
Really?
Their bed is...
ぽかぽか
WARM
WARM
Oh, I'm looking for-ward to sleep-ing♪

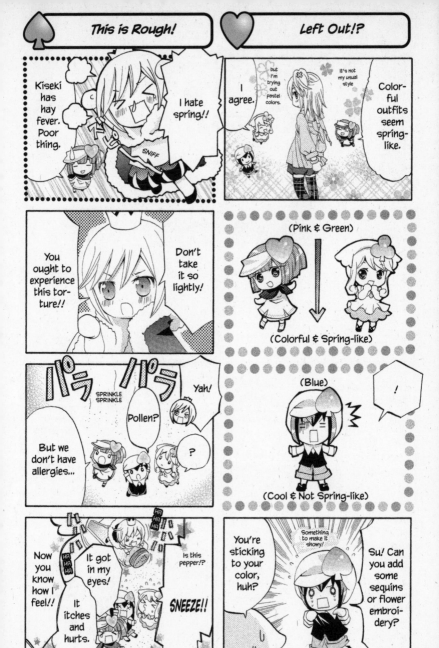

Left Out!?

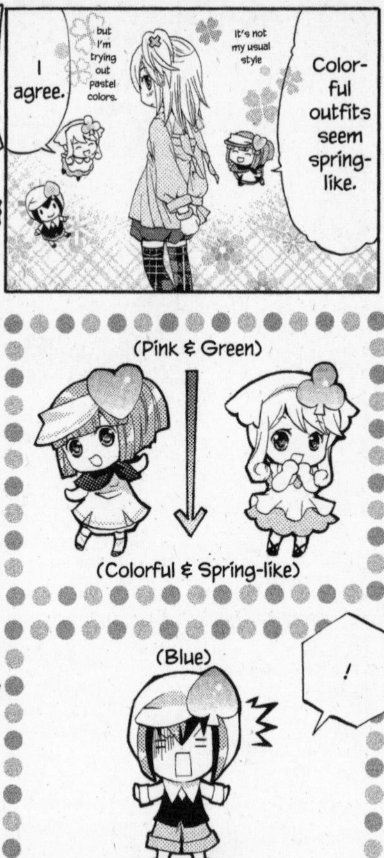

Colorful outfits seem spring-like.
It's not my usual style
but I'm trying out pastel colors.
I agree.
(Pink & Green)
(Colorful & Spring-like)
!
(Blue)
(Cool & Not Spring-like)
Su! Can you add some sequins or flower embroidery?
Something to make it showy!
You're sticking to your color, huh?

This is Rough!

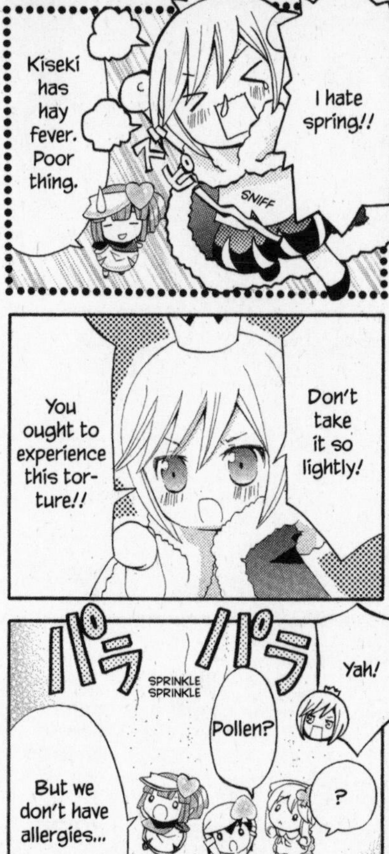

I hate spring!!
SNIFF
Kiseki has hay fever. Poor thing.
Don't take it so lightly!
You ought to experience this torture!!
Yah!
パラ パラ
SPRINKLE SPRINKLE
Pollen?
?
But we don't have allergies...
Is this pepper!?
SNEEZE!!
HA HA HA
It got in my eyes!
It itches and hurts.
HA HA HA
Now you know how I feel!!

Quarantine

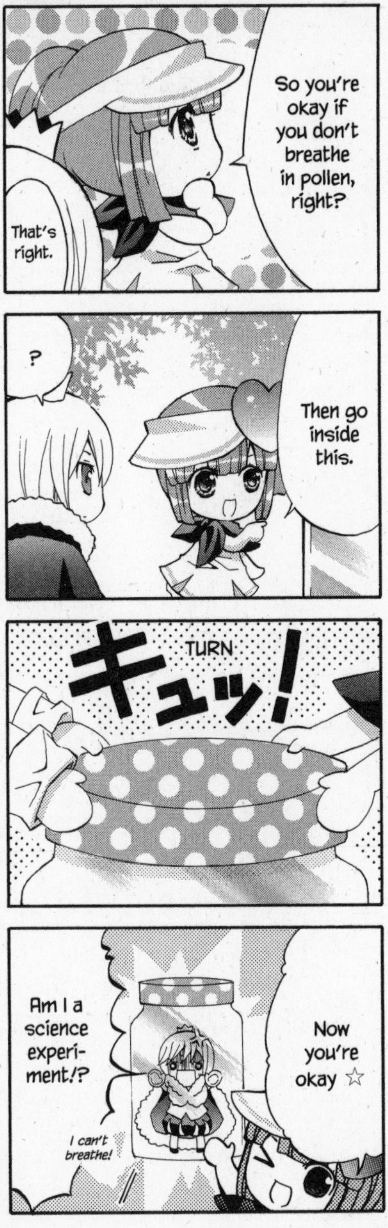
So you're okay if you don't breathe in pollen, right?
That's right.
Then go inside this.
?
TURN
キュッ!
Now you're okay ☆
Am I a science experiment!?
I can't breathe!

Takes Courage

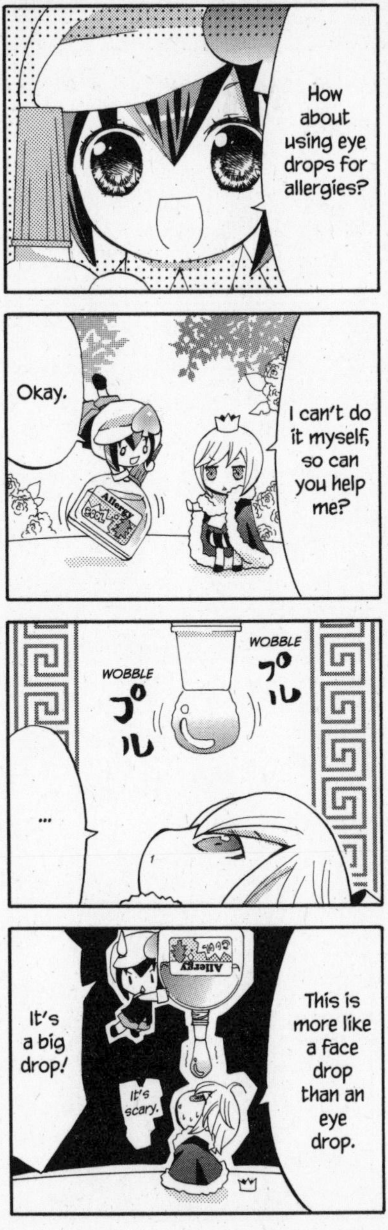
How about using eye drops for allergies?
I can't do it myself, so can you help me?
Okay.
WOBBLE
プル
WOBBLE
プル
...
This is more like a face drop than an eye drop.
It's a big drop!
It's scary.

Oops

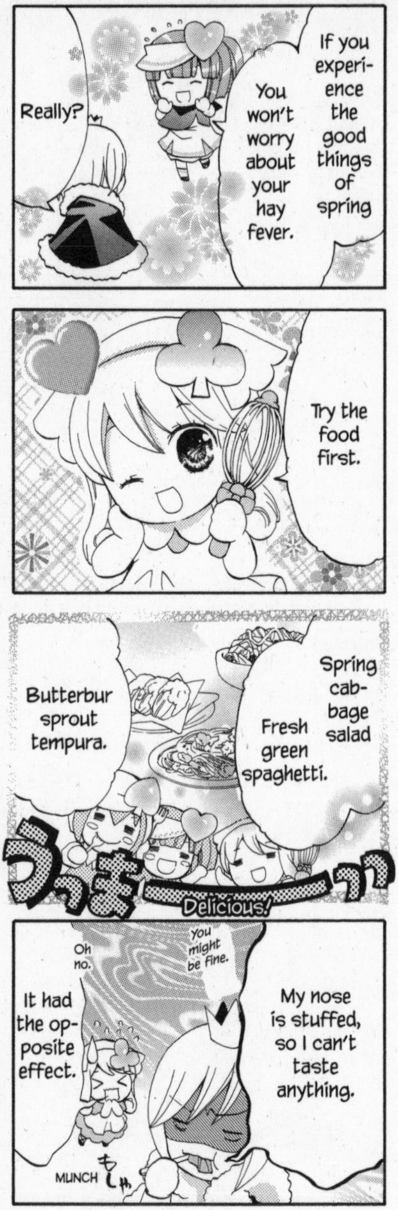
If you experi-ence the good things of spring
You won't worry about your hay fever.
Really?
Try the food first.
Spring cab-bage salad
Fresh green spaghetti.
Butterbur sprout tempura.
うっまーーっ
Delicious!
My nose is stuffed, so I can't taste anything.
You might be fine.
Oh no.
It had the op-posite effect.
MUNCH

First Impression is Important

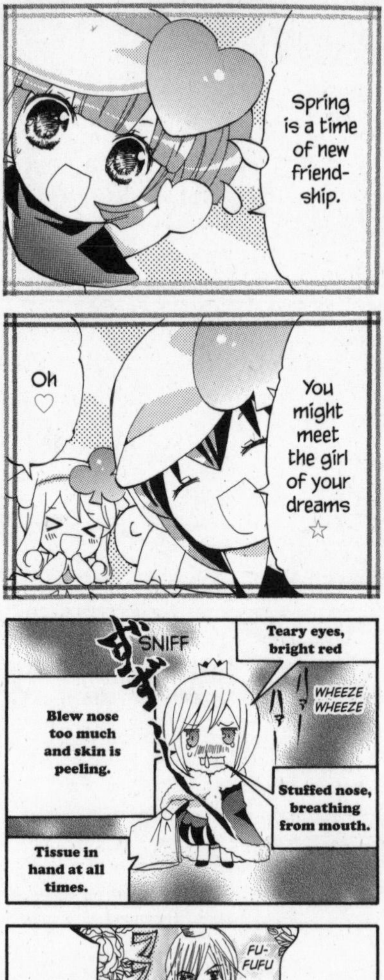
Spring is a time of new friend-ship.
You might meet the girl of your dreams ☆
Oh ♡
Teary eyes, bright red
SNIFF
WHEEZE WHEEZE
Stuffed nose, breathing from mouth.
Blew nose too much and skin is peeling.
Tissue in hand at all times.
FU-FUFU
I want to meet her when I look my usual self.
Who's that!?

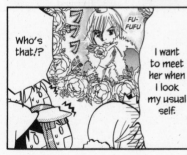

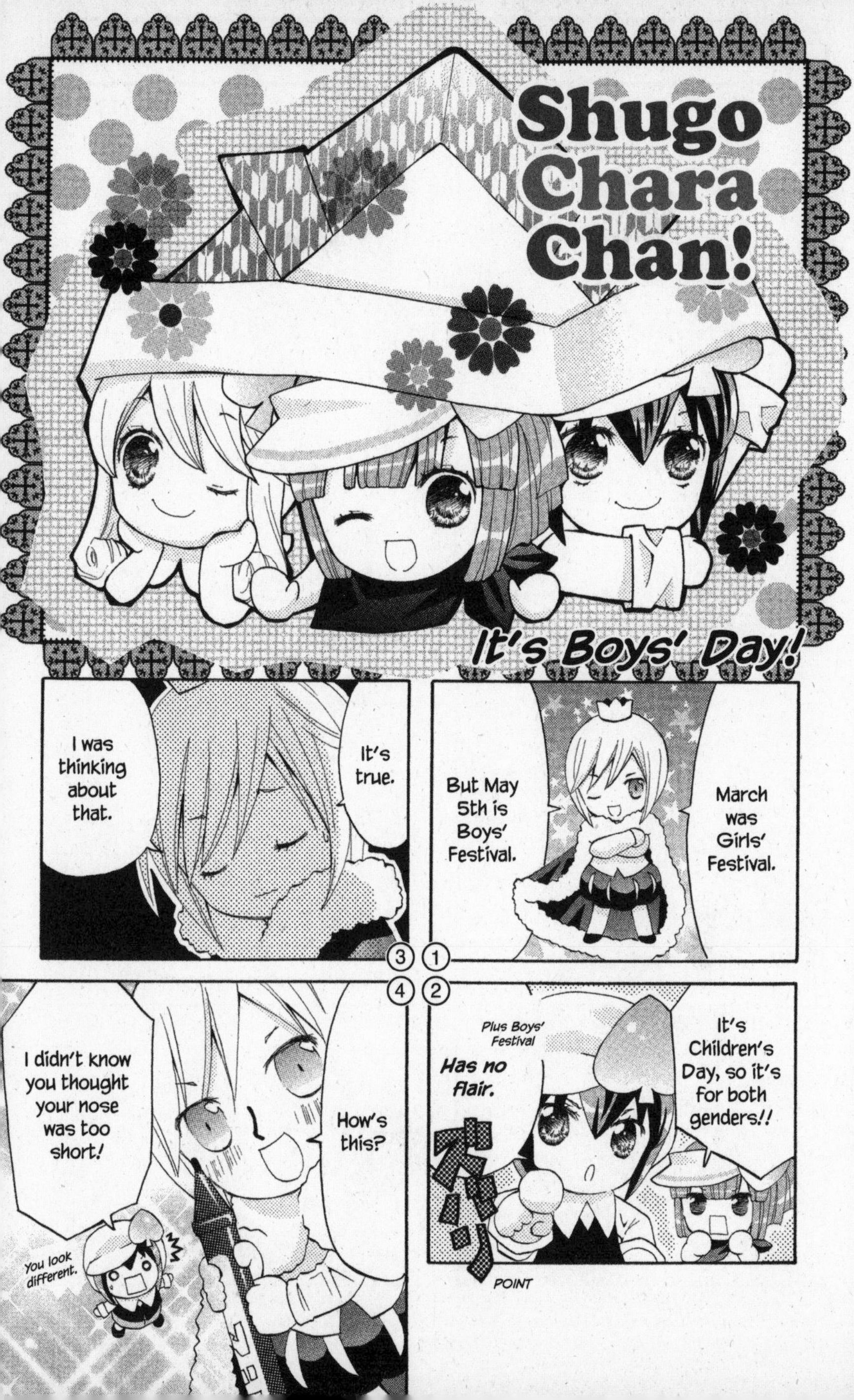

Shugo Chara Chan!
It's Boys' Day!
March was Girls' Festival.
But May 5th is Boys' Festival.
It's Children's Day, so it's for both genders!!
Plus Boys' Festival
Has no flair.
POINT
It's true.
I was thinking about that.
How's this?
I didn't know you thought your nose was too short!
You look different.

Pink vs ?

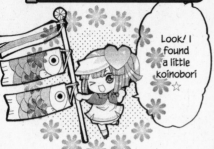

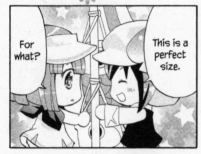

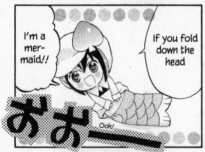

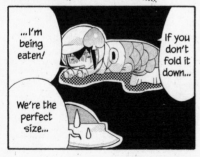

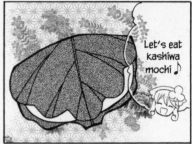

Let's eat kashiwa mochi ♪
Com-pared to the Girls' Festival sakura mochi.
There's no flair.
Com-pletely white.
If theirs was pink.
We should make it a color for boys.
Boy's color would be...
Blue?
It doesn't look tasty at all.

Playing with Koinobori

Look! I found a little koinobori ☆
This is a perfect size.
For what?
If you fold down the head
I'm a mer-maid!!
おおー
Ooh!
If you don't fold it down...
...I'm being eaten!
We're the perfect size...

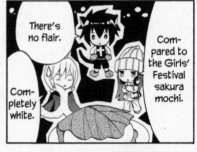

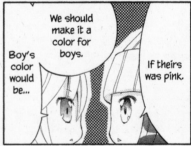

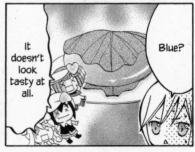

A Special Color

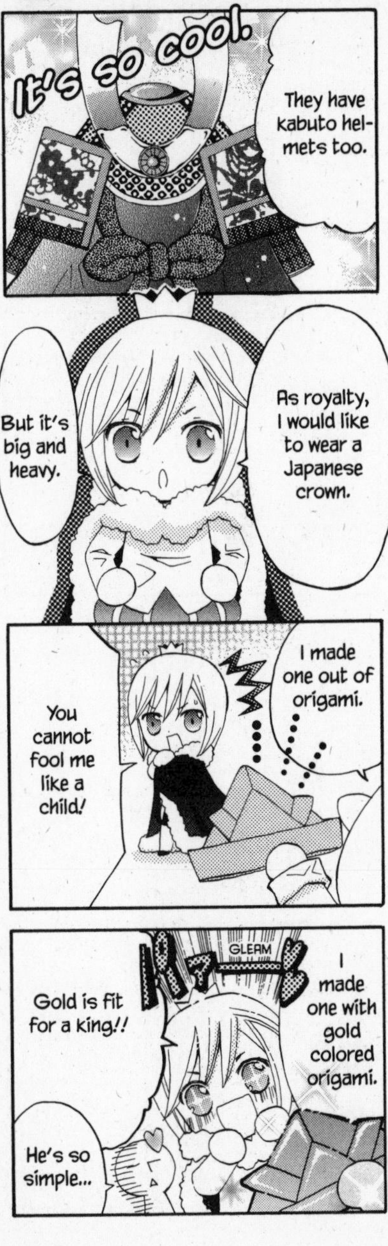
They have kabuto helmets too.
It's so cool.
As royalty, I would like to wear a Japanese crown.
But it's big and heavy.
I made one out of origami.
You cannot fool me like a child!
I made one with gold colored origami.
GLEAM
Gold is fit for a king!!
He's so simple...

Just a Little Taller!

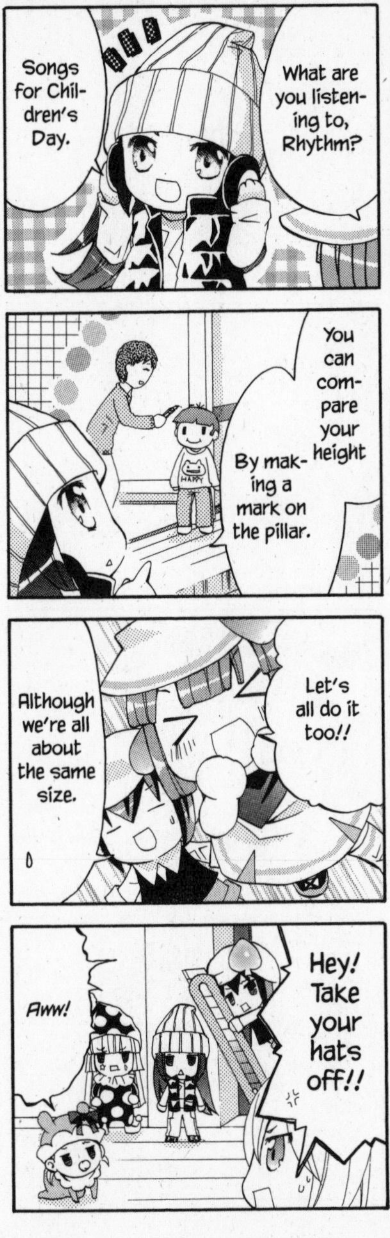
What are you listening to, Rhythm?
Songs for Children's Day.
You can compare your height
By making a mark on the pillar.
HAPPY
Let's all do it too!!
Although we're all about the same size.
Hey! Take your hats off!!
Aww!

Gonna Win Meow

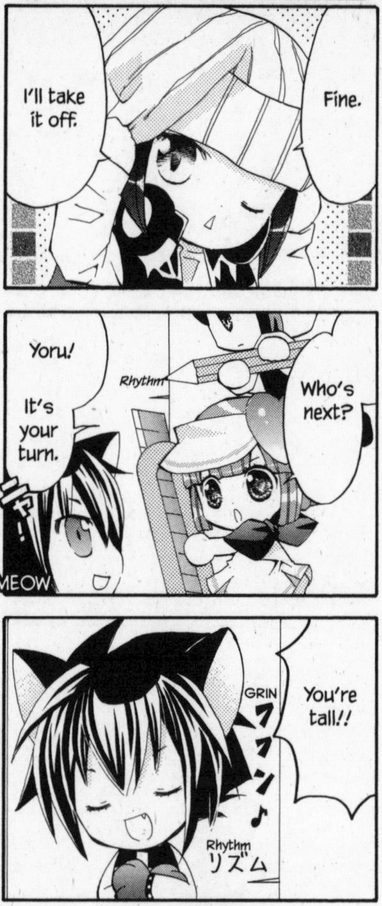

Fine.
I'll take it off.
Who's next?
Rhythm
Yoru!
It's your turn.
MEOW
You're tall!!
GRIN
Rhythm
リズム
Animal lengths include their tail!!
STRETCH
You really want to win!?
And you're calling yourself an animal?

Game of Roulette

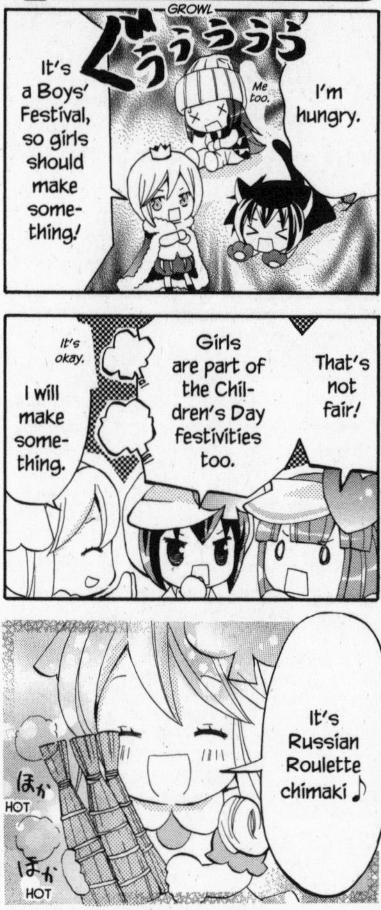

I'm hungry.
Me too.
GROWL
It's a Boys' Festival, so girls should make something!
That's not fair!
Girls are part of the Children's Day festivities too.
It's okay.
I will make something.
It's Russian Roulette chimaki♪
ほか
HOT
ほか
HOT
Each one has either wasabi or mustard or pepper in them ♡
Try your luck.
They're all bad!!!
Don't get Su mad or else!

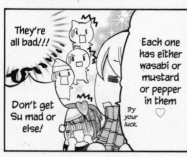

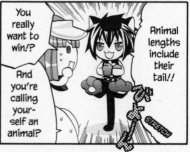

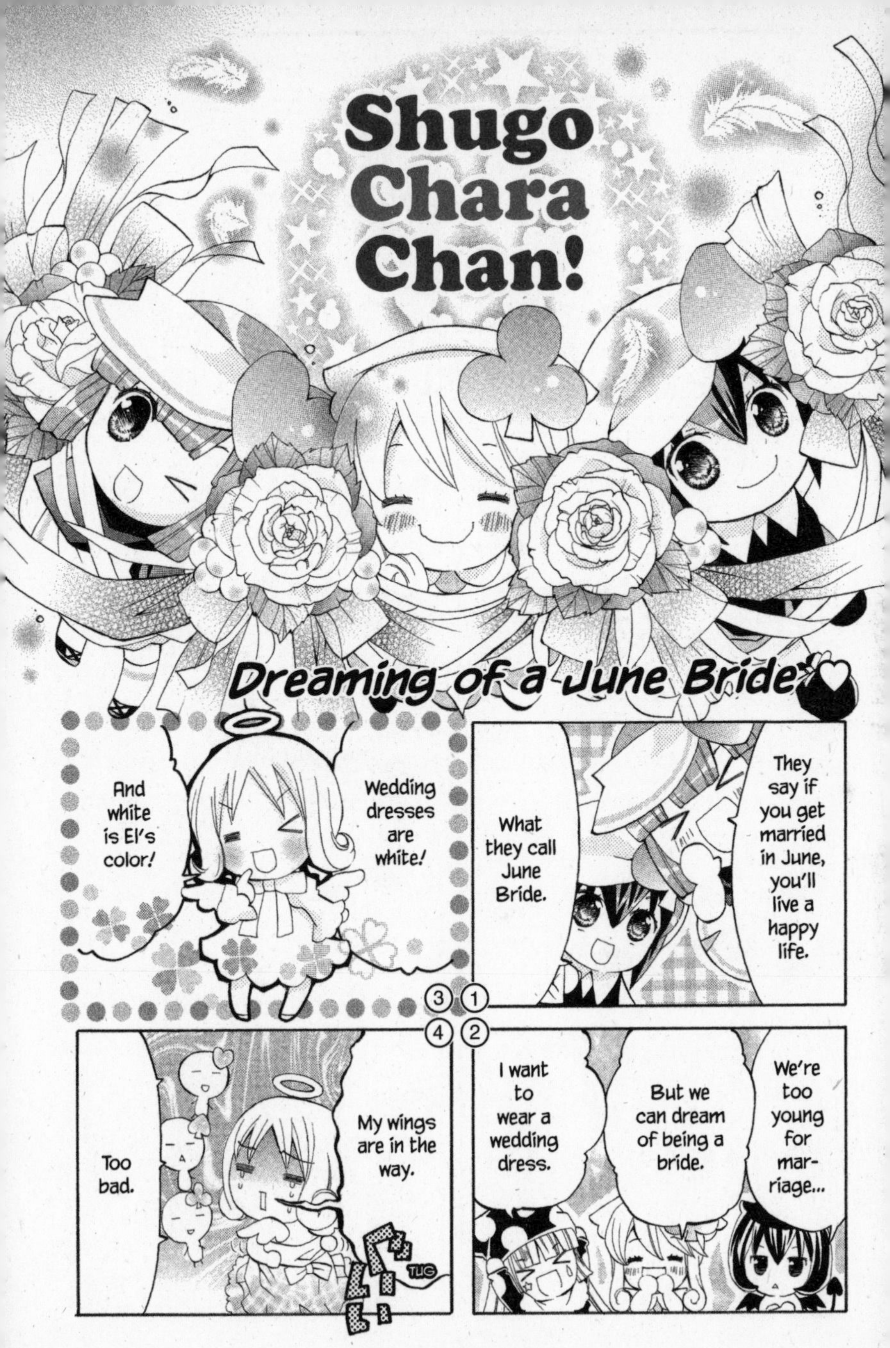
Shugo Chara Chan!
Dreaming of a June Bride
They say if you get married in June, you'll live a happy life.
What they call June Bride.
We're too young for mar-riage...
But we can dream of being a bride.
I want to wear a wedding dress.
Wedding dresses are white!
And white is El's color!
My wings are in the way.
TUG
Too bad.

Her Style

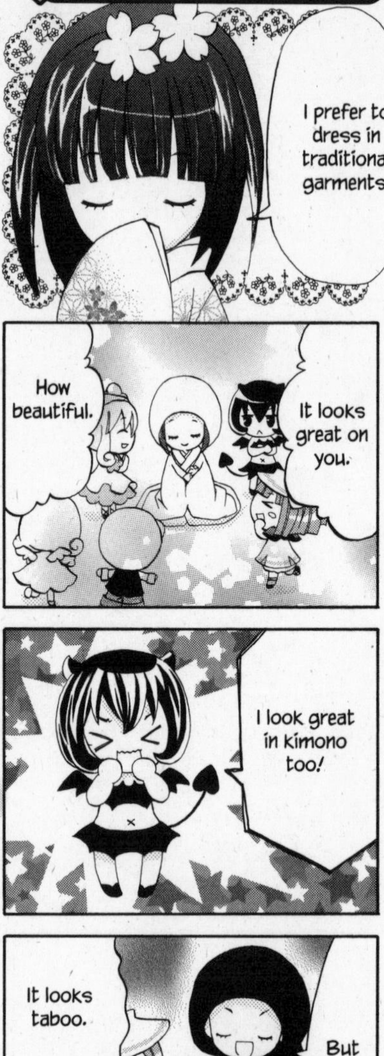
I prefer to dress in traditional garments.
It looks great on you.
How beautiful.
I look great in kimono too!
But it has to be black.
It looks taboo.
Didn't we say this before too?

Hey

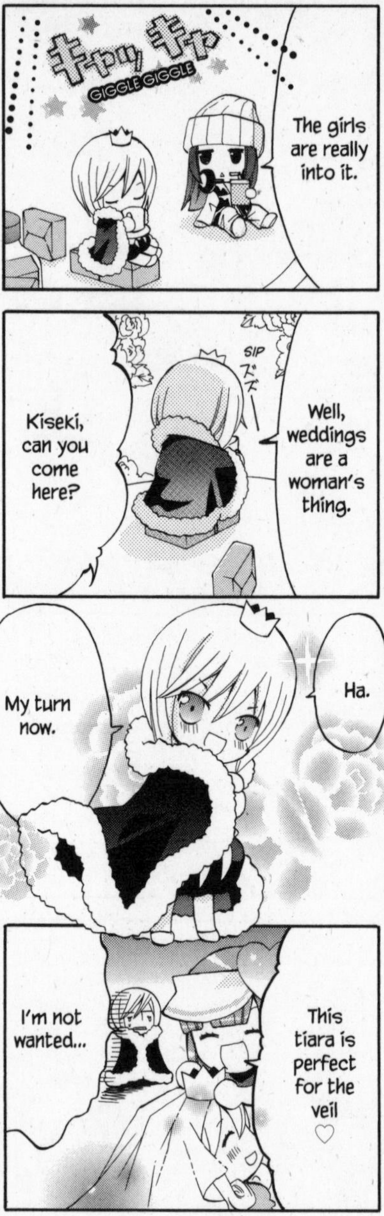
The girls are really into it.
キャッキャ
GIGGLE GIGGLE
Well, weddings are a woman's thing.
SIP
ズズ
Kiseki, can you come here?
Ha.
My turn now.
This tiara is perfect for the veil ♡
I'm not wanted...

Wait a Minute!

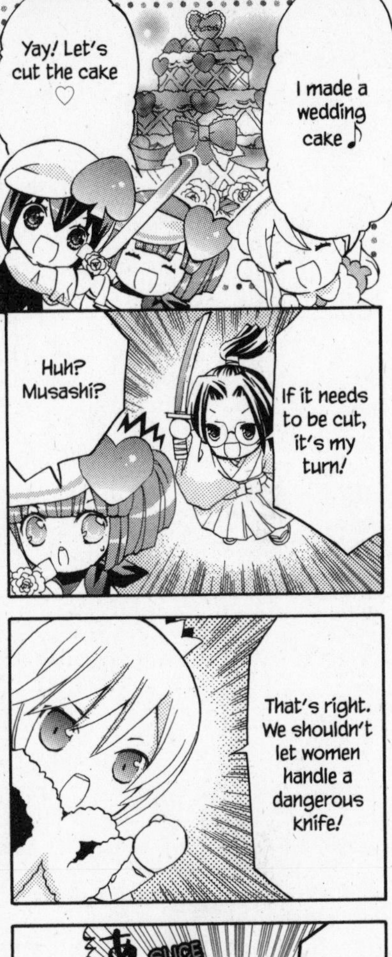
I made a wedding cake ♪
Yay! Let's cut the cake ♡
If it needs to be cut, it's my turn!
Huh? Musashi?
That's right. We shouldn't let women handle a dangerous knife!
One sword double attack!!
SLICE
Aww!
They ruined our dreams!!!

Final Option

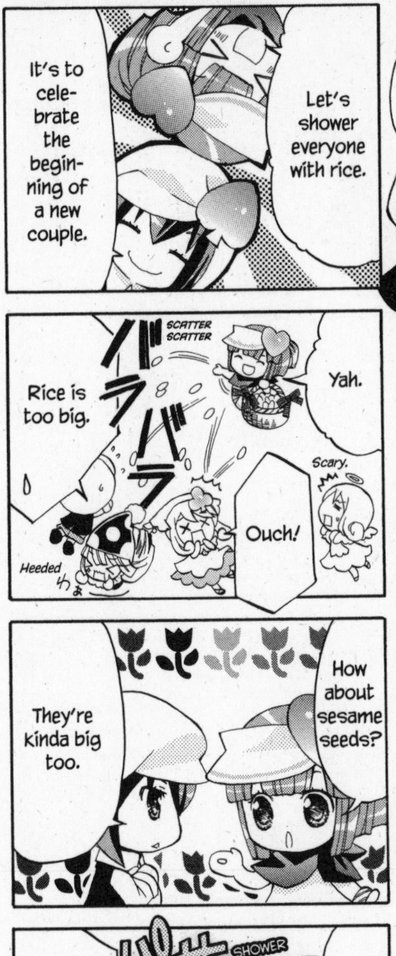
Let's shower everyone with rice.
It's to celebrate the beginning of a new couple.
Yah.
SCATTER SCATTER
Scary.
Rice is too big.
Ouch!
Heeded
How about sesame seeds?
They're kinda big too.
Then we'll use salt ☆
SHOWER
It looks like a sumo wrestling match!!

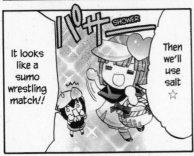

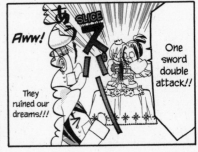

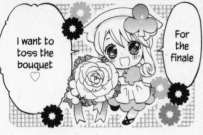

How Small will it Get?

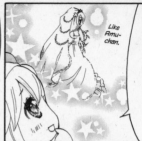

Wedding dresses look better if you're tall and slender.
Like Amu-chan.
I want to be tall and slender.
To be the person you want to be.
Maybe we'll hatch Guardian Eggs too ♪
Wow!
Would they be the size of quail eggs?
And if that Guardian Egg hatched a Guardian Egg...
Like a Matryoshka nesting dolls!!
That's cute.

Yikes!!

For the finale
I want to toss the bouquet ♡
The person who catches the bouquet will be the next bride.
キャー♡
TOSS
!!!
ひょーん
SCREAM♡
ギャー
Ack!!
DROP
PEEK
Why won't anyone catch it?

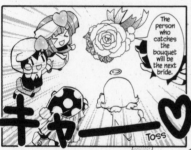

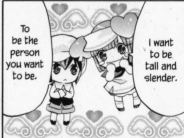

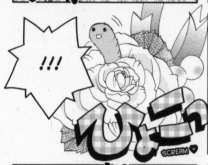

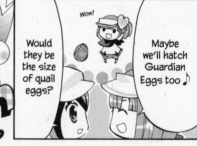

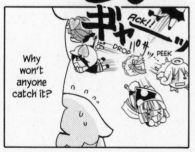

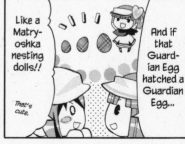

Shugo Chara Chan!

ONE-PANEL MANGA ☆

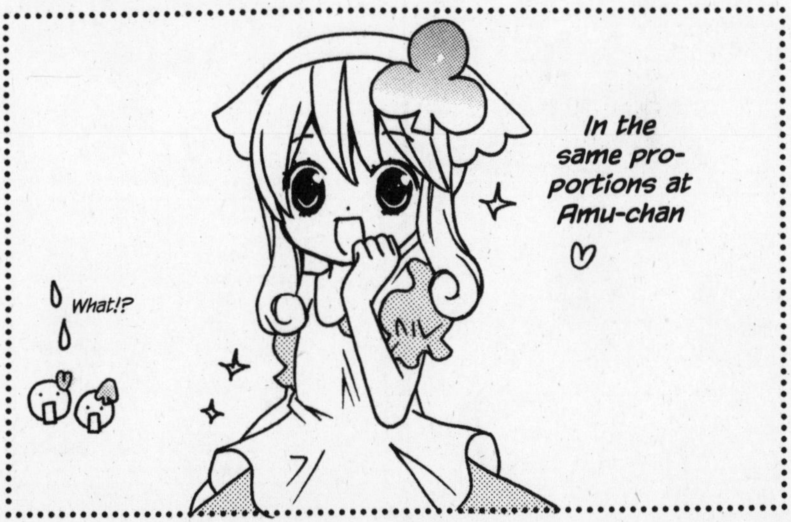
In the same pro-portions at Amu-chan
What!?

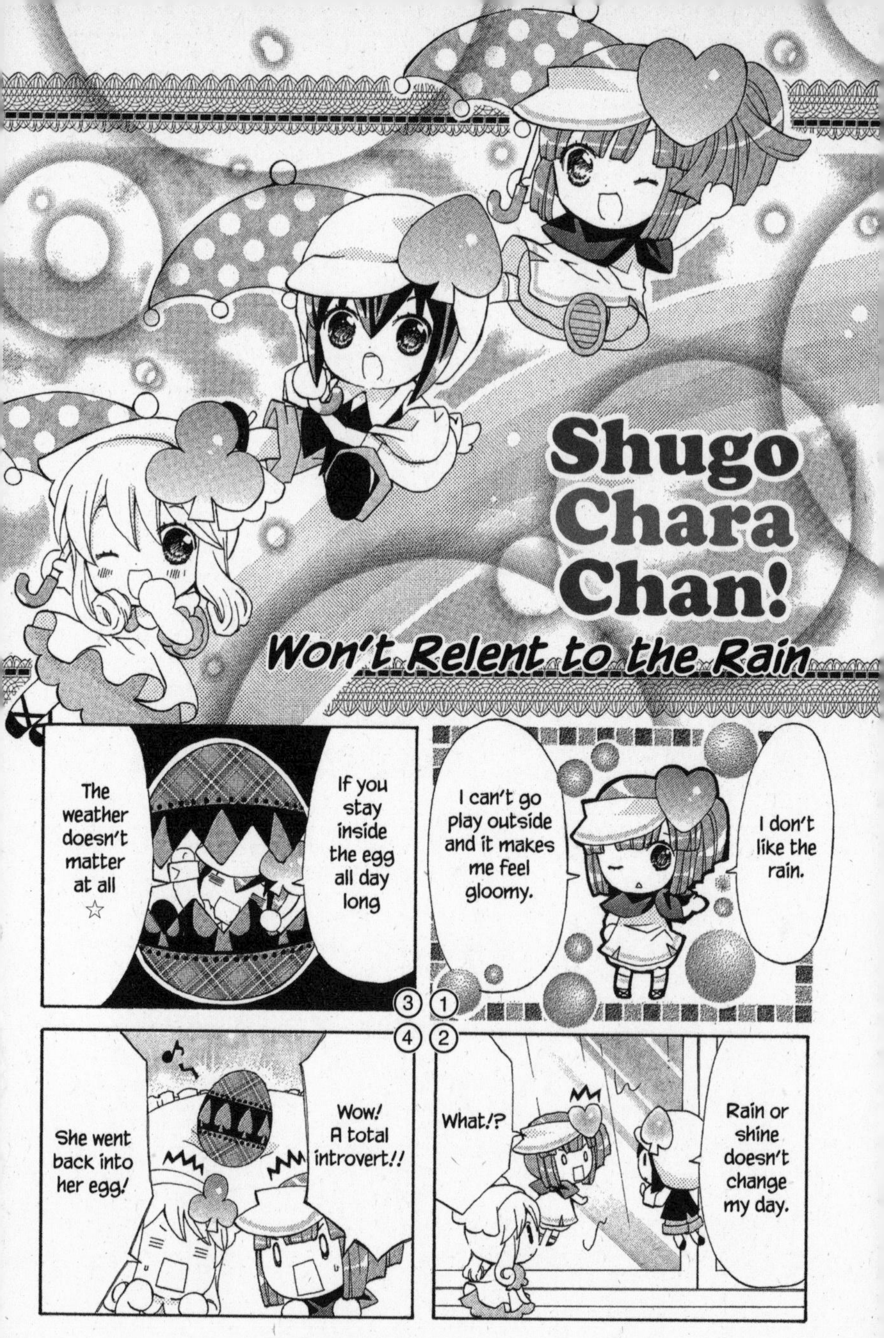
Shugo Chara Chan!
Won't Relent to the Rain
I don't like the rain.
I can't go play outside and it makes me feel gloomy.
Rain or shine doesn't change my day.
What!?
If you stay inside the egg all day long
The weather doesn't matter at all ☆
Wow! A total introvert!!
She went back into her egg!

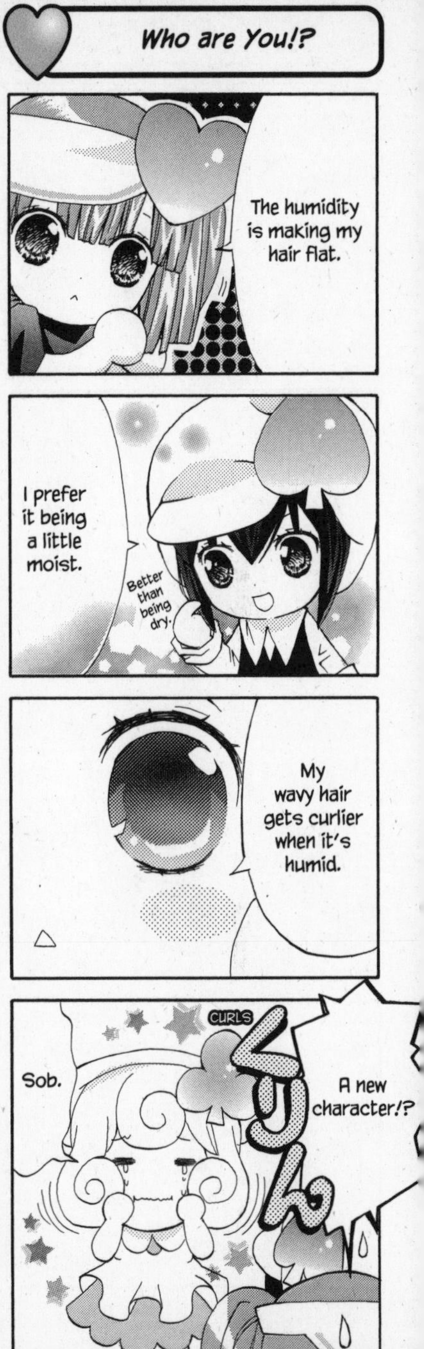
Who are You!?
The humidity is making my hair flat.
I prefer it being a little moist.
Better than being dry.
My wavy hair gets curlier when it's humid.
A new character!?
くりん
CURLS
Sob.

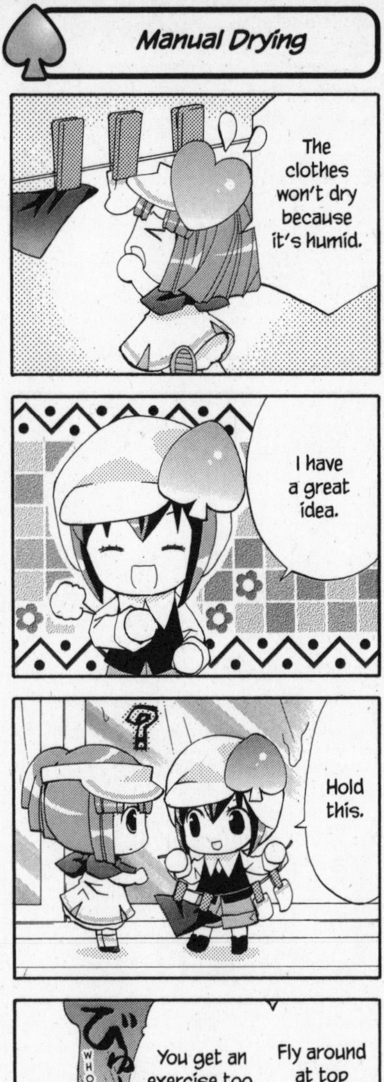
Manual Drying
The clothes won't dry because it's humid.
I have a great idea.
Hold this.
Fly around at top speed, and they'll dry ☆
You get an exercise too, so double awesome!
びゅ〜ん
WHOOSH
I'm tired.

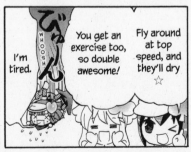

Around Where?

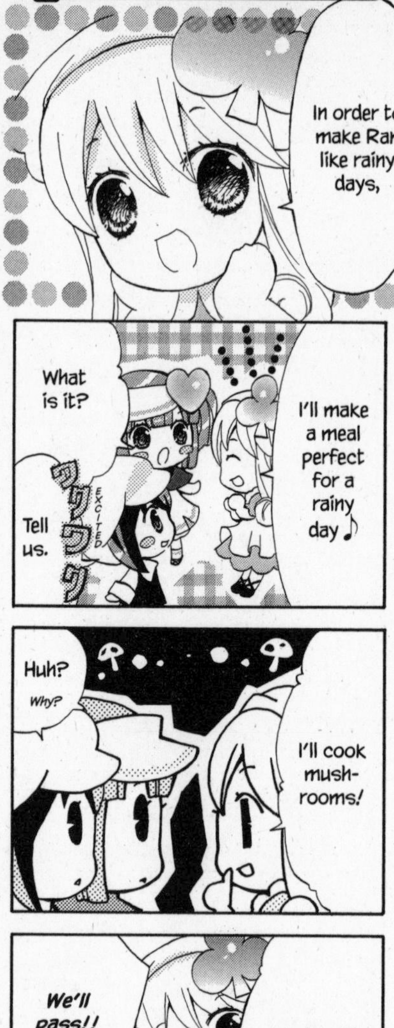
In order to make Ran like rainy days,
I'll make a meal perfect for a rainy day♪
What is it?
Tell us.
ワクワク EXCITED
I'll cook mush-rooms!
Huh?
Why?
It's humid, so I can get them around here ♡
We'll pass!!

Some Fun

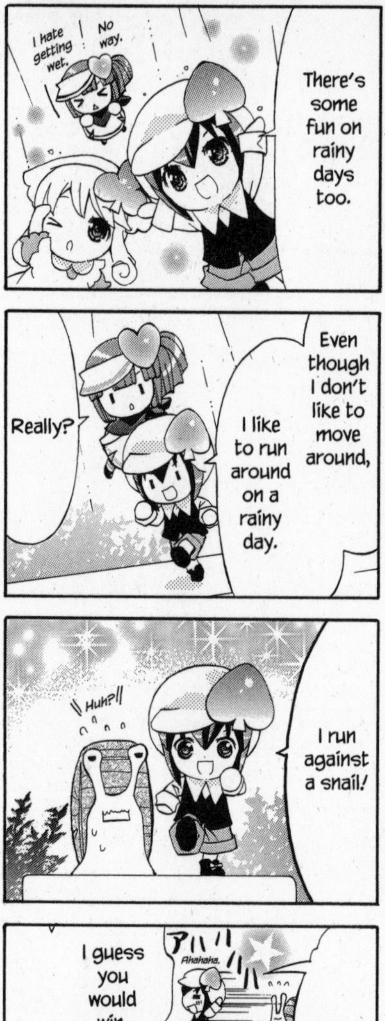
There's some fun on rainy days too.
No way.
I hate getting wet.
Even though I don't like to move around,
I like to run around on a rainy day.
Really?
I run against a snail!
Huh?!
The joy of winning ♡
アハハ Ahahaha.
I guess you would win.
That's sad.

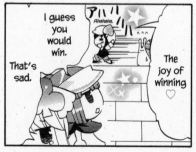

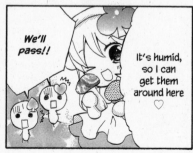

Su's Tragedy

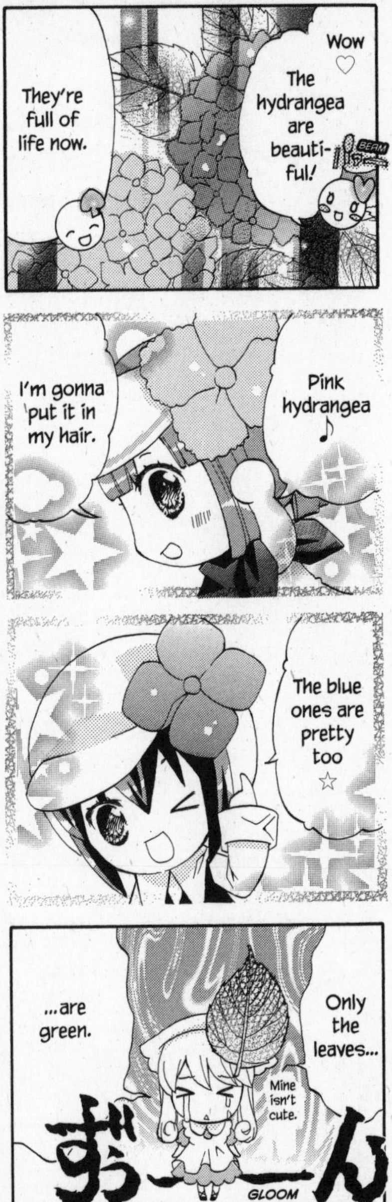
Wow ♡ The hydrangea are beauti-ful!
BEAM
They're full of life now.
Pink hydrangea ♪
I'm gonna put it in my hair.
The blue ones are pretty too ☆
Only the leaves...
...are green.
Mine isn't cute.
ずぅーん
GLOOM

Everyone Happy

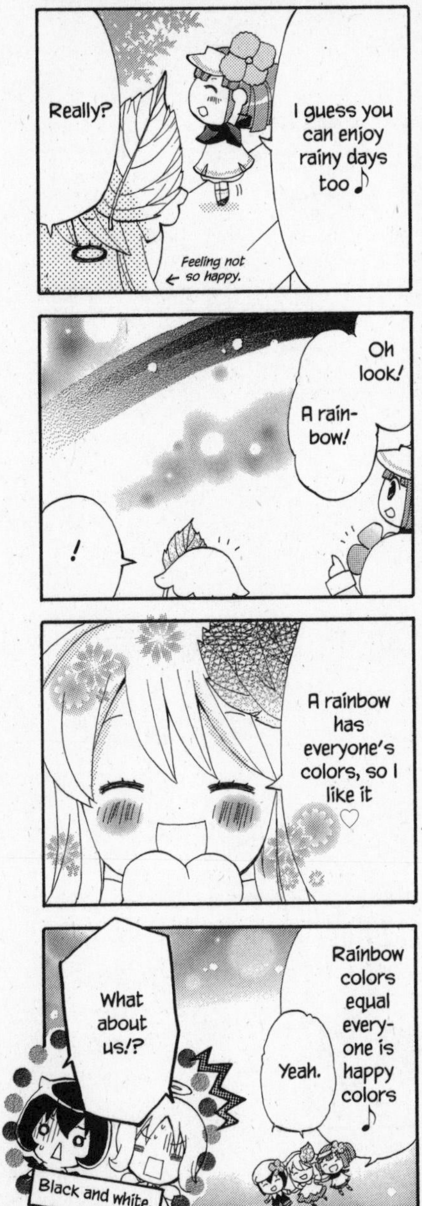
I guess you can enjoy rainy days too ♪
Really?
Feeling not so happy.
Oh look! A rain-bow!
!
A rainbow has everyone's colors, so I like it ♡
Rainbow colors equal every-one is happy colors ♪
Yeah.
What about us!?
Black and white.

Summer Edition Starts on the Next Page!

Shugo Chara Chan!

ONE-PANEL MANGA ☆

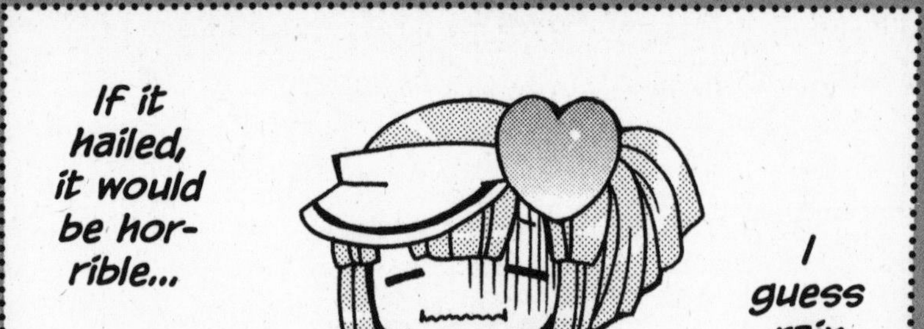

I guess rain isn't so bad.
If it hailed, it would be hor-rible...
Ran thinks further.

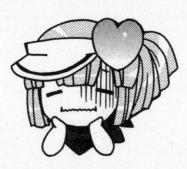

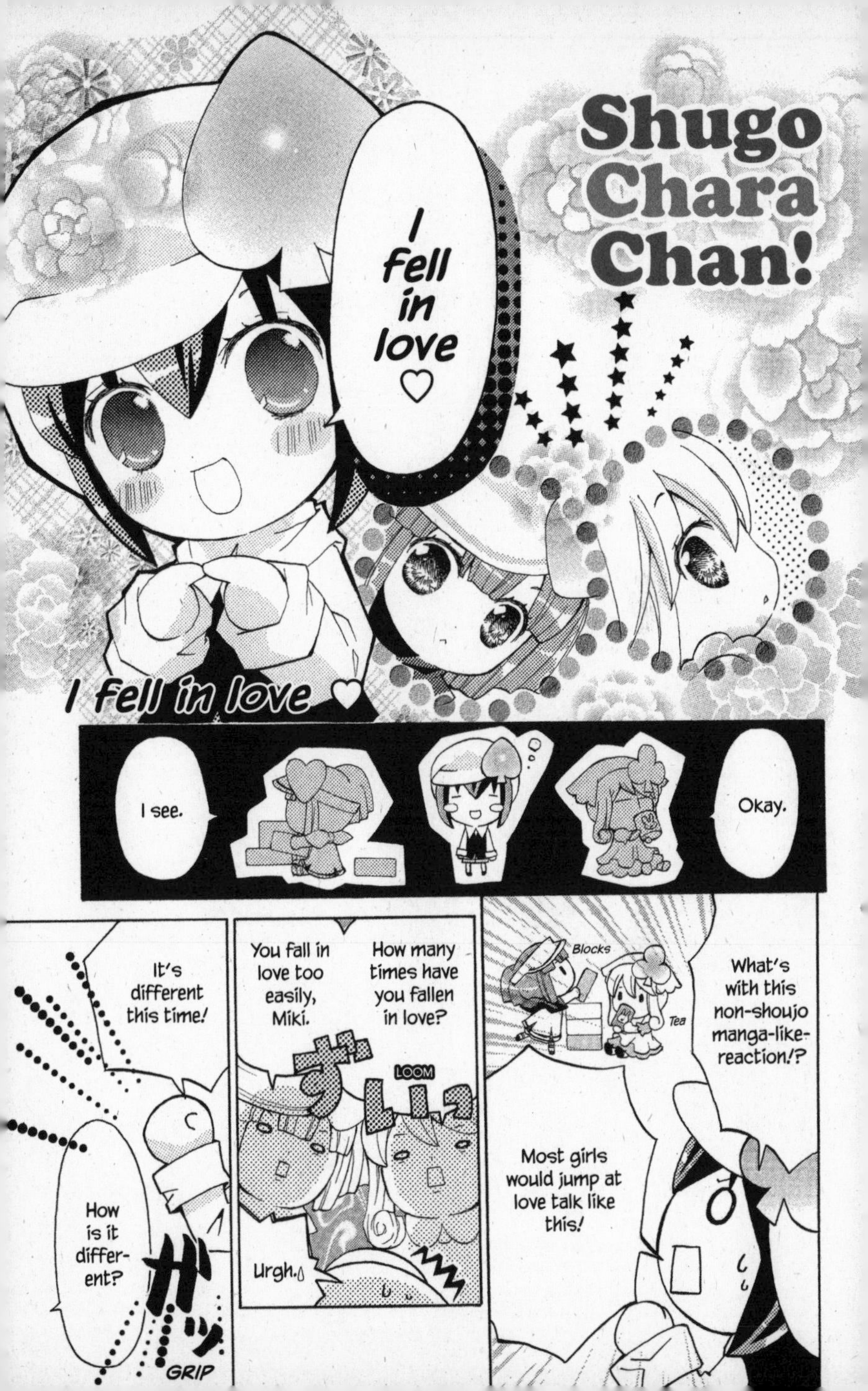

Shugo Chara Chan!
I fell in love ♡
I fell in love ♡
Okay.
I see.
What's with this non-shoujo manga-like-reaction!?
Blocks
Tea
Most girls would jump at love talk like this!
How many times have you fallen in love?
You fall in love too easily, Miki.
LOOM
Urgh.
It's different this time!
How is it different?
GRIP

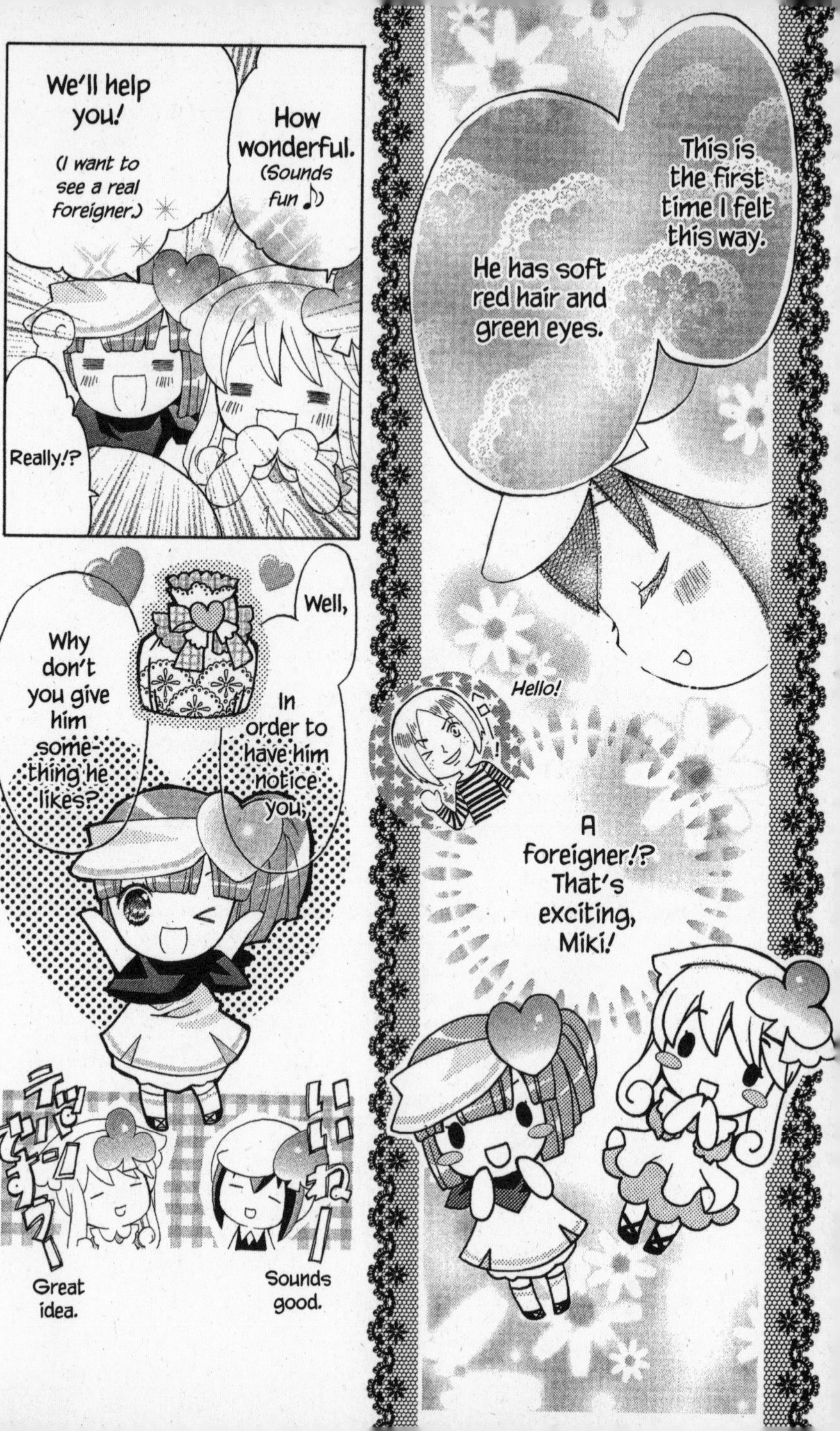
This is the first time I felt this way.
He has soft red hair and green eyes.
Hello!
A foreigner!? That's exciting, Miki!
How wonderful. (Sounds fun ♪)
We'll help you! (I want to see a real foreigner.)
Really!?
Well,
In order to have him notice you,
Why don't you give him something he likes?
いいね！
Sounds good.
Great idea.

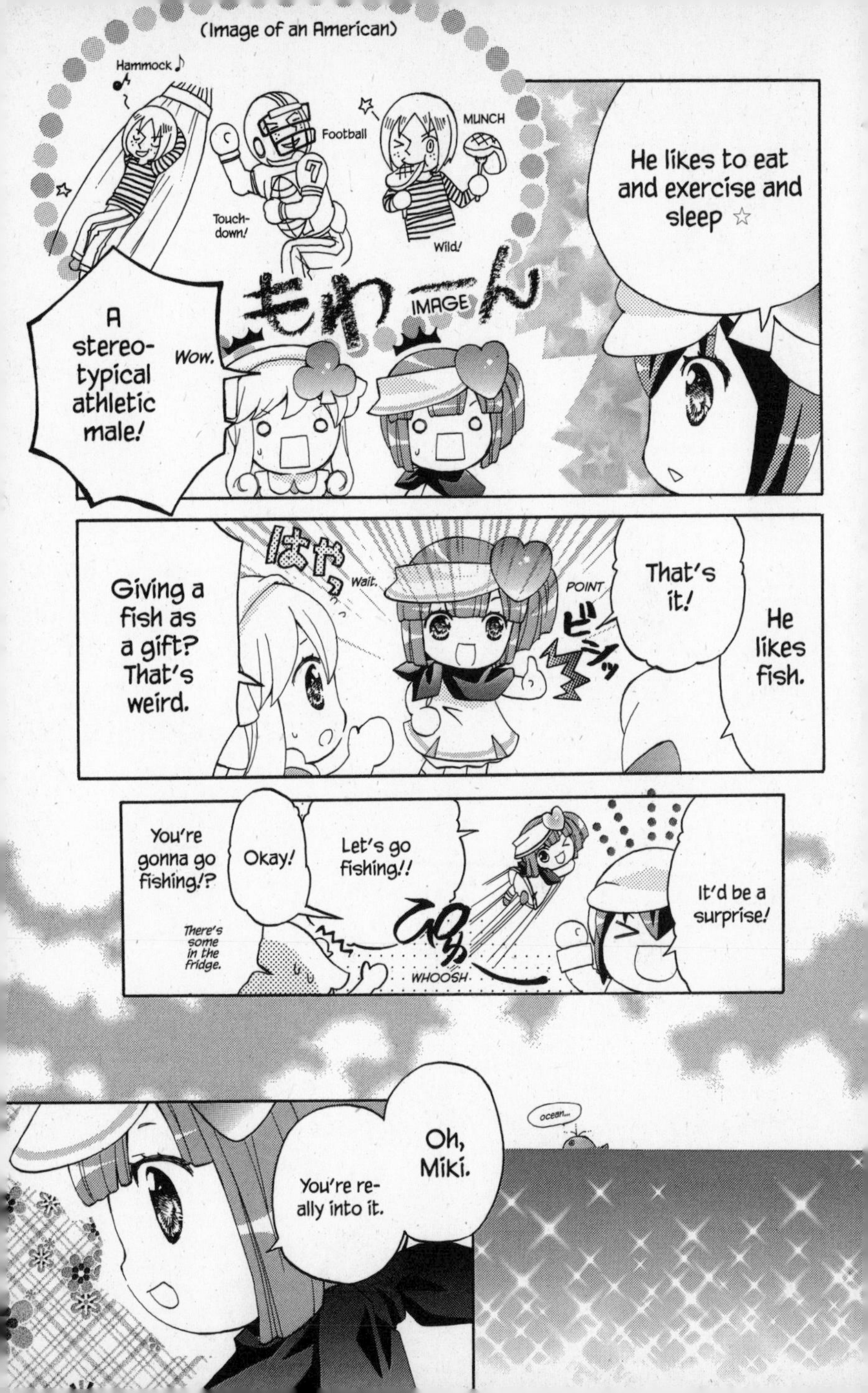
He likes to eat and exercise and sleep ☆
(Image of an American)
Hammock ♪
Football
Touch-down!
MUNCH
Wild!
もわーん
IMAGE
Wow.
A stereo-typical athletic male!
That's it!
He likes fish.
POINT
Wait.
Giving a fish as a gift? That's weird.
It'd be a surprise!
Let's go fishing!!
WHOOSH
Okay!
You're gonna go fishing!?
There's some in the fridge.
Oh, Miki.
You're re-ally into it.
ocean...

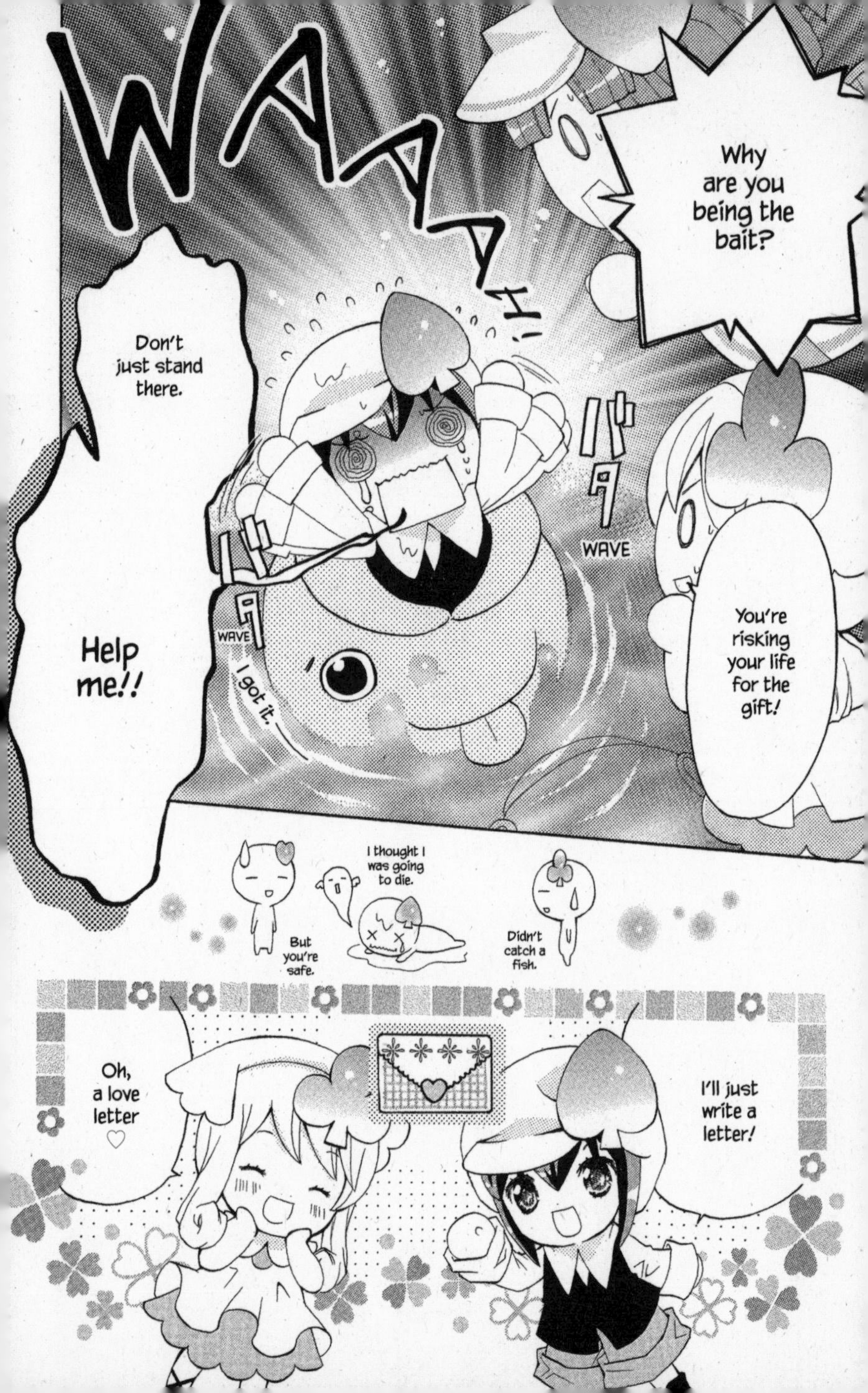
Why are you being the bait?
WAAAAH!!
You're risking your life for the gift!
バタ
WAVE
バタ
WAVE
I got it.
Don't just stand there.
Help me!!
Didn't catch a fish.
I thought I was going to die.
But you're safe.
I'll just write a letter!
Oh, a love letter ♡

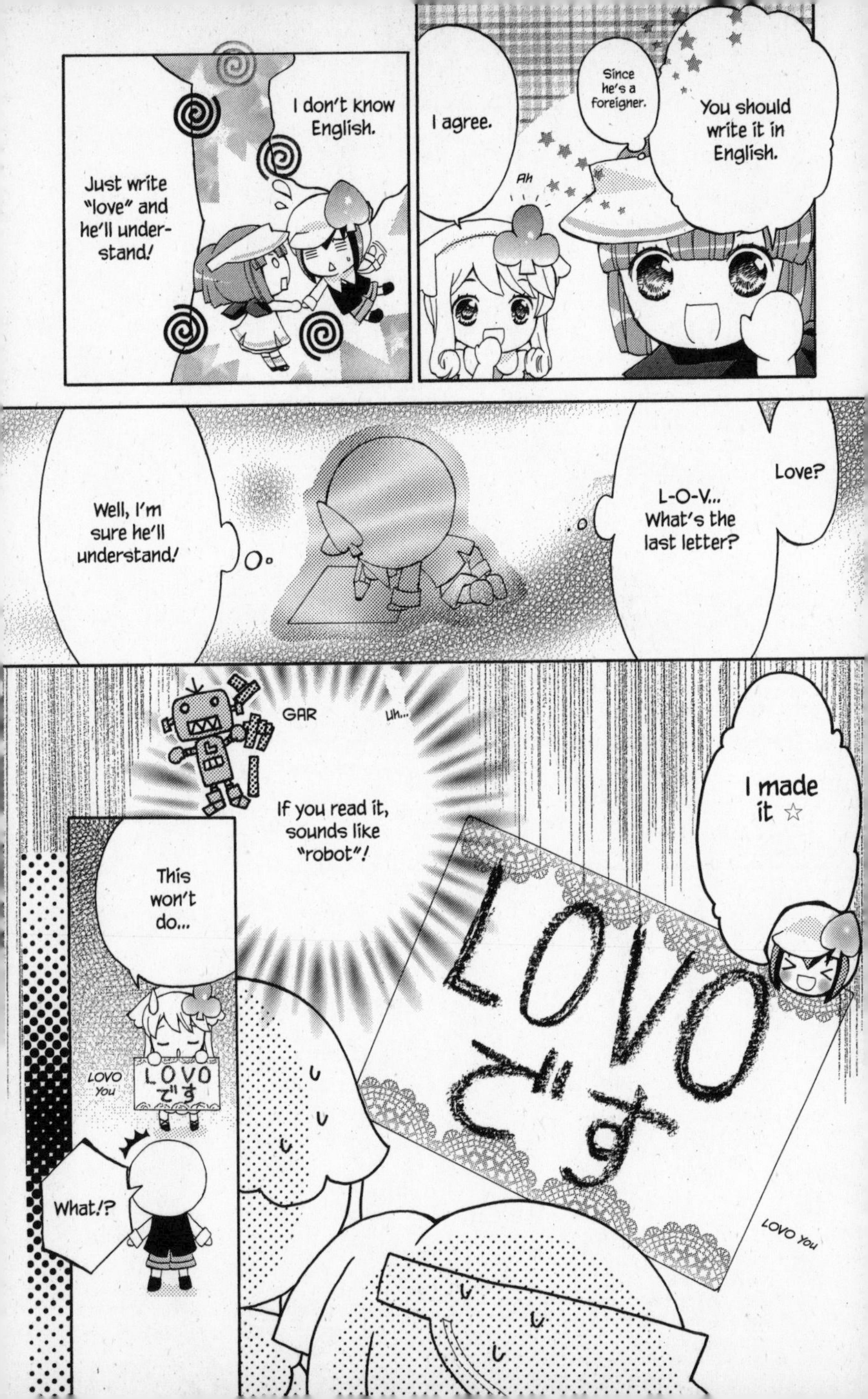
You should write it in English.
Since he's a foreigner.
Ah
I agree.
I don't know English.
Just write "love" and he'll understand!
Love?
L-O-V... What's the last letter?
Well, I'm sure he'll understand!
I made it ☆
LOVO です
LOVO You
Uh...
GAR
If you read it, sounds like "robot"!
This won't do...
LOVO です
LOVO You
What!?

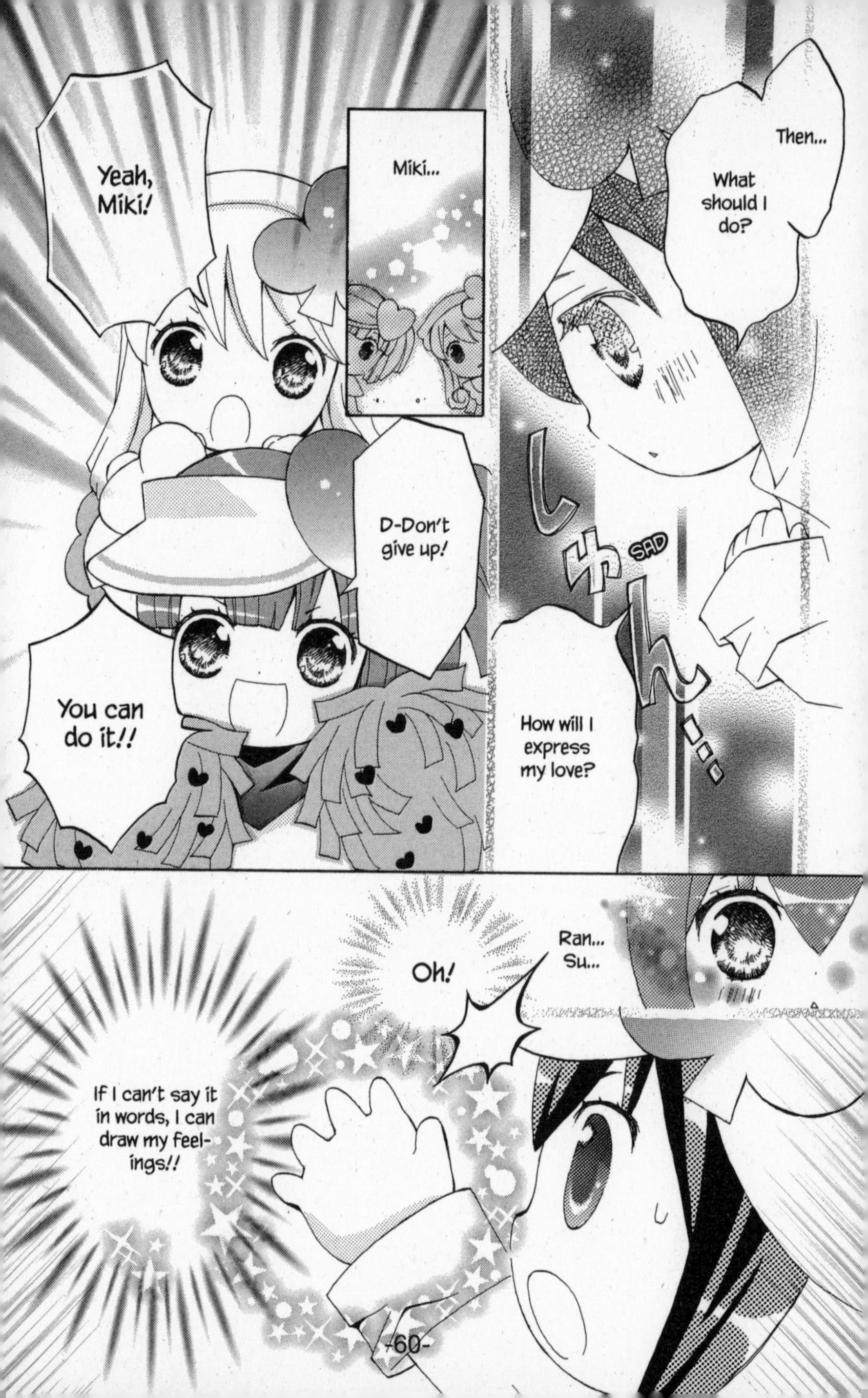
Then...
What should I do?
しゅん SAD
How will I express my love?
Miki...
Yeah, Miki!
D-Don't give up!
You can do it!!
Ran... Su...
Oh!
If I can't say it in words, I can draw my feel-ings!!

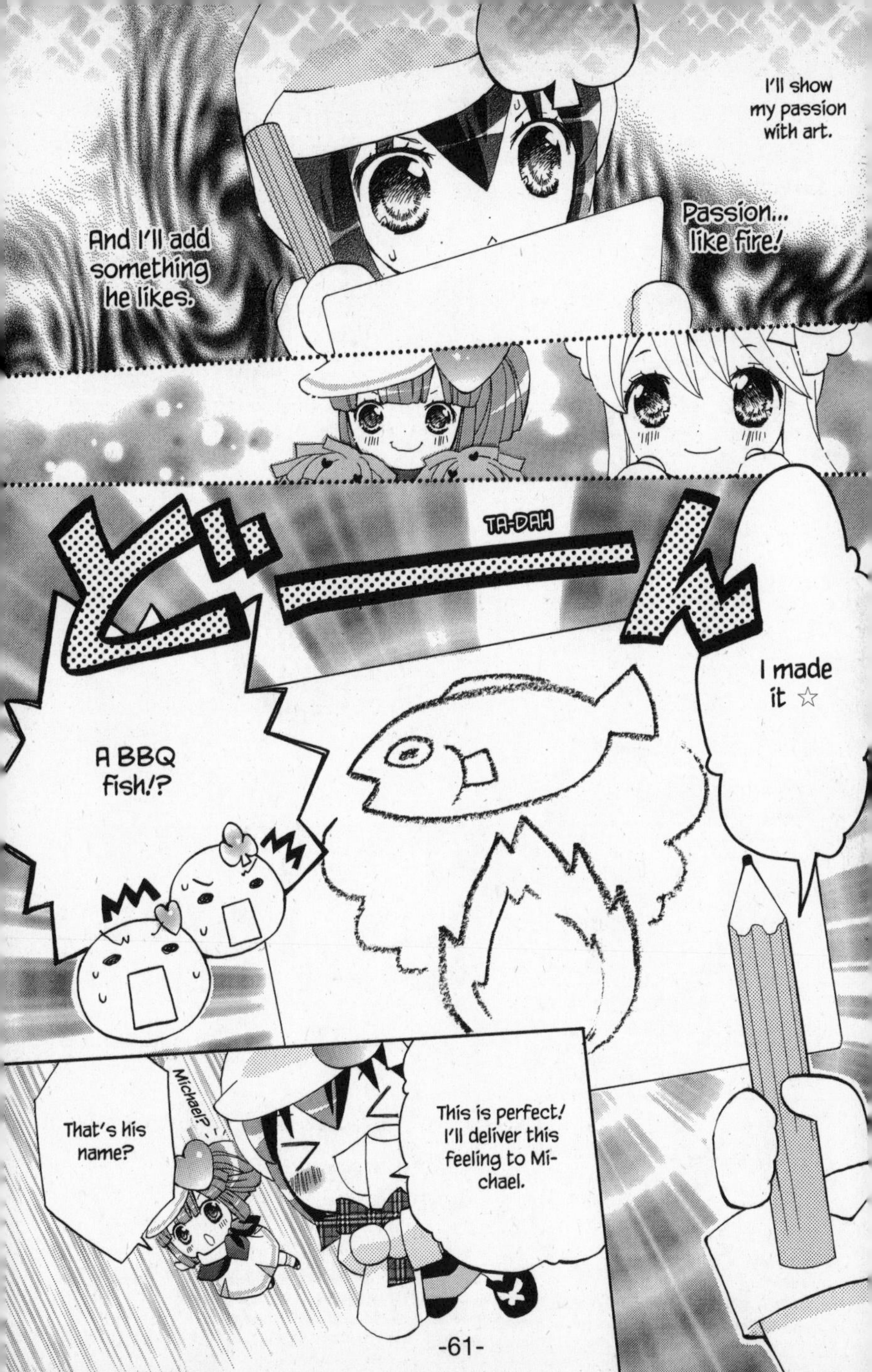
I'll show my passion with art.
Passion... like fire!
And I'll add something he likes.
どーん
TA-DAH
I made it ☆
A BBQ fish!?
This is perfect! I'll deliver this feeling to Mi-chael.
Michael!?
That's his name?

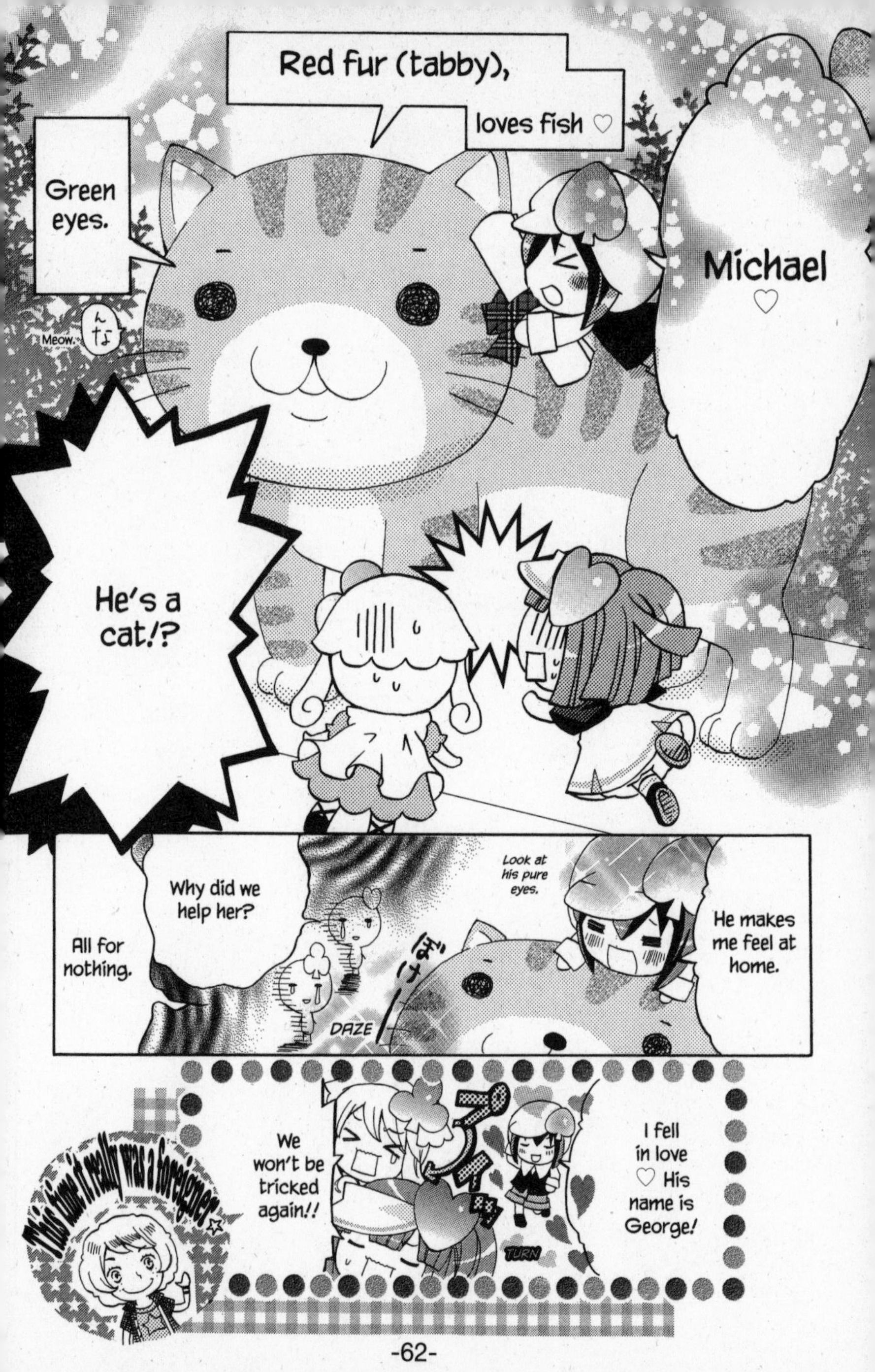
Red fur (tabby),
loves fish ♡
Michael ♡
Green eyes.
んな
Meow.
He's a cat!?
He makes me feel at home.
Look at his pure eyes.
ぽけー
DAZE
Why did we help her?
All for nothing.
I fell in love ♡ His name is George!
TURN
We won't be tricked again!!
This time it really was a foreigner☆

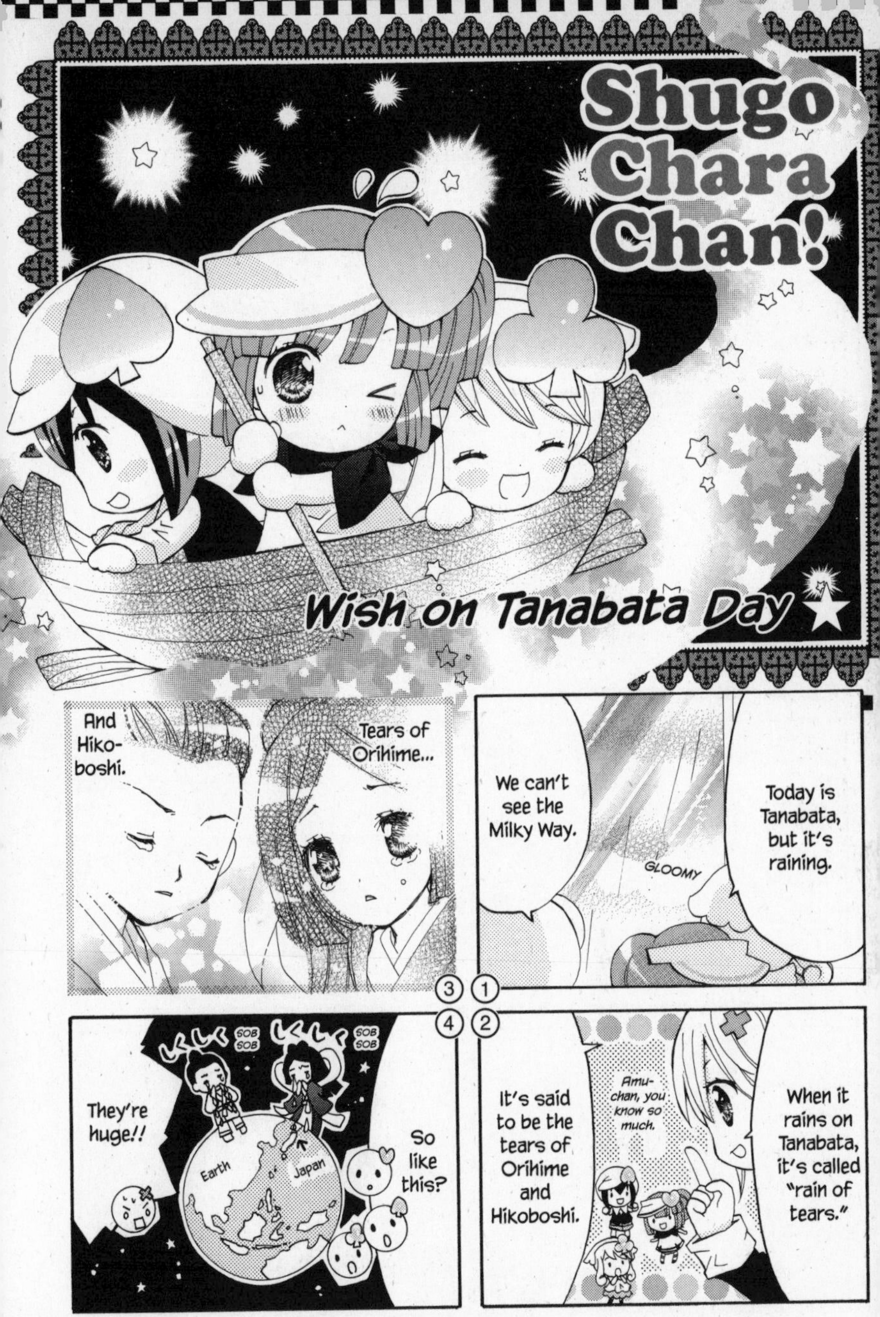
Shugo Chara Chan!
Wish on Tanabata Day
Today is Tanabata, but it's raining.
GLOOMY
We can't see the Milky Way.
When it rains on Tanabata, it's called "rain of tears."
Amu-chan, you know so much.
It's said to be the tears of Orihime and Hikoboshi.
Tears of Orihime...
And Hiko-boshi.
So like this?
しくしく
SOB SOB
しくしく
SOB SOB
Earth
Japan
They're huge!!

Stars are...

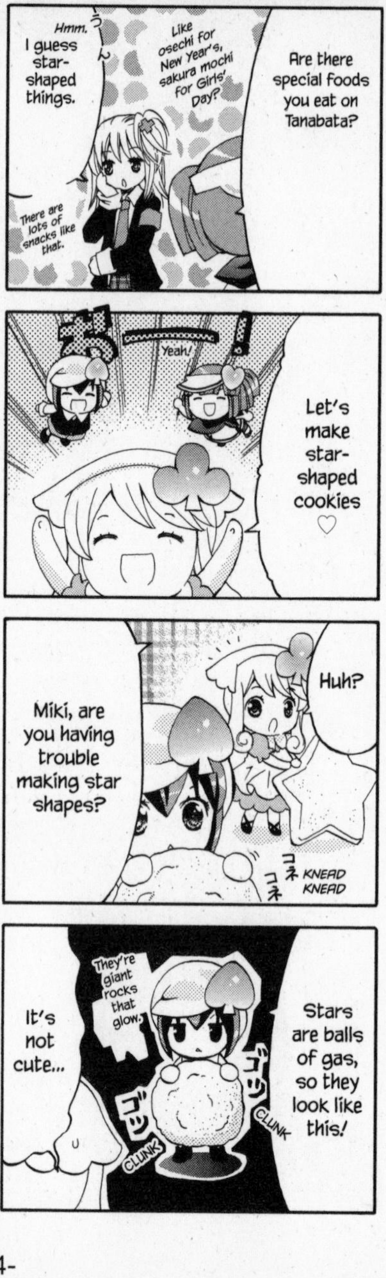
Are there special foods you eat on Tanabata?
Like osechi for New Year's, sakura mochi for Girls' Day?
Hmm. うん
I guess star-shaped things.
There are lots of snacks like that.
Let's make star-shaped cookies ♡
Yeah!
Huh?
Miki, are you having trouble making star shapes?
コネ コネ KNEAD KNEAD
Stars are balls of gas, so they look like this!
ゴツ CLUNK
ゴツ CLUNK
They're giant rocks that glow.
It's not cute...

These are Starfish

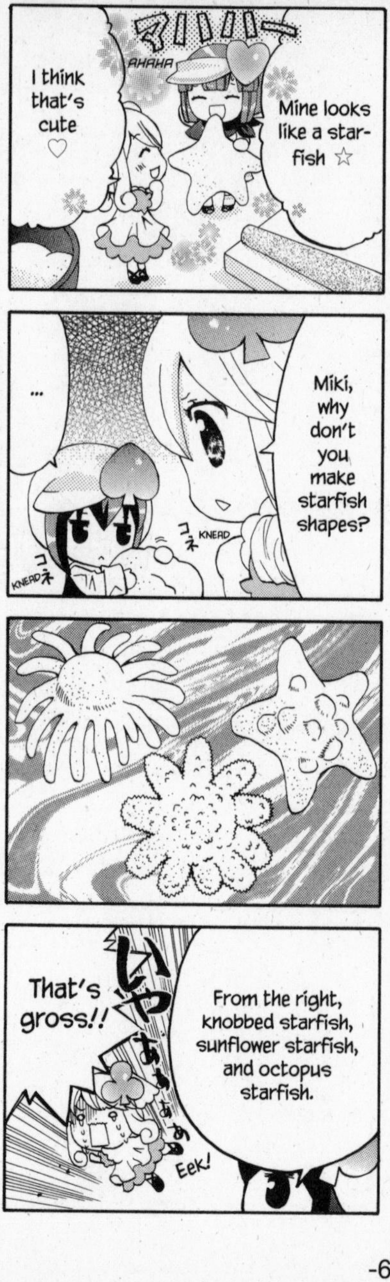
Mine looks like a star-fish ☆
AHAHA
I think that's cute ♡
Miki, why don't you make starfish shapes?
コネ KNEAD
コネ KNEAD
...
From the right, knobbed starfish, sunflower starfish, and octopus starfish.
いやああああ
Eek!
That's gross!!

Alone Time

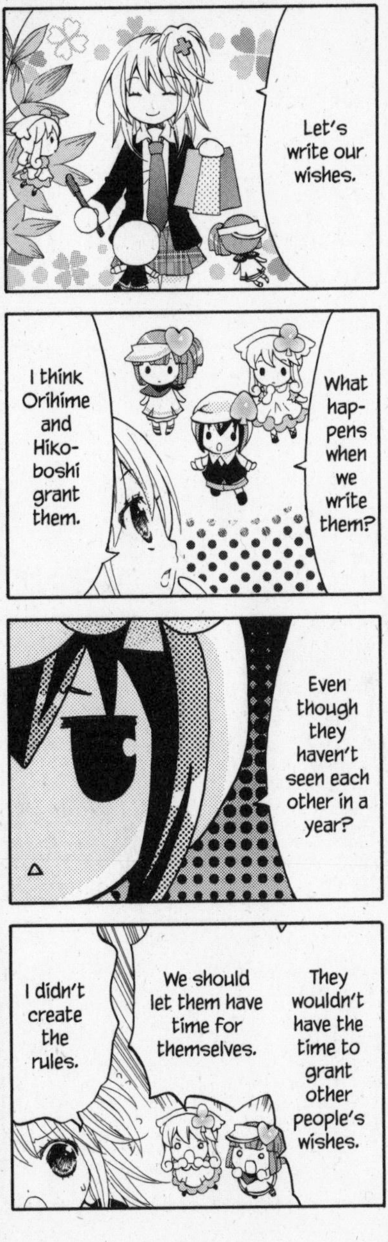
Let's write our wishes.
What hap-pens when we write them?
I think Orihime and Hiko-boshi grant them.
Even though they haven't seen each other in a year?
They wouldn't have the time to grant other people's wishes.
We should let them have time for themselves.
I didn't create the rules.

Similar

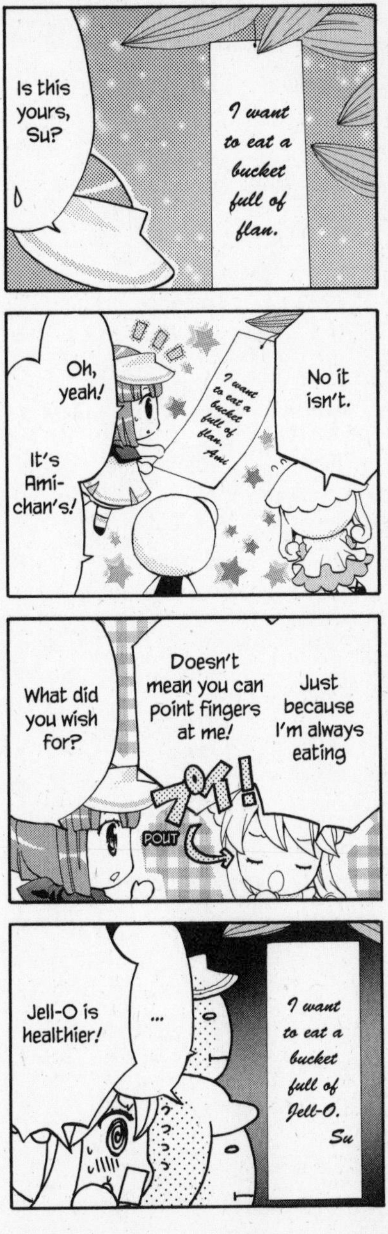
I want to eat a bucket full of flan.
Is this yours, Su?
No it isn't.
I want to eat a bucket full of flan. Ami
Oh, yeah!
It's Ami-chan's!
Just because I'm always eating
Doesn't mean you can point fingers at me!
POUT
What did you wish for?
I want to eat a bucket full of Jell-O. Su
...
Jell-O is healthier!

To the Details

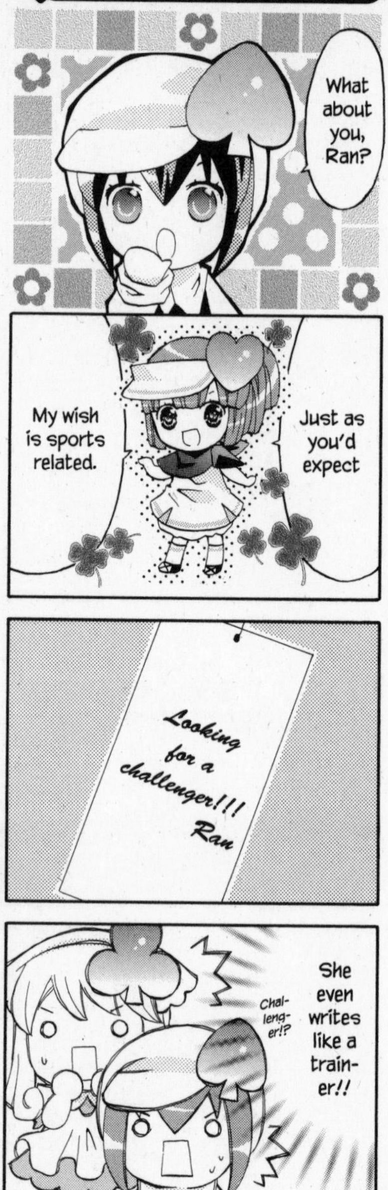

What about you, Ran?
Just as you'd expect
My wish is sports related.
Looking for a challenger!!! Ran
She even writes like a trainer!!
Challenger!?

Nonchalant

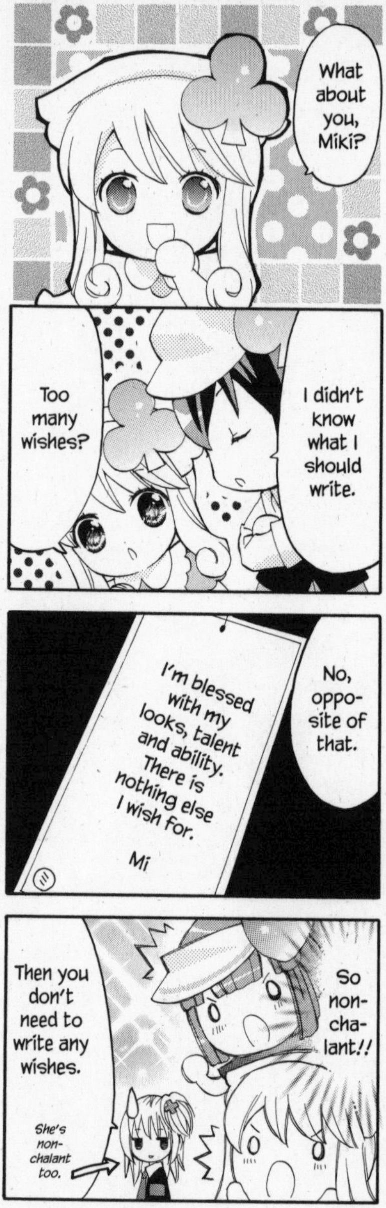

What about you, Miki?
I didn't know what I should write.
Too many wishes?
No, opposite of that.
I'm blessed with my looks, talent and ability. There is nothing else I wish for. Mi
So non-chalant!!
Then you don't need to write any wishes.
She's non-chalant too.

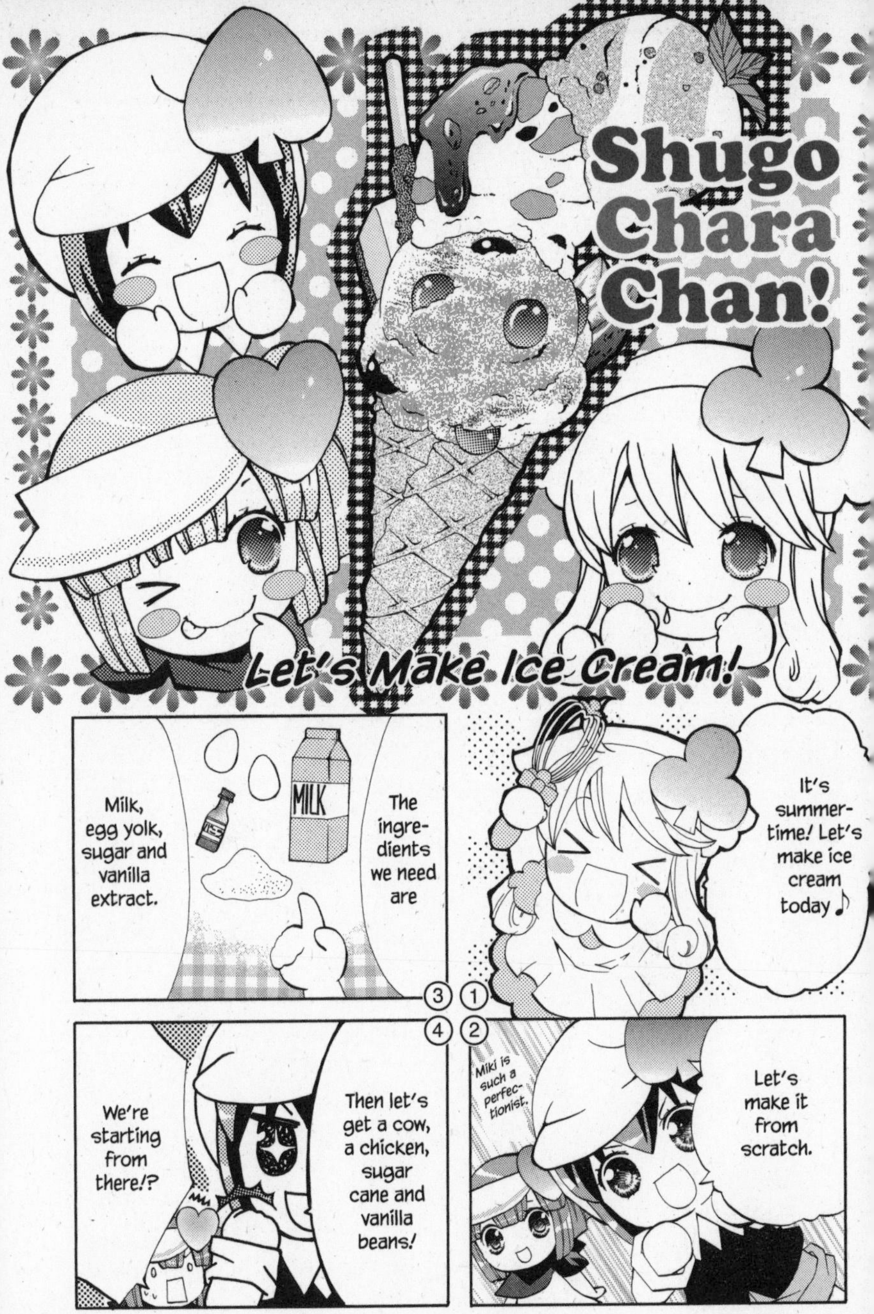
Shugo Chara Chan!
Let's Make Ice Cream!
It's summer-time! Let's make ice cream today♪
Let's make it from scratch.
Miki is such a perfec-tionist.
The ingre-dients we need are
Milk, egg yolk, sugar and vanilla extract.
MILK
Then let's get a cow, a chicken, sugar cane and vanilla beans!
We're starting from there!?

Have to be Careful

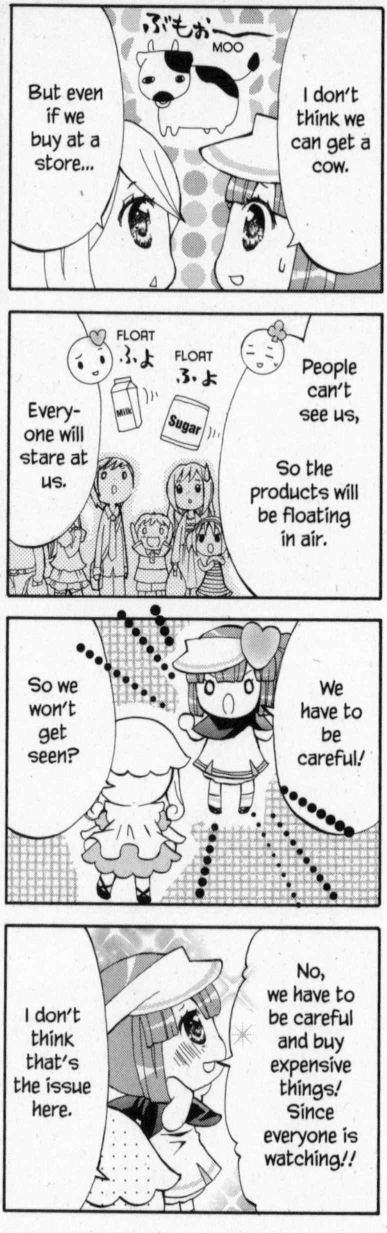
ぶもぉ〜
MOO
I don't think we can get a cow.
But even if we buy at a store...
People can't see us,
So the products will be floating in air.
FLOAT
ふよ
FLOAT
ふよ
Milk
Sugar
Every-one will stare at us.
We have to be careful!
So we won't get seen?
No, we have to be careful and buy expensive things! Since everyone is watching!!
I don't think that's the issue here.

Cracking Eggs

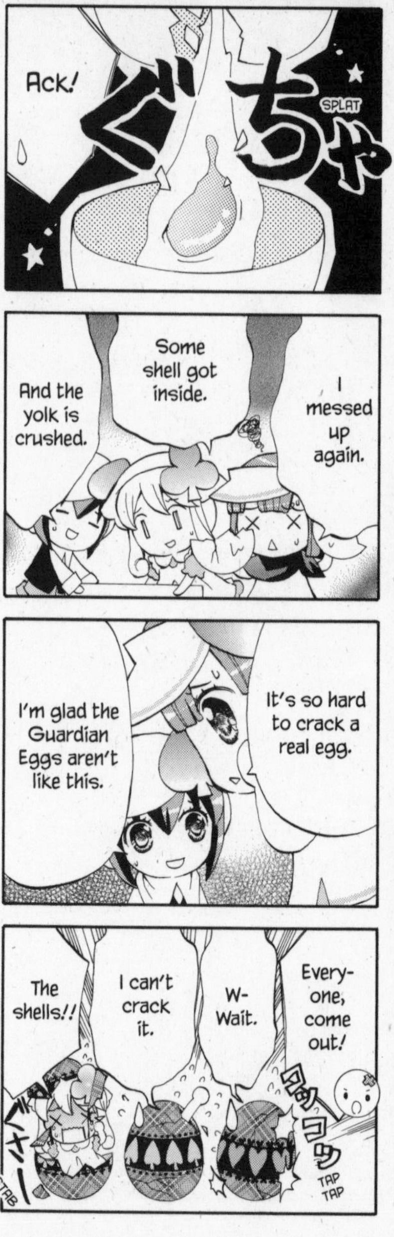
ぐちゃ
SPLAT
Ack!
I messed up again.
Some shell got inside.
And the yolk is crushed.
It's so hard to crack a real egg.
I'm glad the Guardian Eggs aren't like this.
Every-one, come out!
TAP TAP
W-Wait.
I can't crack it.
The shells!!
STAB

That's the Plan

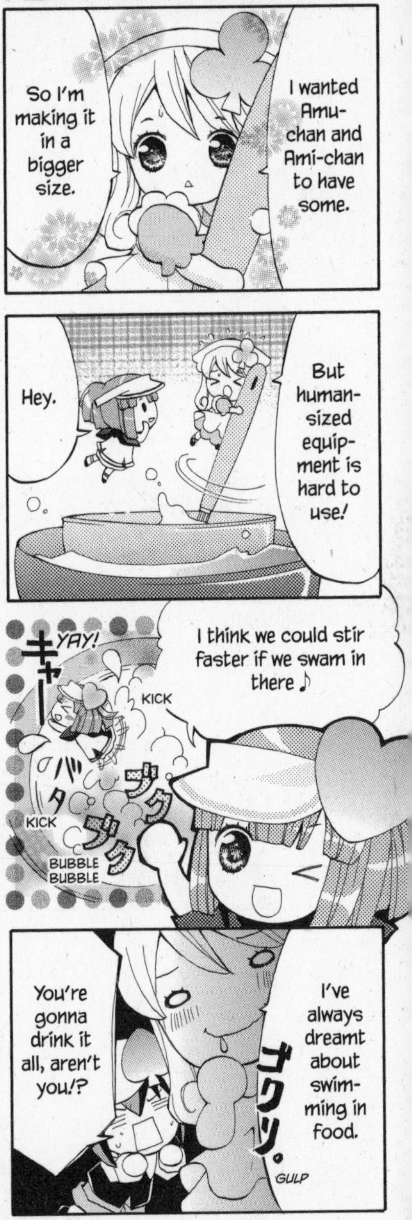
I wanted Amu-chan and Ami-chan to have some.
So I'm making it in a bigger size.
But human-sized equipment is hard to use!
Hey.
I think we could stir faster if we swam in there♪
YAY!
KICK
KICK
BUBBLE BUBBLE
I've always dreamt about swimming in food.
GULP
You're gonna drink it all, aren't you!?

Easy Way Out

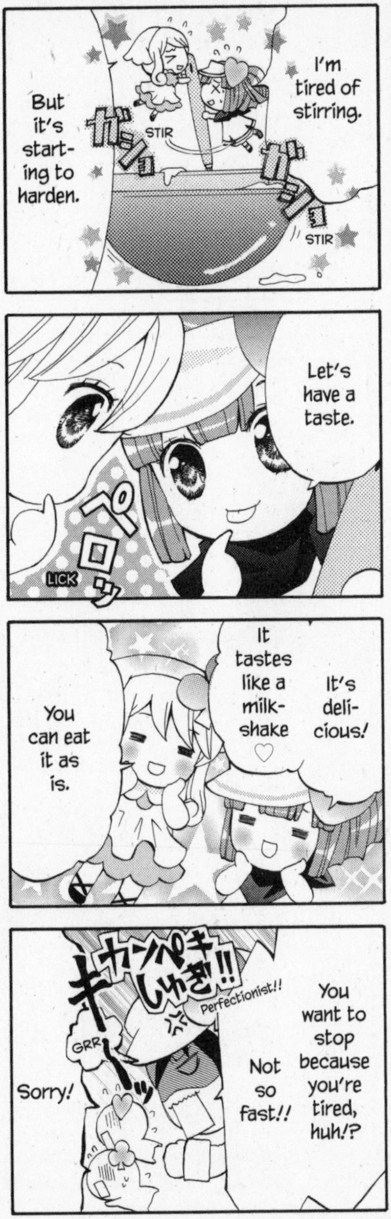
I'm tired of stirring.
STIR
STIR
But it's starting to harden.
Let's have a taste.
LICK
It's delicious!
It tastes like a milkshake ♡
You can eat it as is.
You want to stop because you're tired, huh!?
Not so fast!!
Perfectionist!!
GRR
Sorry!

Ack!

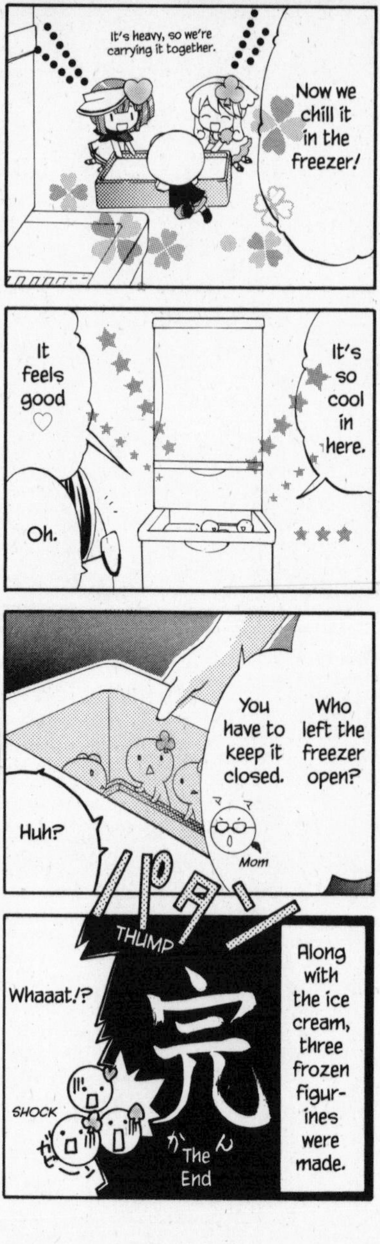
Now we chill it in the freezer!
It's heavy, so we're carrying it together.
It's so cool in here.
It feels good ♡
Oh.
Who left the freezer open?
You have to keep it closed.
Mom
Huh?
Along with the ice cream, three frozen figurines were made.
THUMP
完
かん
The End
Whaaat!?
SHOCK

You Saved Us

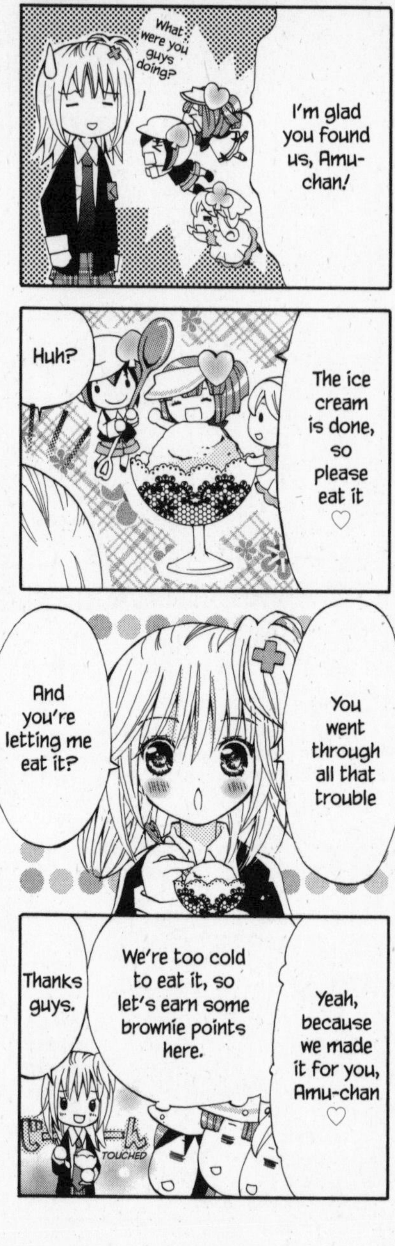
I'm glad you found us, Amu-chan!
What were you guys doing?
The ice cream is done, so please eat it ♡
Huh?
You went through all that trouble
And you're letting me eat it?
Yeah, because we made it for you, Amu-chan ♡
We're too cold to eat it, so let's earn some brownie points here.
Thanks guys.
TOUCHED

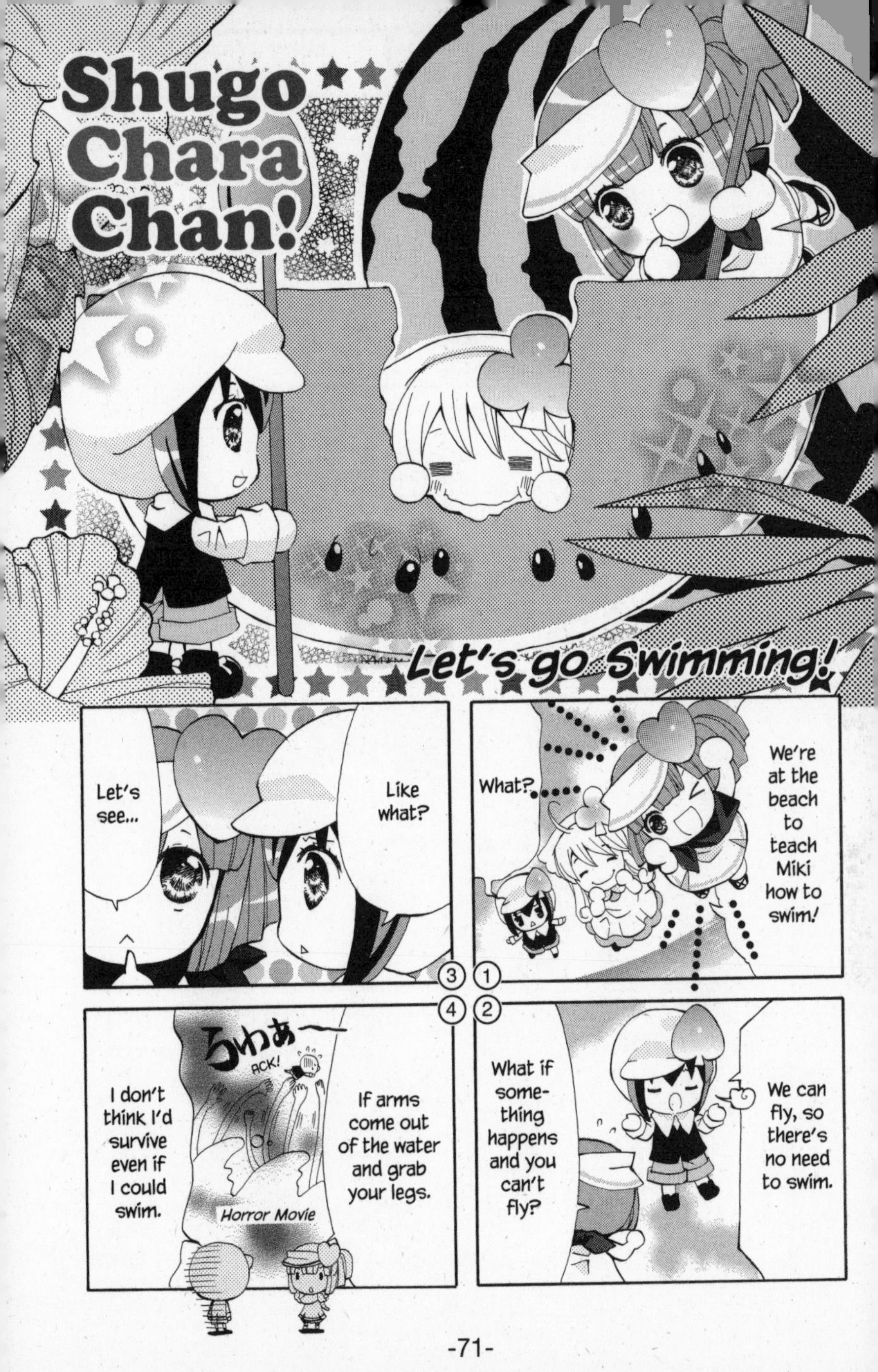
Shugo Chara Chan!
Let's go Swimming!
We're at the beach to teach Miki how to swim!
What?
We can fly, so there's no need to swim.
What if something happens and you can't fly?
Like what?
Let's see...
If arms come out of the water and grab your legs.
うわあ〜
ACK!
Horror Movie
I don't think I'd survive even if I could swim.

Won't Chase After Lost Ones

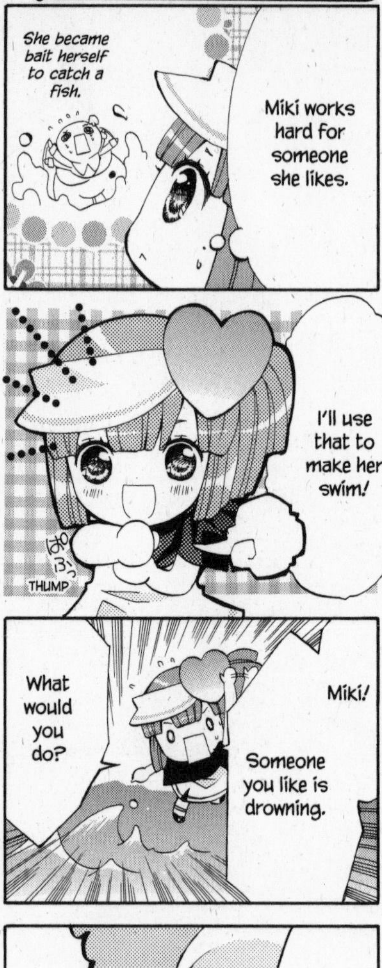
Miki works hard for someone she likes.
She became bait herself to catch a fish.
I'll use that to make her swim!
ぽふっ
THUMP
Miki!
Someone you like is drowning.
What would you do?
I'll find someone else to fall in love with.
ガビ
SHOCK
So cold!

Hidden Talent

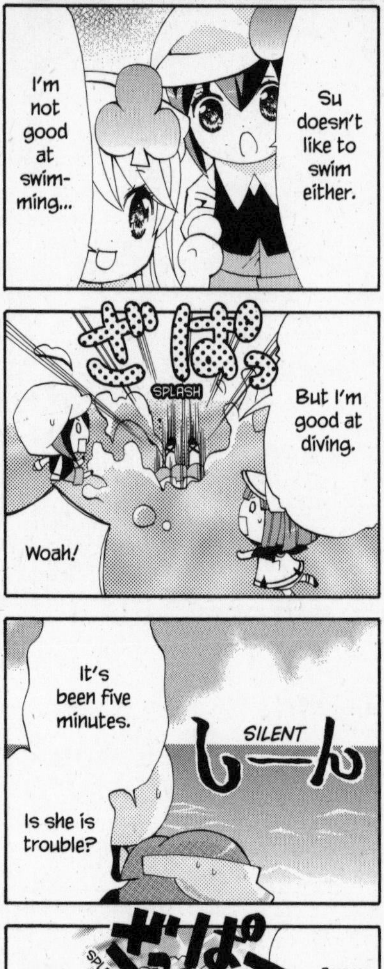
Su doesn't like to swim either.
I'm not good at swimming...
ざばっ
SPLASH
But I'm good at diving.
Woah!
It's been five minutes.
しーん
SILENT
Is she is trouble?
Because
I can get luxury ingredients ♡
Abalone, sea urchin, giant shrimp!
ざぱー
SPLASH
She's a diving fisherman!!

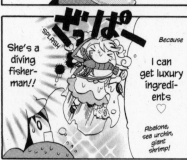

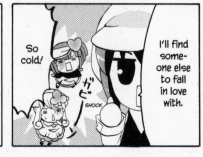

No Soup for You

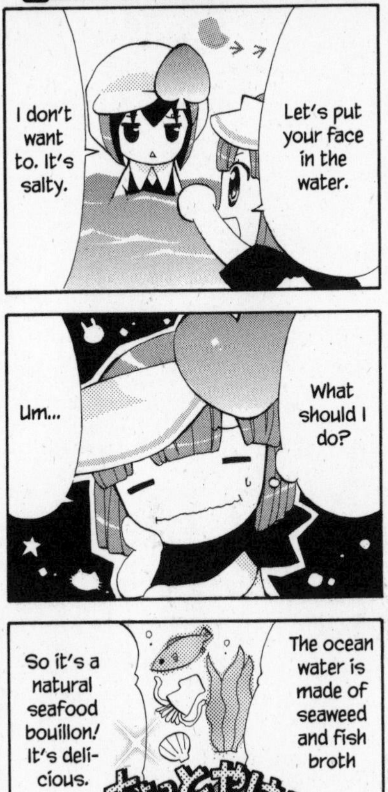
Let's put your face in the water.
I don't want to. It's salty.
What should I do?
Um...
The ocean water is made of seaweed and fish broth
So it's a natural seafood bouillon! It's delicious.
ちょっとやけ!
がぶがぶがぶ
GULP GULP GULP
Oops, the wrong one reacted!!
GULP GULP GULP

Bouillon = broth

Different Tastes?

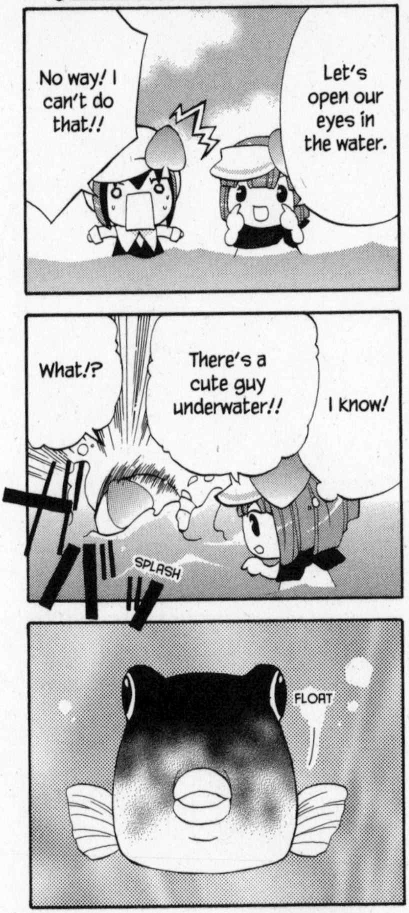
Let's open our eyes in the water.
No way! I can't do that!!
I know!
There's a cute guy underwater!!
What!?
SPLASH
FLOAT
Huh?
Puffer fish is a good looking fish in the water!
You have bad taste, Ran.
....

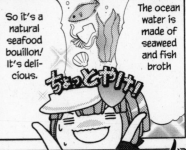

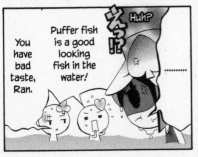

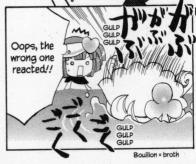

No Motivation

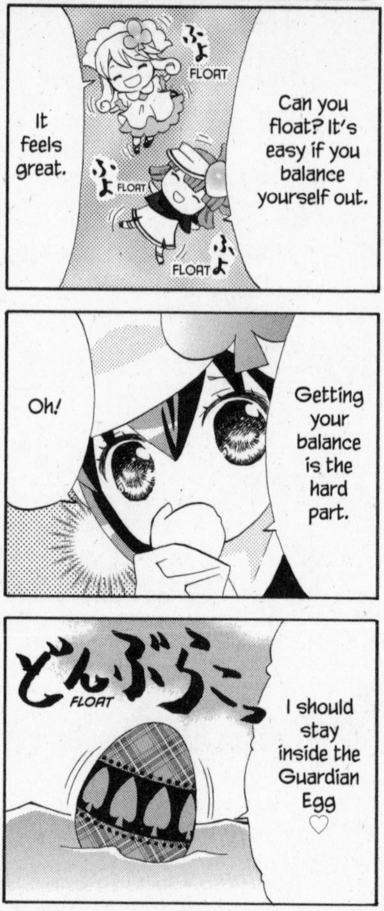
Can you float? It's easy if you balance yourself out.
It feels great.
ふよ FLOAT
ふよ FLOAT
ふよ FLOAT
Getting your balance is the hard part.
Oh!
どんぶらこっ FLOAT
I should stay inside the Guardian Egg ♡
You'll never learn to swim that way.

No Peel?

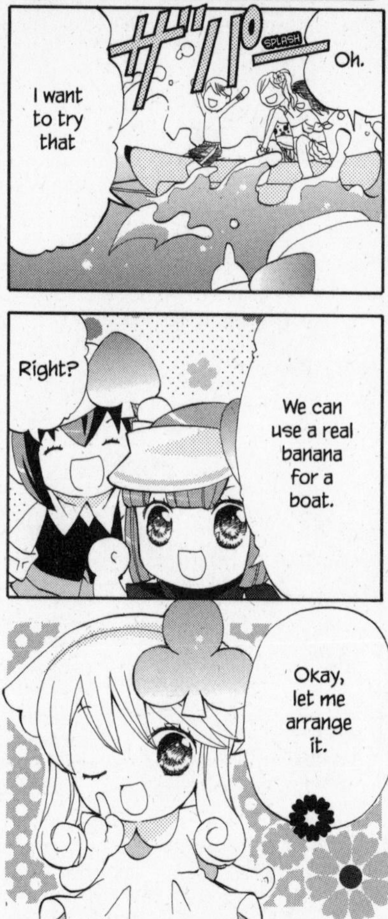
ザパー SPLASH
Oh.
I want to try that
We can use a real banana for a boat.
Right?
Okay, let me arrange it.
I made it more summer-like.
Chocolate banana ♥
Like a summer festival.
There's no need to do that!!
The chocolate is melting too.

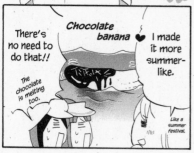

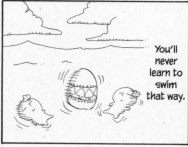

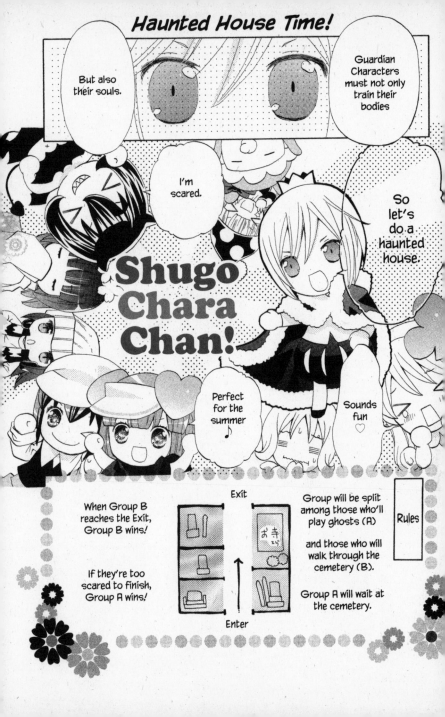

Haunted House Time!

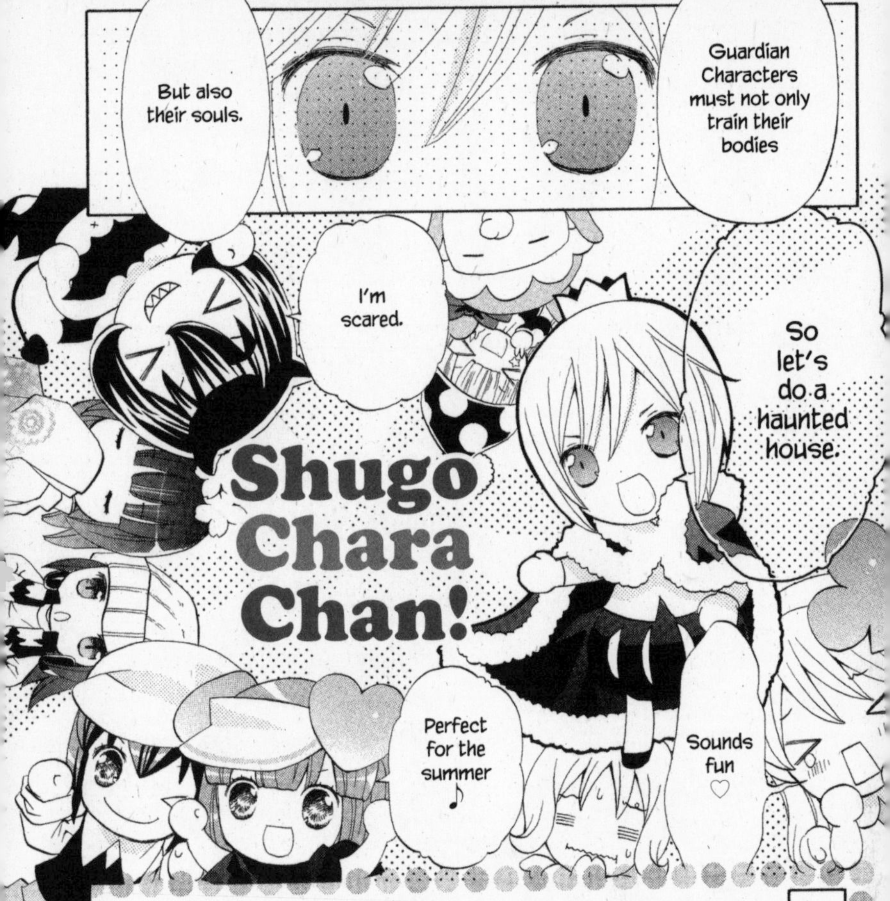

Guardian Characters must not only train their bodies
But also their souls.
So let's do a haunted house.
I'm scared.
Shugo Chara Chan!
Sounds fun ♡
Perfect for the summer ♪

Rules

Group will be split among those who'll play ghosts (A) and those who will walk through the cemetery (B).

Group A will wait at the cemetery.

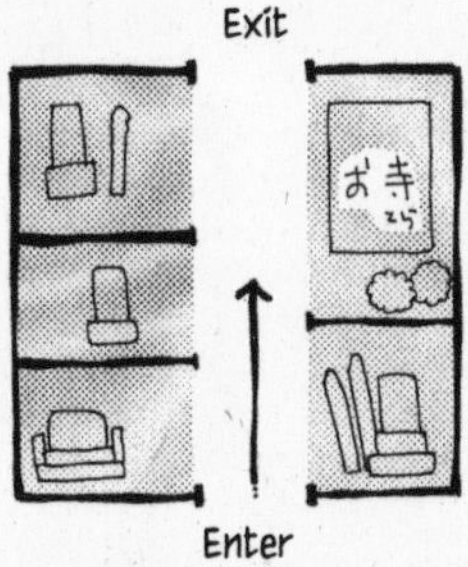

Exit
お寺
Enter

When Group B reaches the Exit, Group B wins!

If they're too scared to finish, Group A wins!

Group selected by rock paper scissors.

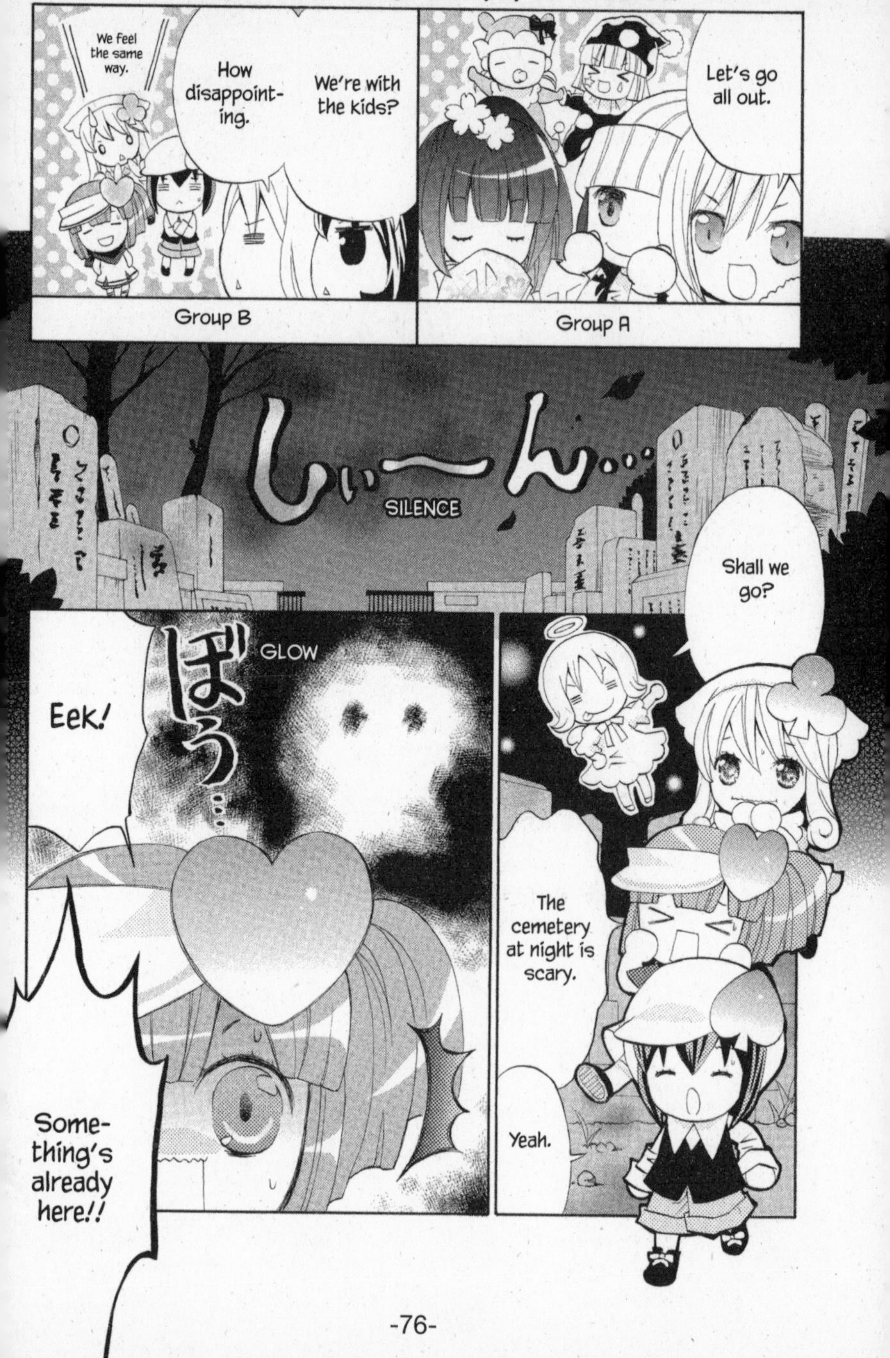
Let's go all out.
Group A
We're with the kids?
How disappoint-ing.
We feel the same way.
Group B
しぃ〜ん…
SILENCE
Shall we go?
The cemetery at night is scary.
Yeah.
ぽう…
GLOW
Eek!
Some-thing's already here!!

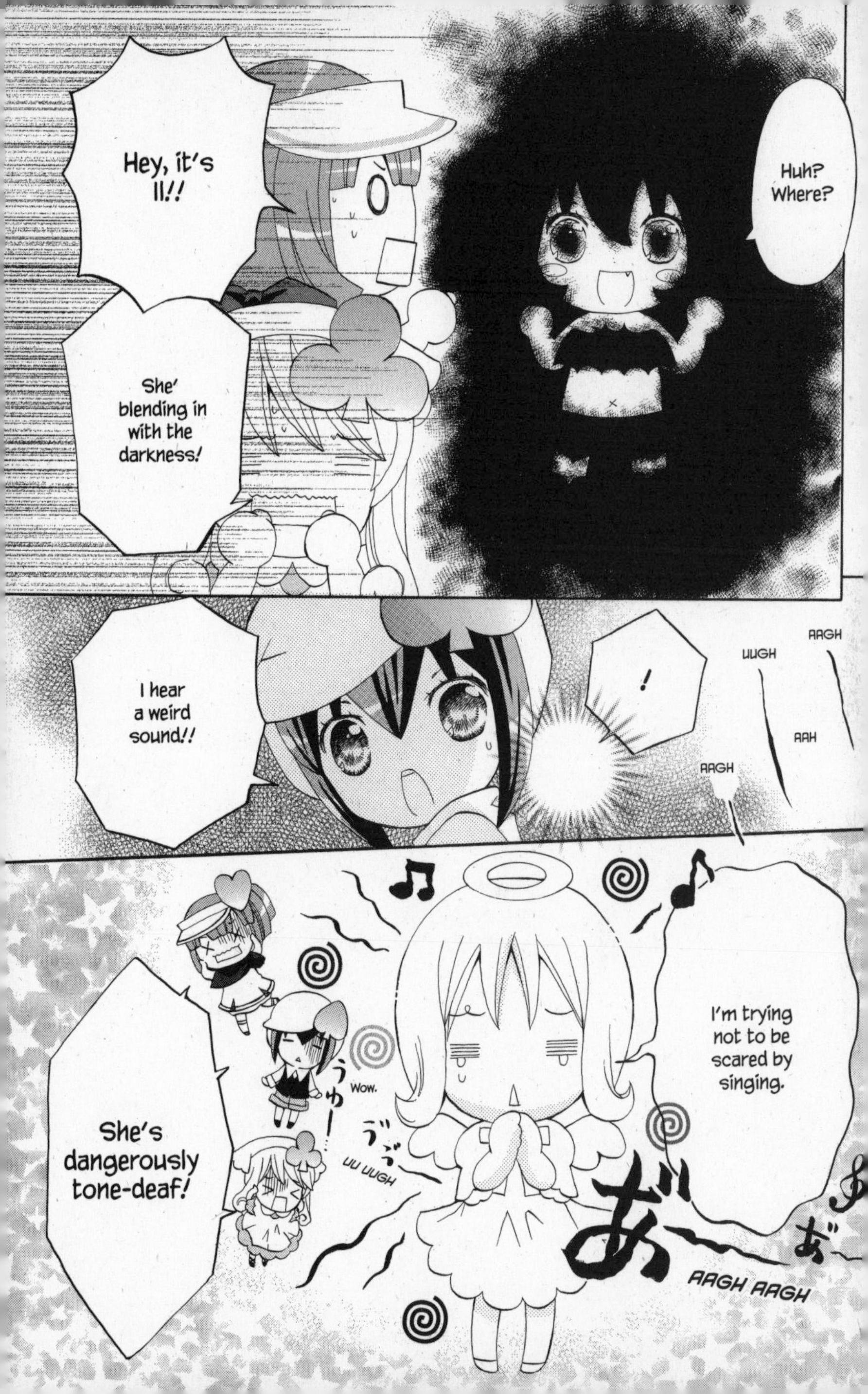
Huh? Where?
Hey, it's Il!!
She' blending in with the darkness!
AAGH
UUGH
AAH
AAGH
!
I hear a weird sound!!
I'm trying not to be scared by singing.
あ~~
あ~
AAGH AAGH
うゅ~!
WOW.
ヴ…
UU UUGH
She's dangerously tone-deaf!

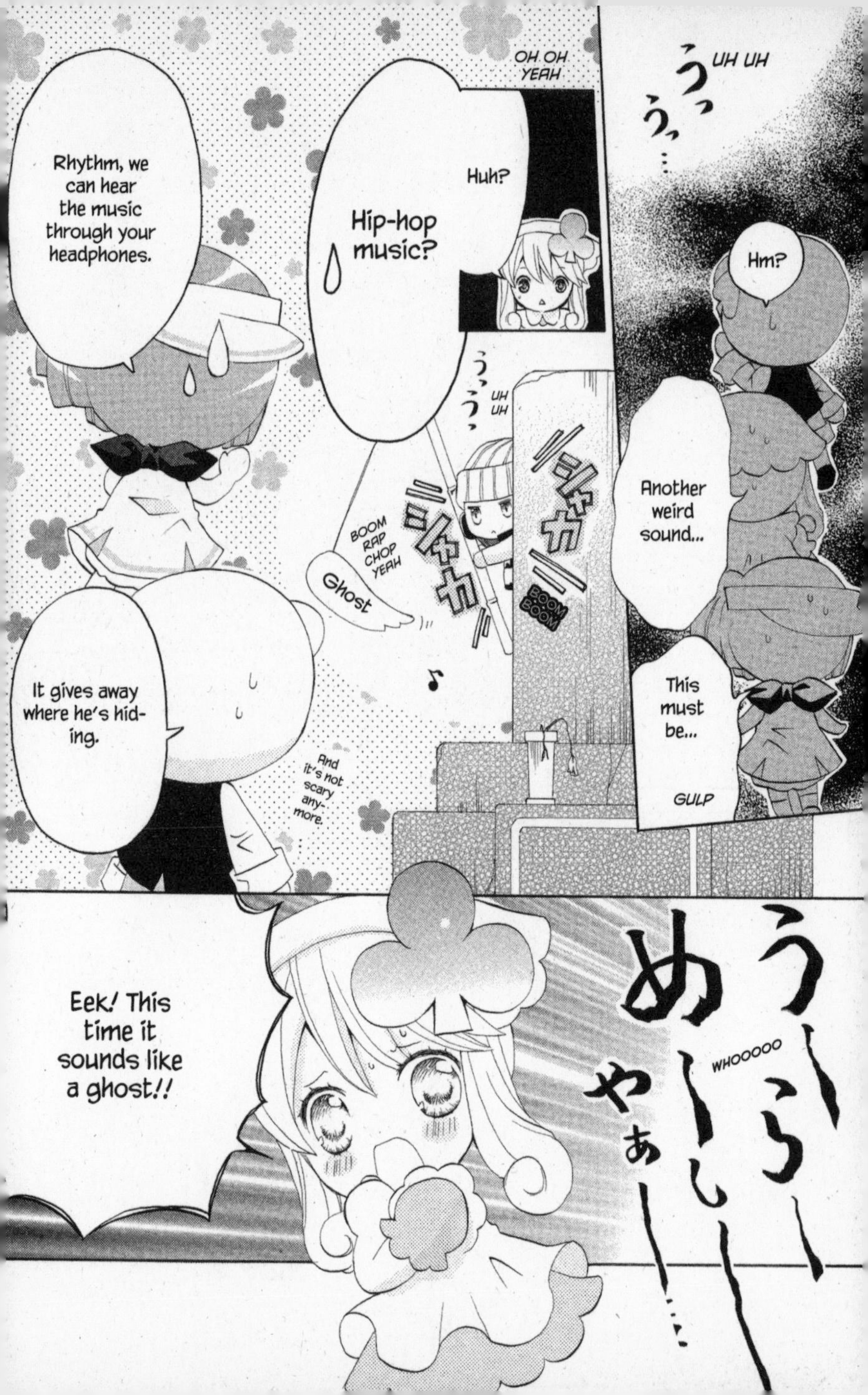

うっうっ…
UH UH
Hm?
Another weird sound...
This must be...
GULP
OH OH YEAH
Huh?
Hip-hop music?
うっうっ
UH UH
シャカ
シャカ
BOOM BOOM
BOOM RAP CHOP YEAH
Ghost
Rhythm, we can hear the music through your headphones.
It gives away where he's hiding.
And it's not scary anymore.
うらめしやぁ…
WHOOOOO
Eek! This time it sounds like a ghost!!

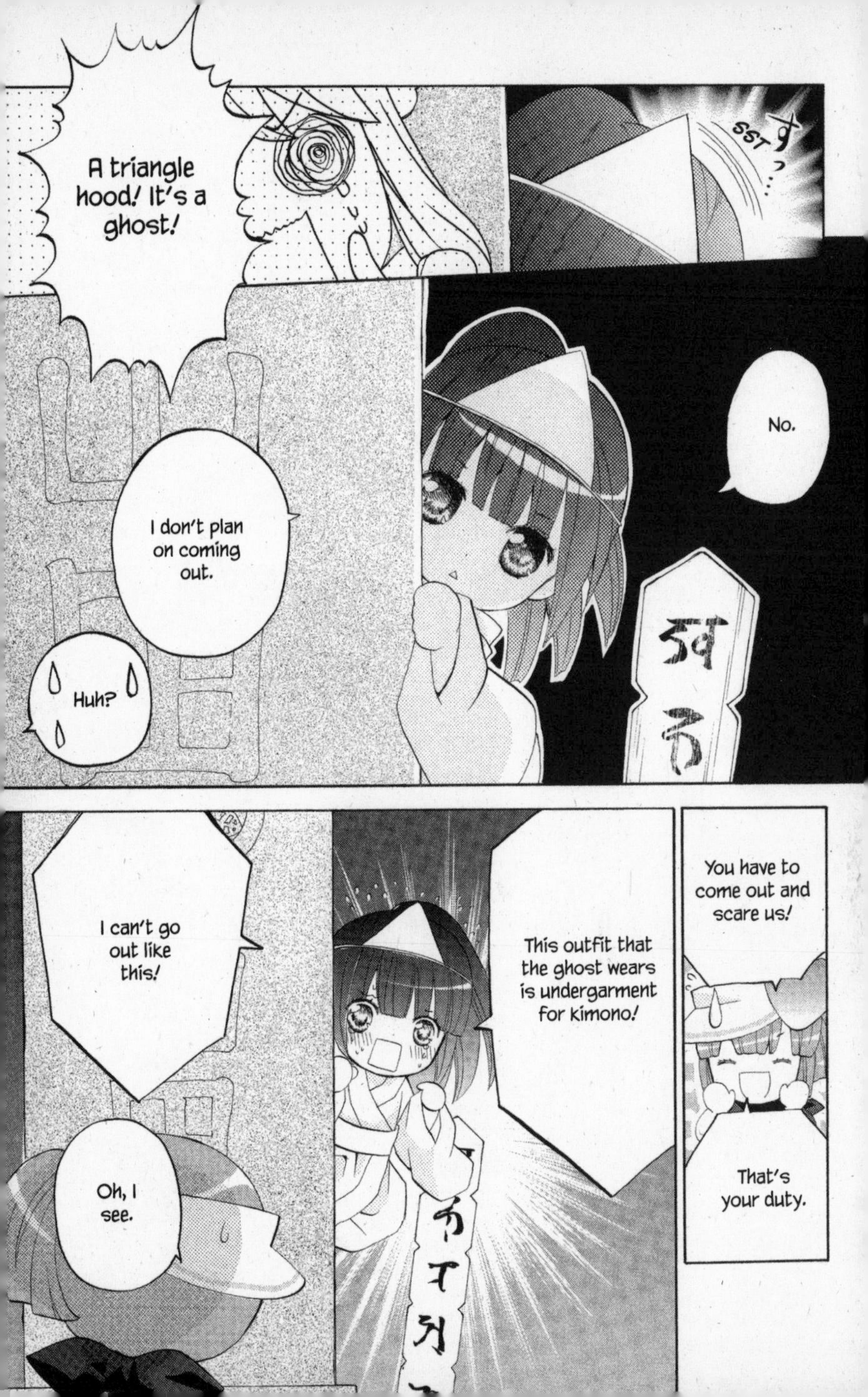
SST
A triangle hood! It's a ghost!
No.
I don't plan on coming out.
Huh?
You have to come out and scare us!
That's your duty.
This outfit that the ghost wears is undergarment for kimono!
I can't go out like this!
Oh, I see.

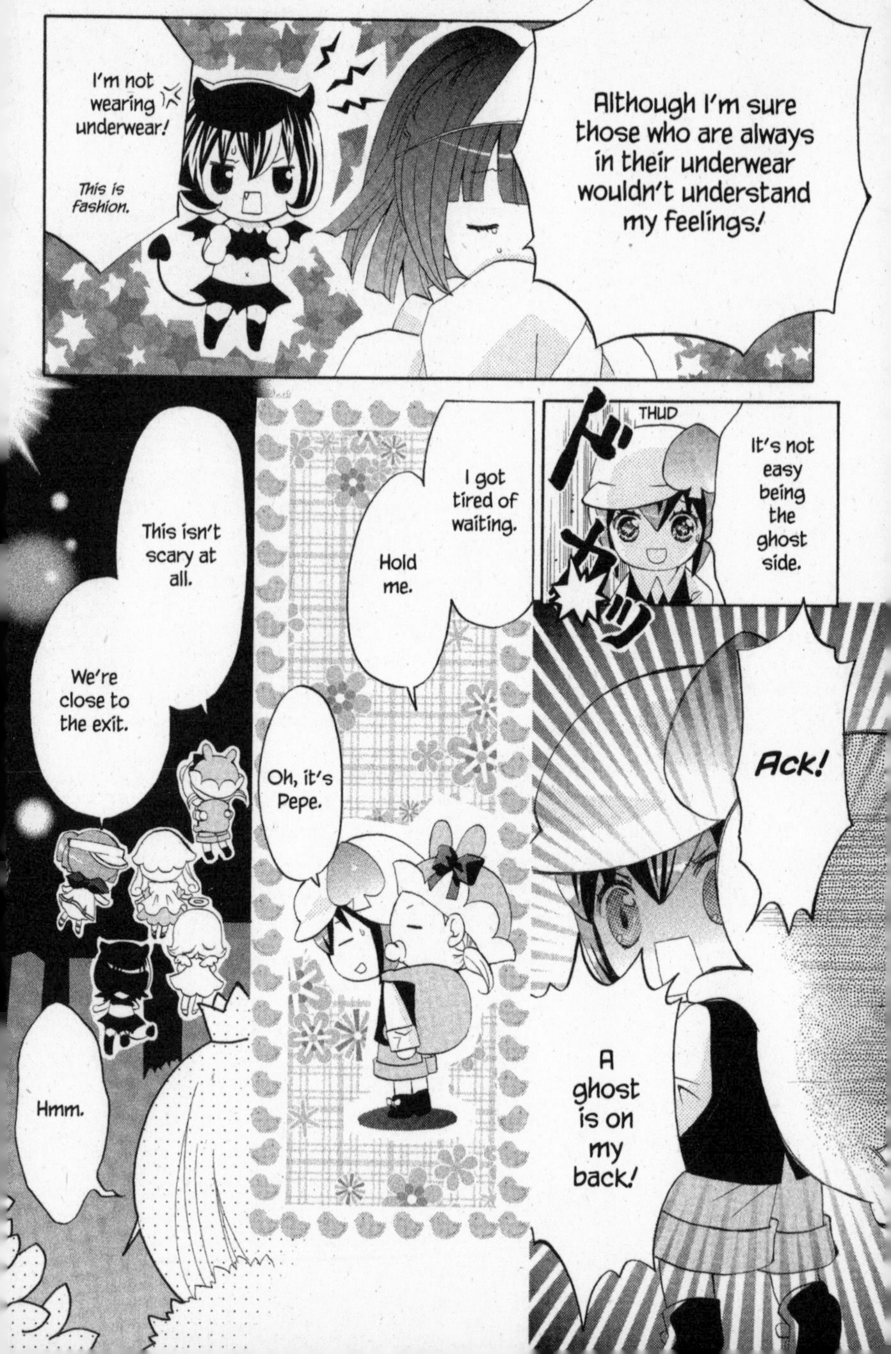
Although I'm sure those who are always in their underwear wouldn't understand my feelings!
I'm not wearing underwear!
This is fashion.
THUD
It's not easy being the ghost side.
Ack!
A ghost is on my back!
I got tired of waiting.
Hold me.
Oh, it's Pepe.
This isn't scary at all.
We're close to the exit.
Hmm.

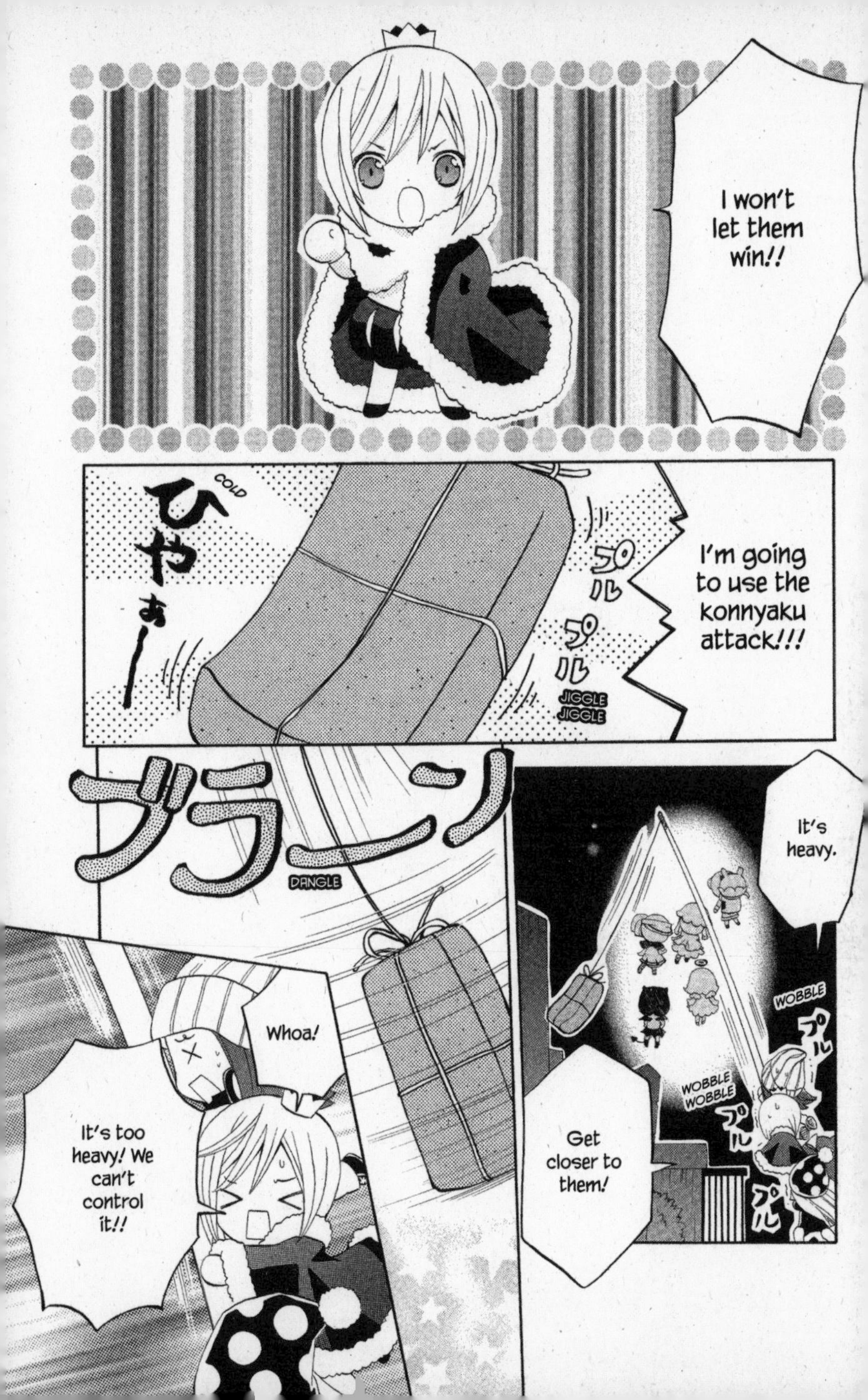
I won't let them win!!
I'm going to use the konnyaku attack!!!
プルプル
JIGGLE JIGGLE
ひやぁー
COLD
It's heavy.
WOBBLE
プル
WOBBLE WOBBLE
プル
プル
Get closer to them!
ブラーン
DANGLE
Whoa!
It's too heavy! We can't control it!!

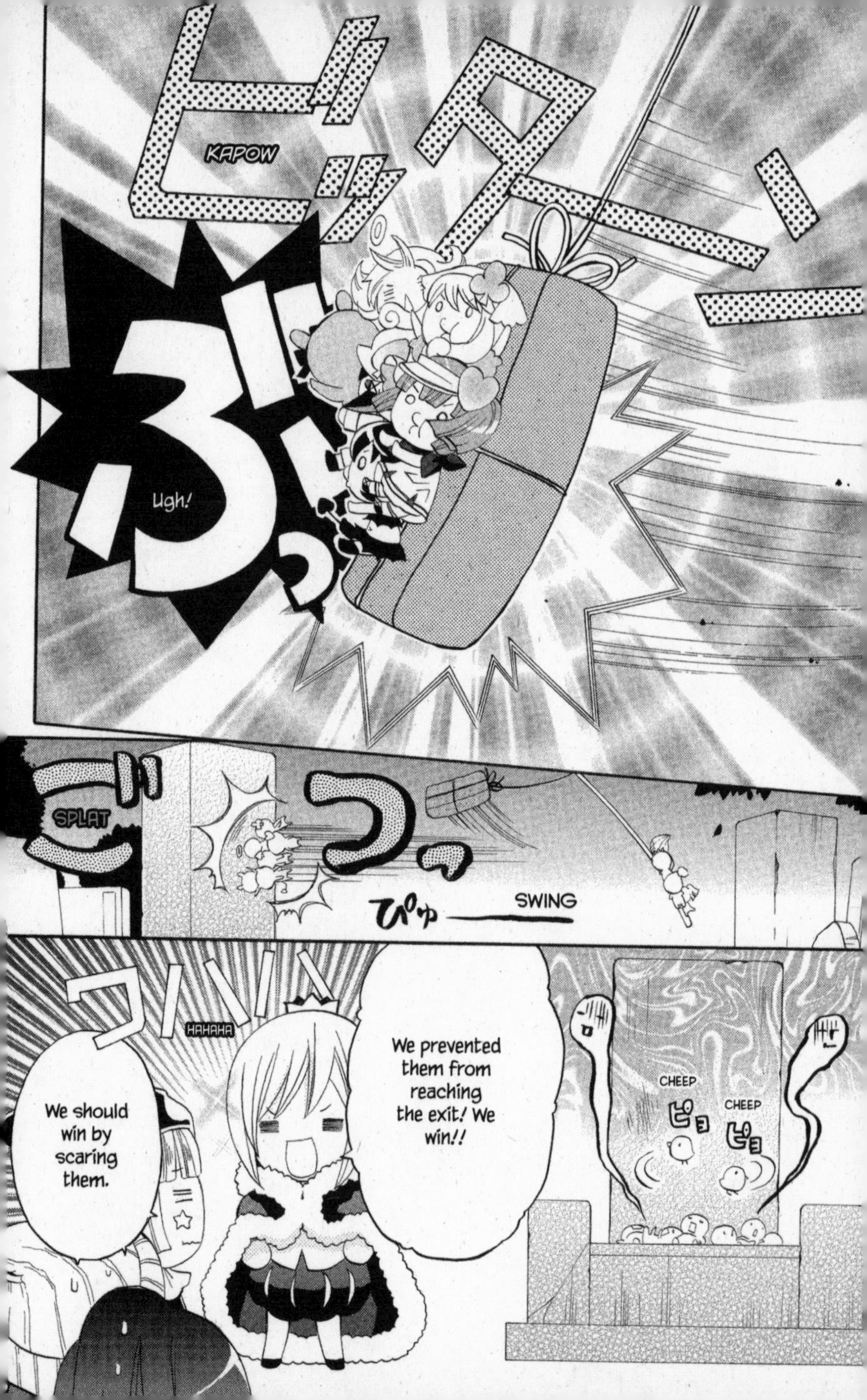
KAPOW
Ugh!
SWING
SPLAT
CHEEP
CHEEP
We prevented them from reaching the exit! We win!!
HAHAHA
We should win by scaring them.

Shugo Chara Chan!

ONE-PANEL MANGA ☆

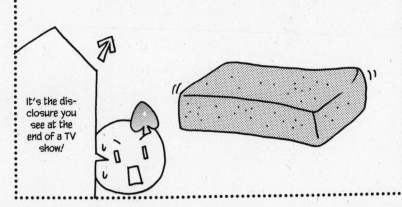

※ *We ate the konnyaku afterwards.*

It's the disclosure you see at the end of a TV show!

Autumn Edition Starts on the Next Page!

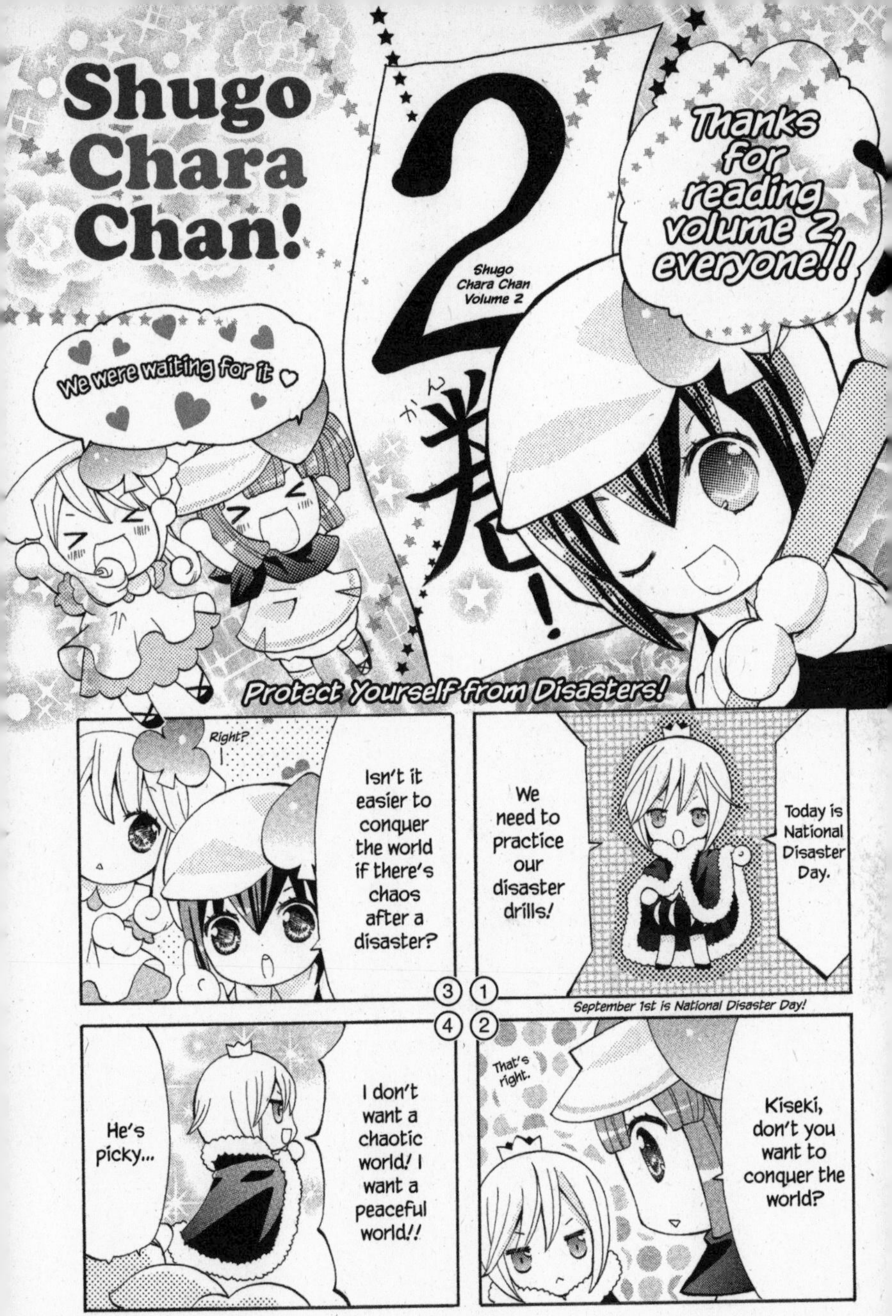
Shugo Chara Chan!
Thanks for reading volume 2, everyone!!
Shugo Chara Chan Volume 2
We were waiting for it ♡
Protect Yourself from Disasters!
Today is National Disaster Day.
We need to practice our disaster drills!
September 1st is National Disaster Day!
Kiseki, don't you want to conquer the world?
That's right.
Isn't it easier to conquer the world if there's chaos after a disaster?
Right?
I don't want a chaotic world! I want a peaceful world!!
He's picky...

No Need to Come

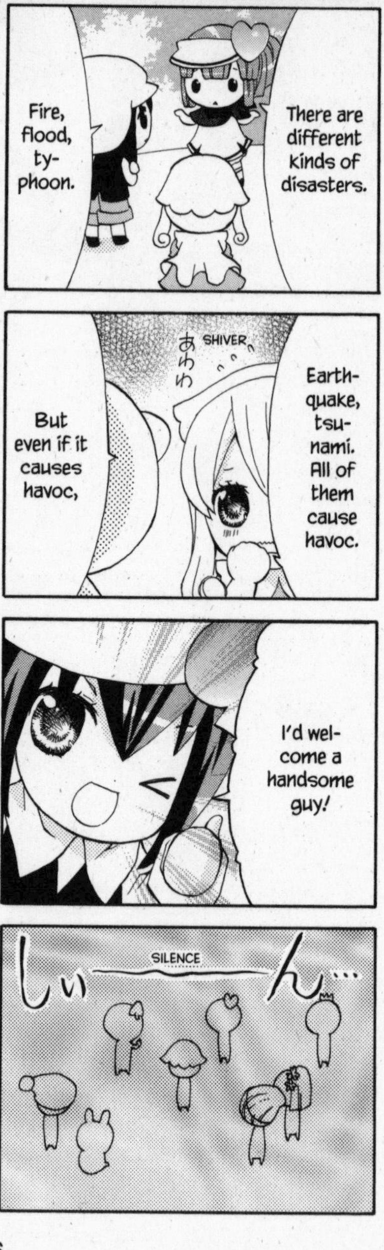
There are different kinds of disasters.
Fire, flood, ty-phoon.
Earth-quake, tsu-nami. All of them cause havoc.
あわわ
SHIVER
But even if it causes havoc,
I'd wel-come a handsome guy!
しぃーーーん…
SILENCE

Be Careful!

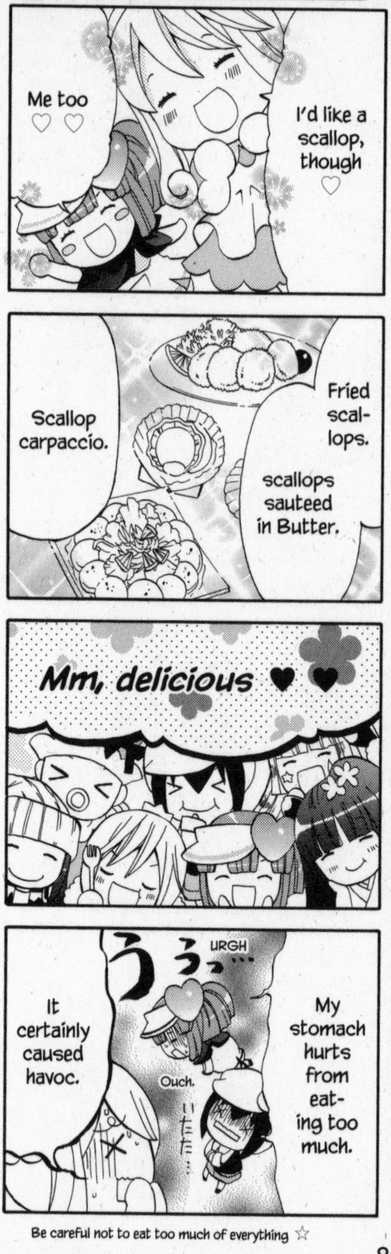
I'd like a scallop, though ♡
Me too ♡ ♡
Fried scal-lops.
scallops sauteed in Butter.
Scallop carpaccio.
Mm, delicious ♥ ♥
うぅっ…
URGH
My stomach hurts from eat-ing too much.
Ouch.
いたた…
It certainly caused havoc.

Be careful not to eat too much of everything ☆

Correct Answer?

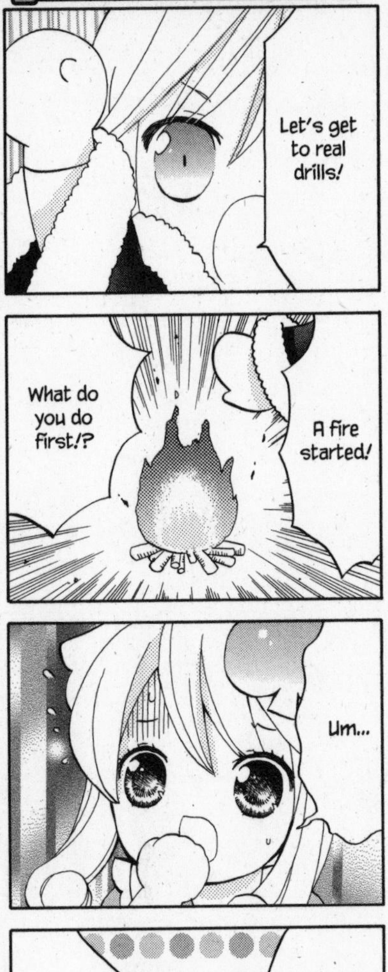
Let's get to real drills!
A fire started!
What do you do first!?
Um...
I'll prepare a sweet potato!
Hey!!

Be Careful About Fire

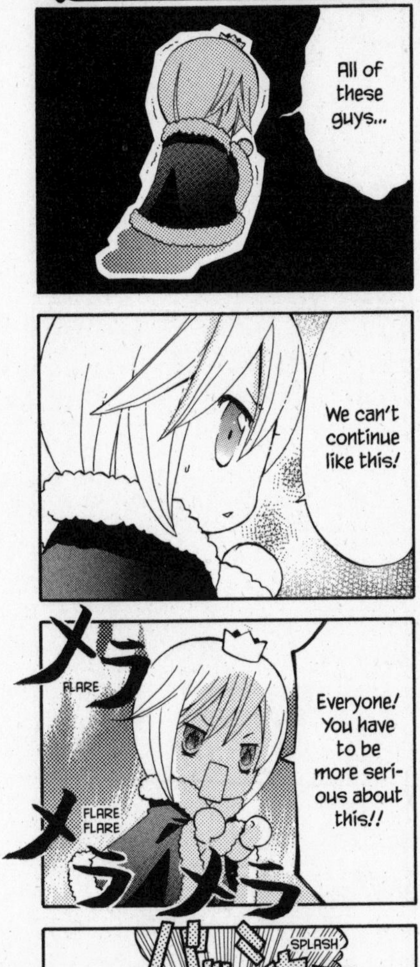
All of these guys...
We can't continue like this!
Everyone! You have to be more serious about this!!
メラ
FLARE
メラメラ
FLARE FLARE
メラメラ
バッシャー
SPLASH
Fire!!
That's only a manga way of expression...
びっしょり…
WET

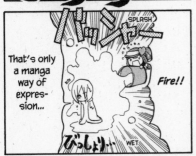

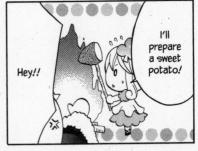

Risking Their Lives

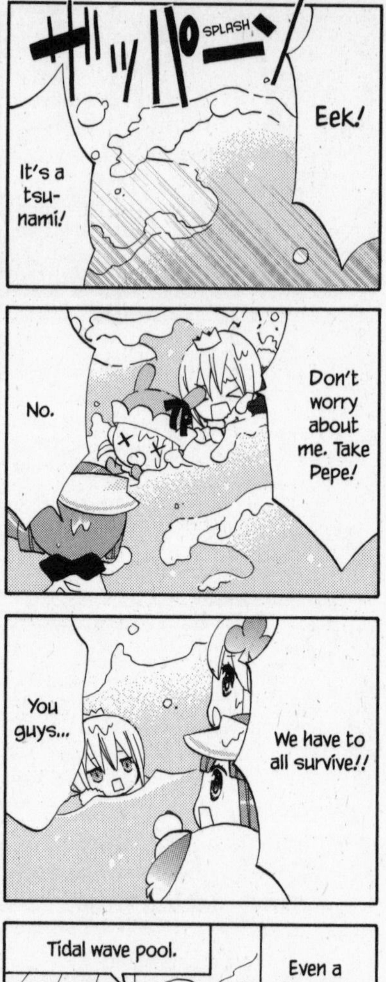
SPLASH
Eek!
It's a tsunami!
Don't worry about me. Take Pepe!
No.
We have to all survive!!
You guys...
Even a fun pool is like a natural disaster to the Guardian Characters!
Tidal wave pool.
We will survive the disaster!

This May be on a Test☆

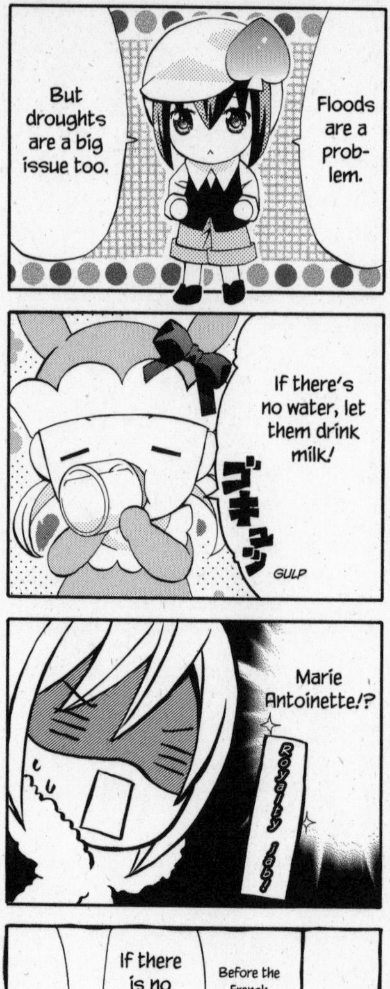
Floods are a problem.
But droughts are a big issue too.
If there's no water, let them drink milk!
GULP
Marie Antoinette!?
Royalty jab!
Shugo Chara Chan Historical Trivia!
Before the French Revolution, when the citizens of France were starving, Marie Antoinette famously said
If there is no bread, let them eat cake.
According to history.
Educational four-panel manga.
HO HO HO

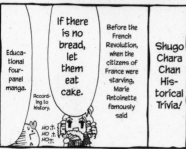

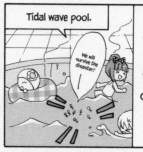

Shugo Chara Chan!

Let's be Friends with Animals ☆

ガオー ROAR

Animal Issue!

Only on TV or photos.

③ ①

| 20 20日～26日 動物愛護週間 20th ~ 26th Animal Appreciation Week | 21 敬老の日 Elderly Day | 22 国民 Citizen | September has Animal Appreciation Week too. |
| 27 | 28 | | |

④ ②

Can they learn to love animals?

The fleas might jump onto us too.

They're as big as dinosaurs for us!!

Because real ones are huge!

Yeah.

We like animals.

-89-

Separation Line

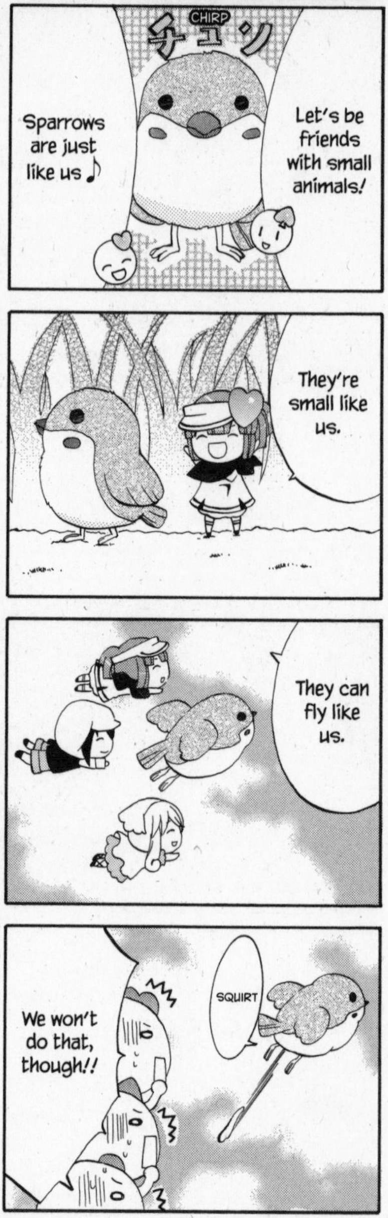

CHIRP
チュン
Let's be friends with small animals!
Sparrows are just like us♪
They're small like us.
They can fly like us.
SQUIRT
We won't do that, though!!

Always Munching

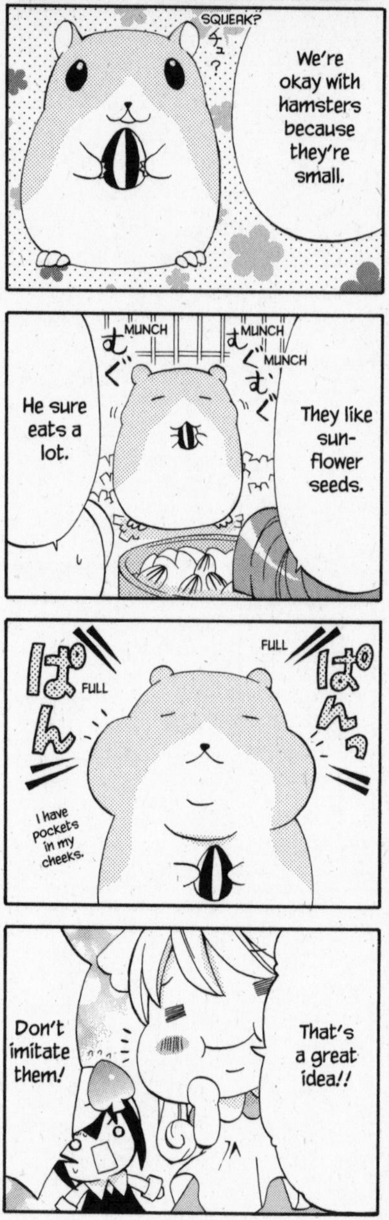

SQUEAK?
チュ?
We're okay with hamsters because they're small.
MUNCH
むぐ
MUNCH
むぐ
MUNCH
むぐ
They like sunflower seeds.
He sure eats a lot.
FULL
ぱんっ
FULL
ぱん
I have pockets in my cheeks.
That's a great idea!!
Don't imitate them!

Bonus Item

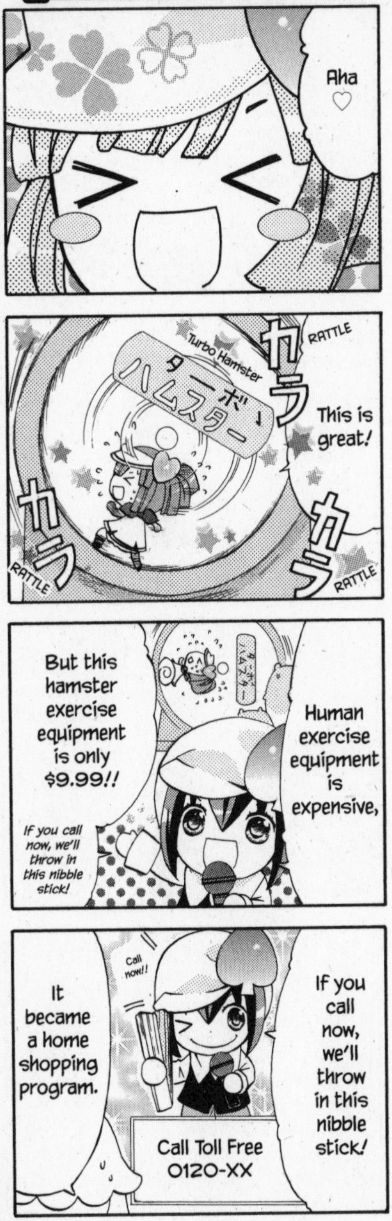
Aha ♡
RATTLE
カラ
This is great!
Turbo Hamster
ターボハムスター
カラ
RATTLE
カラ
RATTLE
Human exercise equipment is expensive,
But this hamster exercise equipment is only $9.99!!
If you call now, we'll throw in this nibble stick!
If you call now, we'll throw in this nibble stick!
Call now!!
It became a home shopping program.
Call Toll Free 0120-XX

To be Alive...

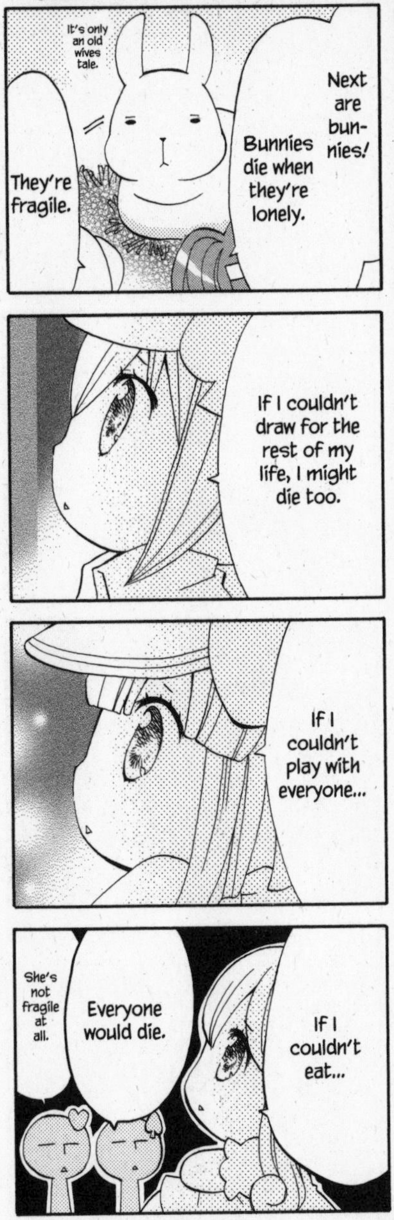
Next are bun-nies!
Bunnies die when they're lonely.
It's only an old wives tale.
They're fragile.
If I couldn't draw for the rest of my life, I might die too.
If I couldn't play with everyone...
If I couldn't eat...
Everyone would die.
She's not fragile at all.

Three Pets?

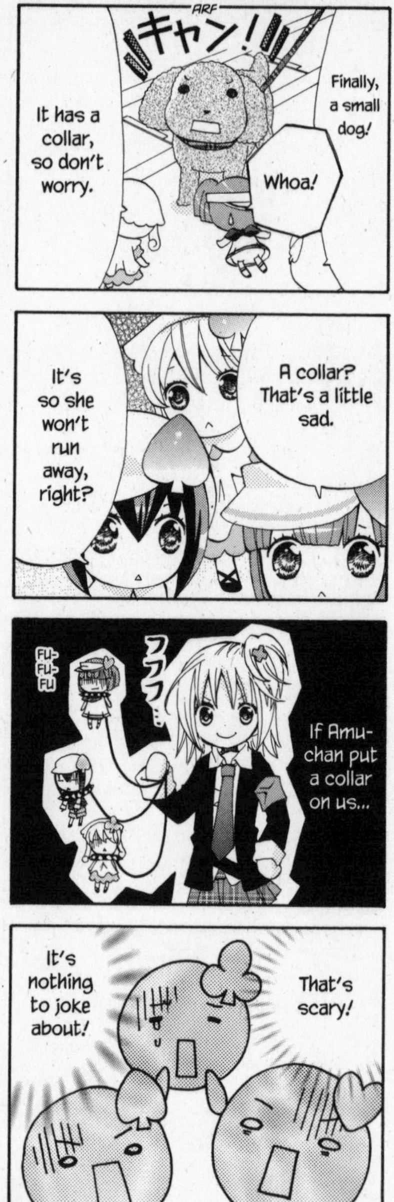
ARF
キャン!
Finally, a small dog!
Whoa!
It has a collar, so don't worry.
A collar? That's a little sad.
It's so she won't run away, right?
フフフ…
FU-FU-FU
If Amu-chan put a collar on us...
That's scary!
It's nothing to joke about!

We're Loved

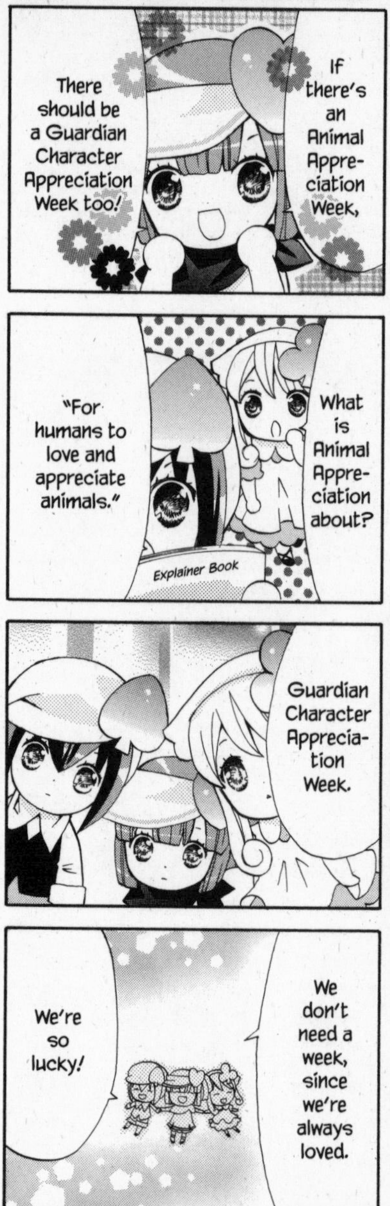
If there's an Animal Appreciation Week,
There should be a Guardian Character Appreciation Week too!
What is Animal Appreciation about?
"For humans to love and appreciate animals."
Explainer Book
Guardian Character Appreciation Week.
We don't need a week, since we're always loved.
We're so lucky!

Shugo Chara Chan!

ONE-PANEL MANGA ☆

But the manga still continues ☆

Shugo Chara Chan! One-Panel Manga ends here!

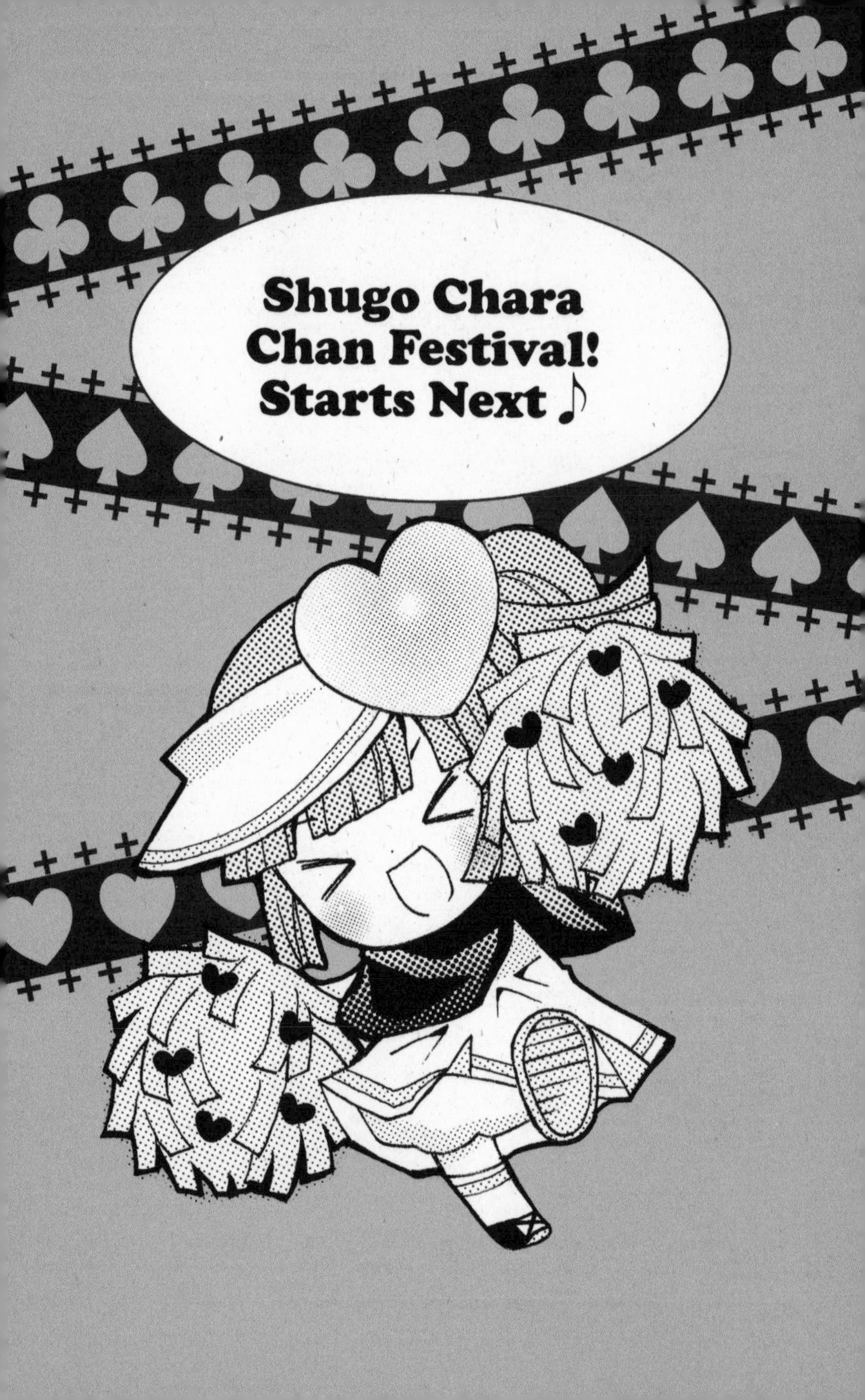
Shugo Chara Chan Festival! Starts Next ♪

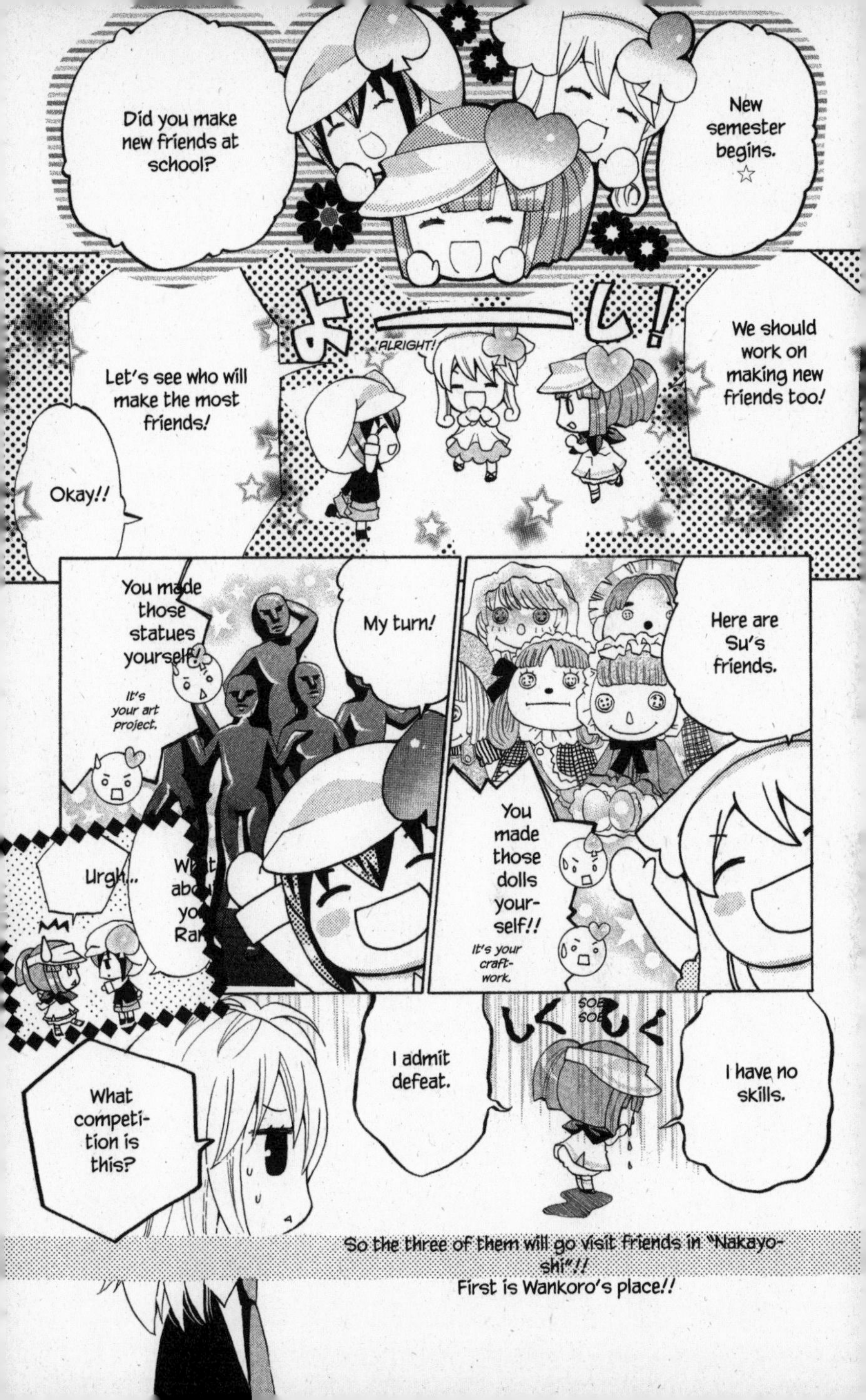
New semester begins. ☆
Did you make new friends at school?
We should work on making new friends too!
よーーし!
ALRIGHT!
Let's see who will make the most friends!
Okay!!
Here are Su's friends.
You made those dolls yourself!!
It's your craftwork.
My turn!
You made those statues yourself!!
It's your art project.
Urgh...
I have no skills.
しくしく
SOB SOB
I admit defeat.
What competition is this?
So the three of them will go visit friends in "Nakayoshi"!!
First is Wankoro's place!!

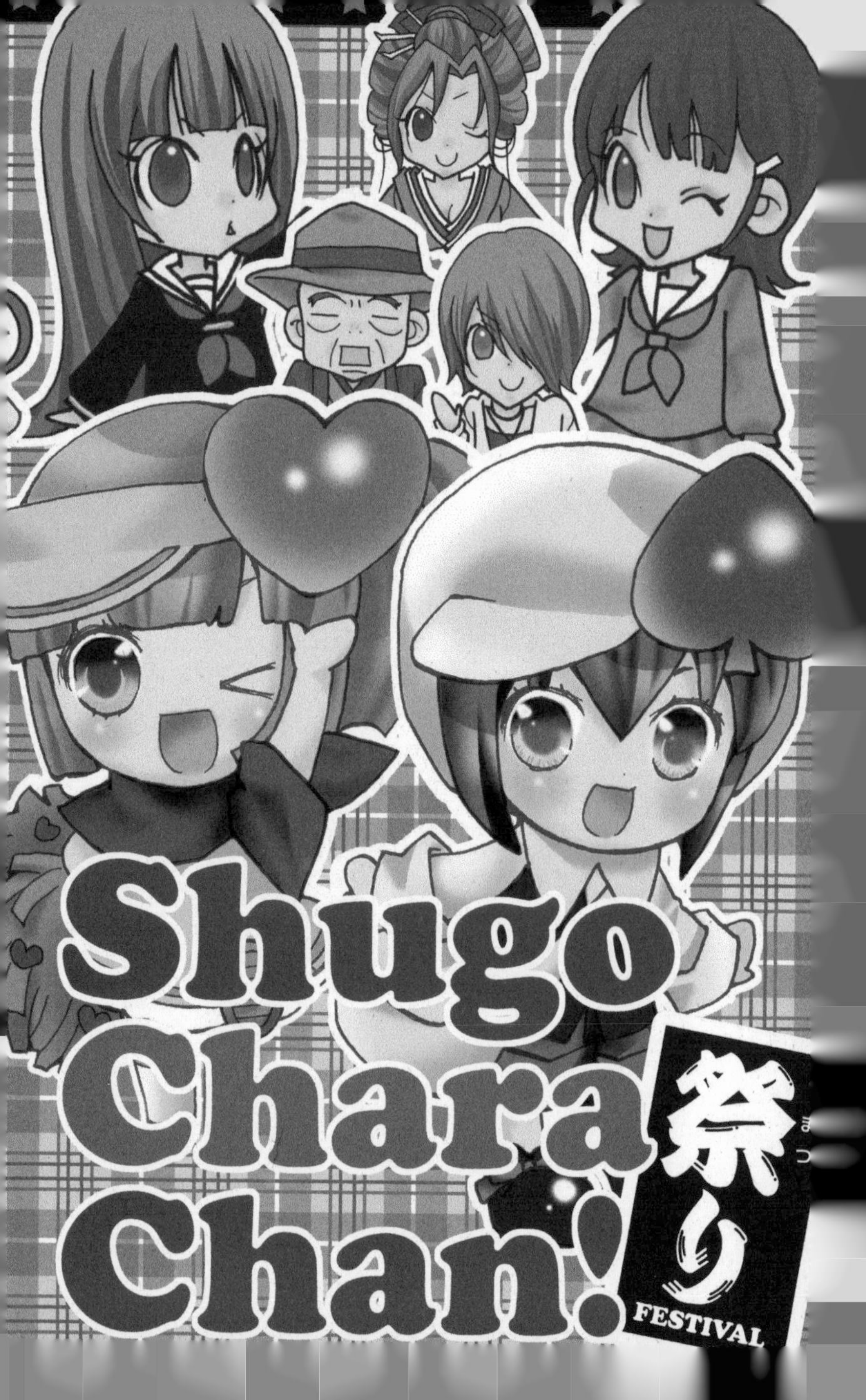

Shugo Chara Chan!
祭り
FESTIVAL

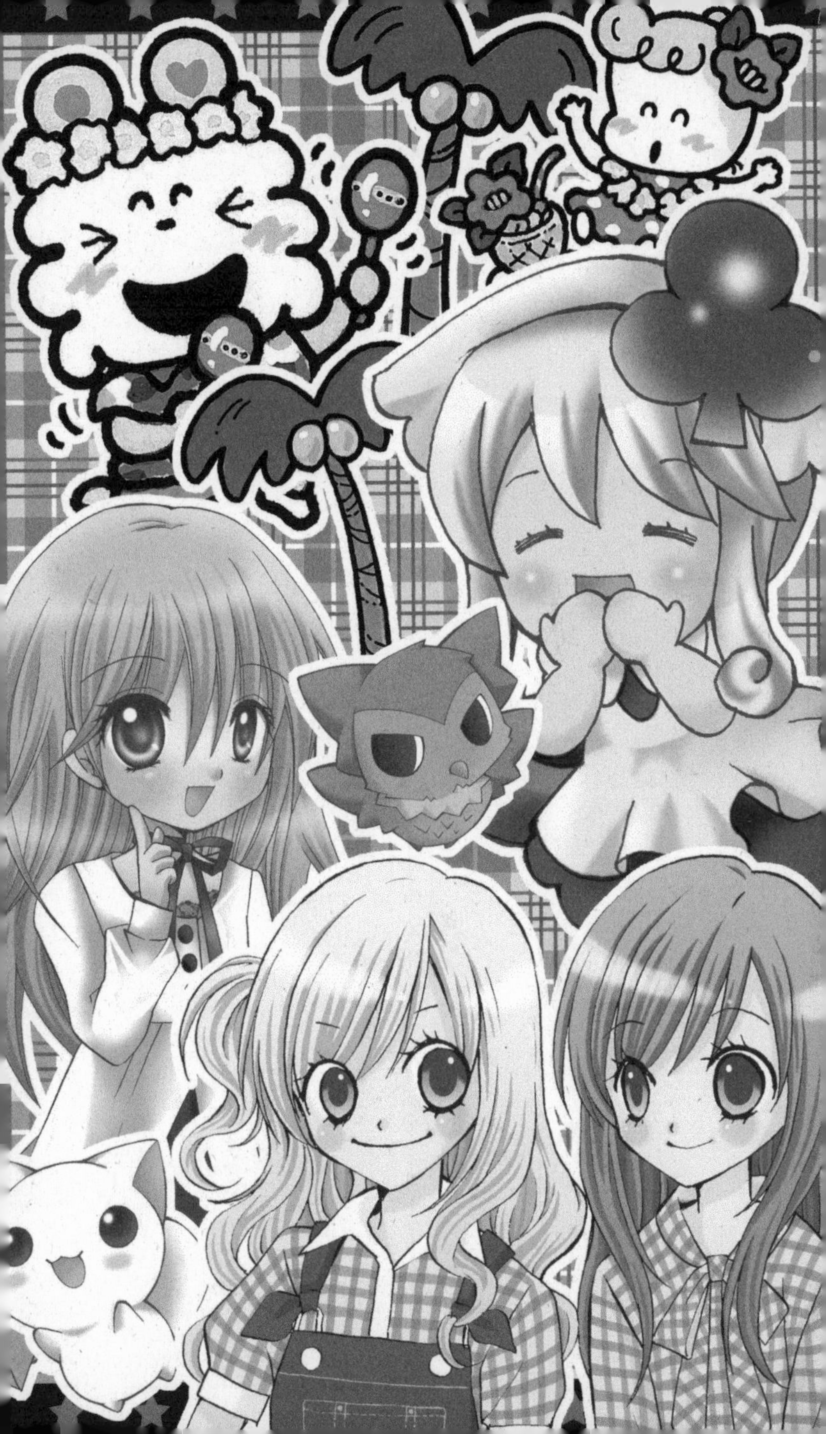

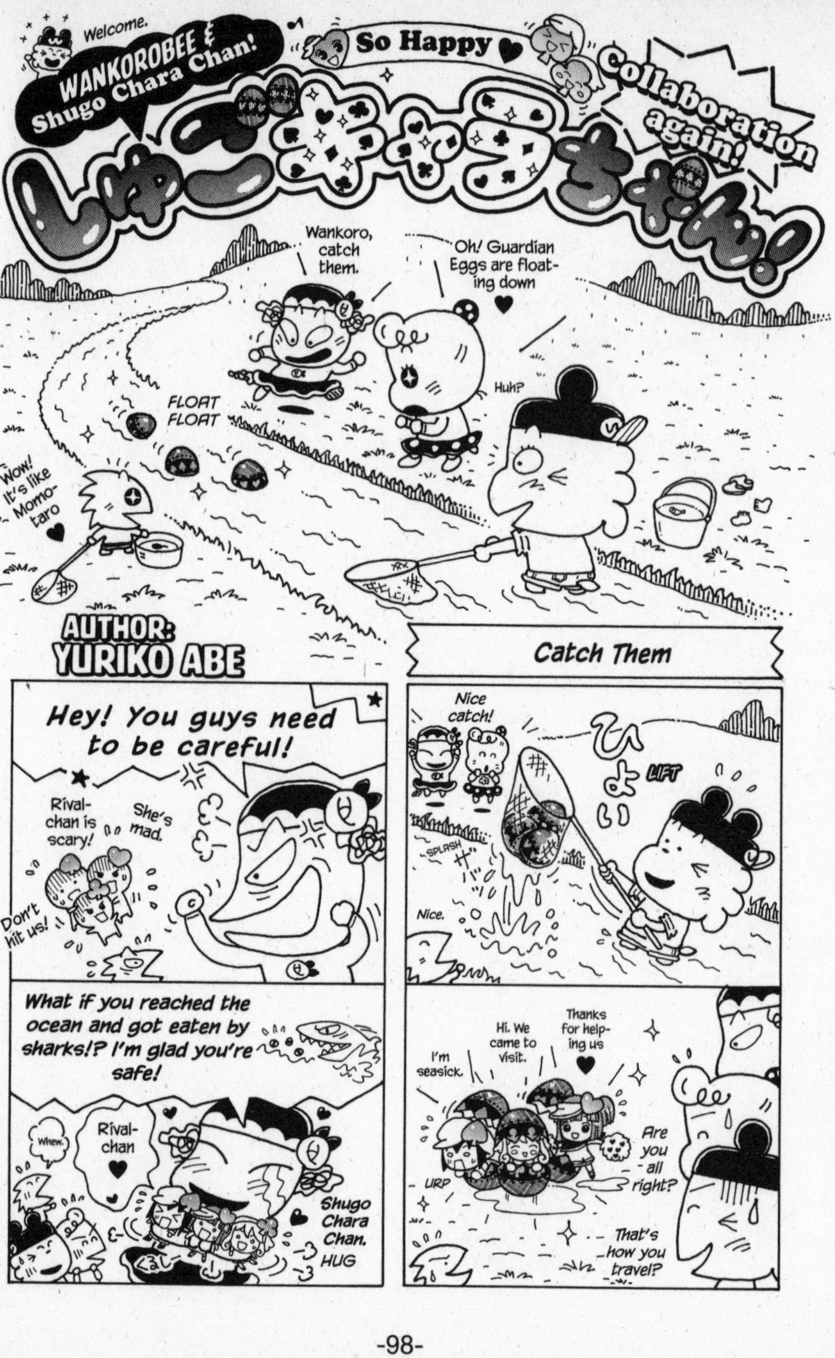

Collaboration again!
So Happy ♥
Welcome.
WANKOROBEE & Shugo Chara Chan!
しゅごキャラちゃん!
Oh! Guardian Eggs are floating down ♥
Wankoro, catch them.
Huh?
FLOAT FLOAT
Wow! It's like Momotaro ♥
AUTHOR: YURIKO ABE
Catch Them
Nice catch!
LIFT
SPLASH
Nice.
Thanks for helping us ♥
Hi. We came to visit.
I'm seasick.
Are you all right?
URP
That's how you travel?
Hey! You guys need to be careful!
She's mad.
Rival-chan is scary!
Don't hit us!
What if you reached the ocean and got eaten by sharks!? I'm glad you're safe!
Rival-chan ♥
Whew.
Shugo Chara Chan.
HUG

Egg

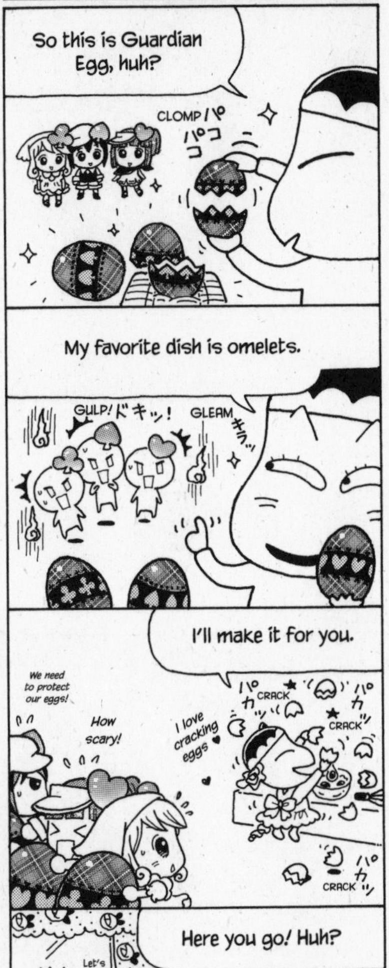
So this is Guardian Egg, huh?
CLOMP パコ
My favorite dish is omelets.
GULP! ドキッ!
GLEAM キラッ
I'll make it for you.
We need to protect our eggs!
How scary!
I love cracking eggs ♥
パカッ CRACK
CRACK
パカッ CRACK
Here you go! Huh?
Let's leave our eggs behind.
Run!
Where did they go?

Guardian Egg Fan ♡

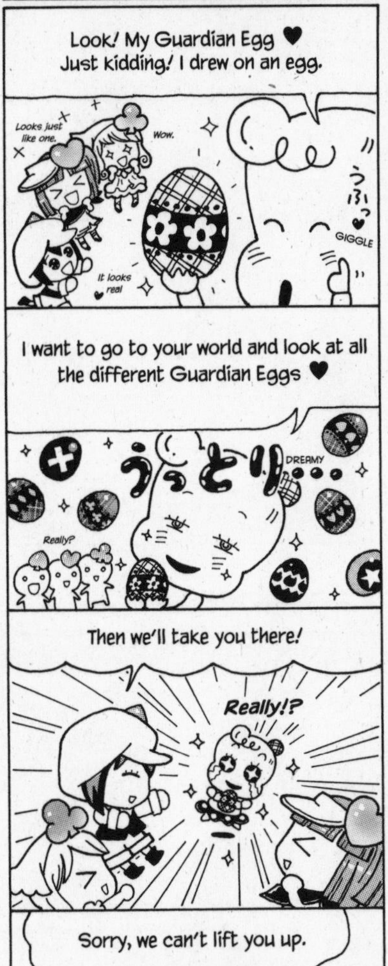
Look! My Guardian Egg ♥ Just kidding! I drew on an egg.
Looks just like one.
Wow.
It looks real ♥
うふっ♥ GIGGLE
I want to go to your world and look at all the different Guardian Eggs ♥
うっとり DREAMY
Really?
Then we'll take you there!
Really!?
Sorry, we can't lift you up.
Yikes.
Of course.
Ouch...
URGH

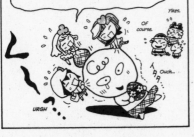

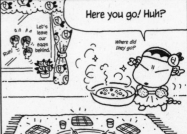

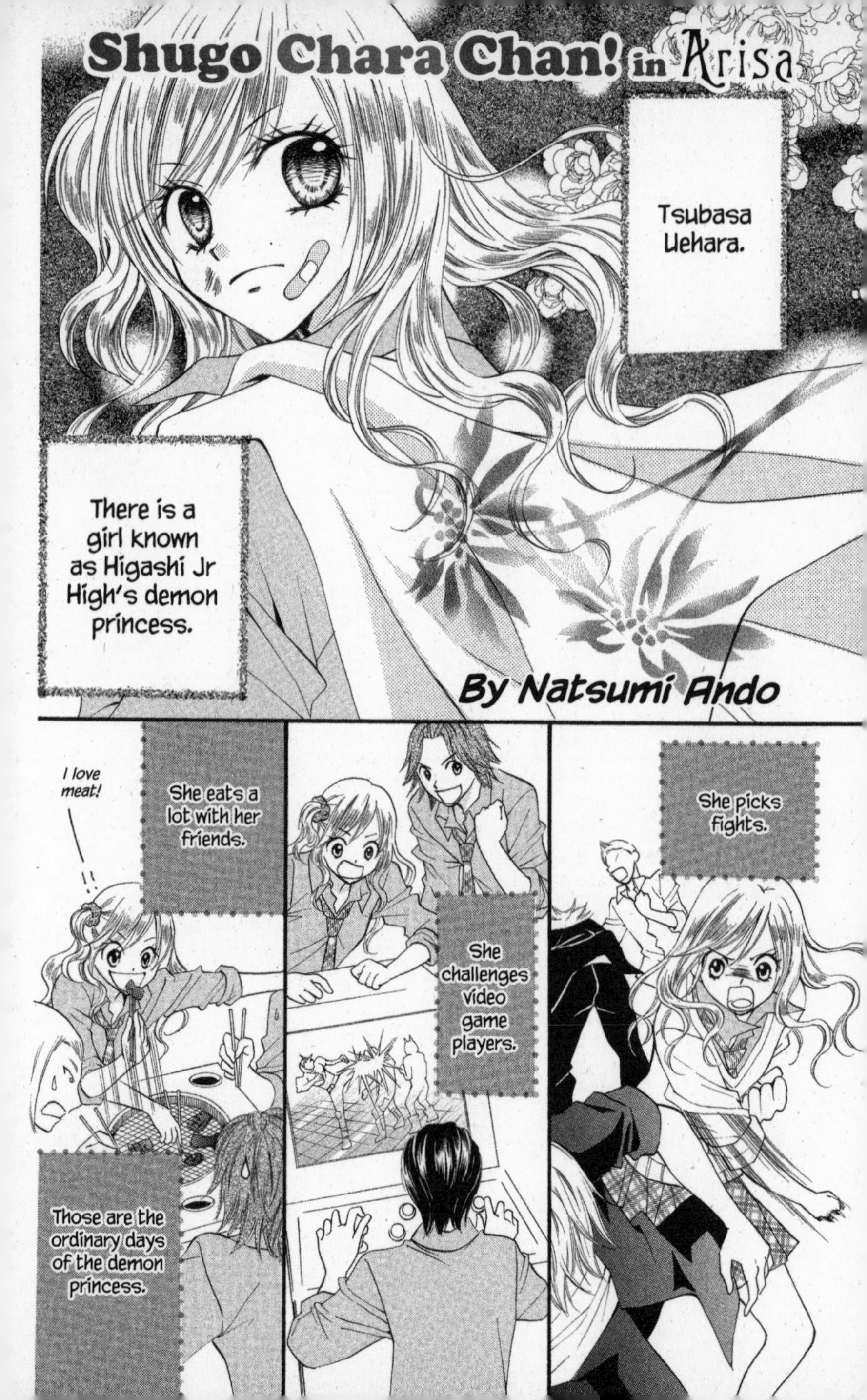
Shugo Chara Chan! in Arisa
Tsubasa Uehara.
There is a girl known as Higashi Jr High's demon princess.
By Natsumi Ando
She picks fights.
She challenges video game players.
I love meat!
!!
She eats a lot with her friends.
Those are the ordinary days of the demon princess.

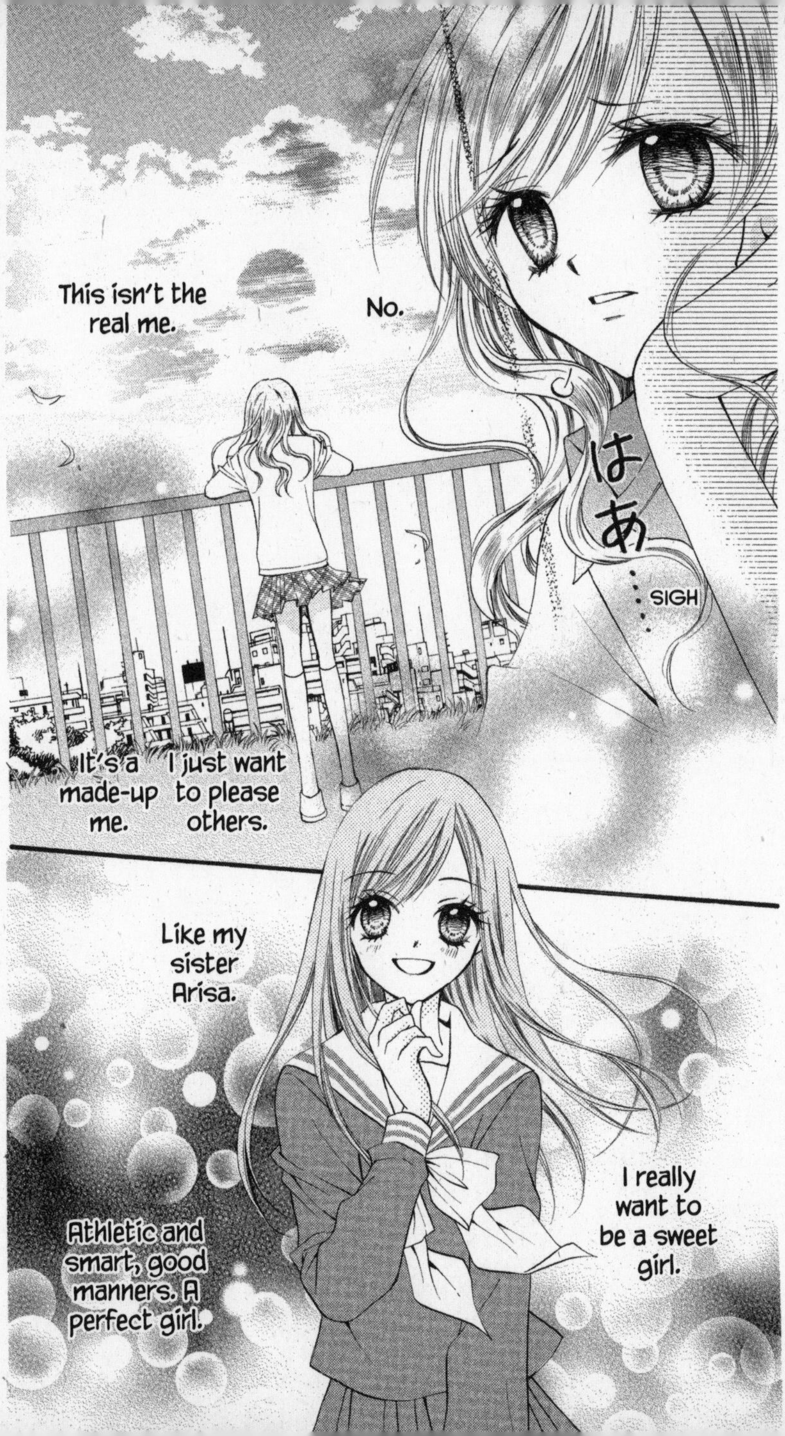
No.
はあ…
SIGH
This isn't the real me.
I just want to please others.
It's a made-up me.
I really want to be a sweet girl.
Like my sister Arisa.
Athletic and smart, good manners. A perfect girl.

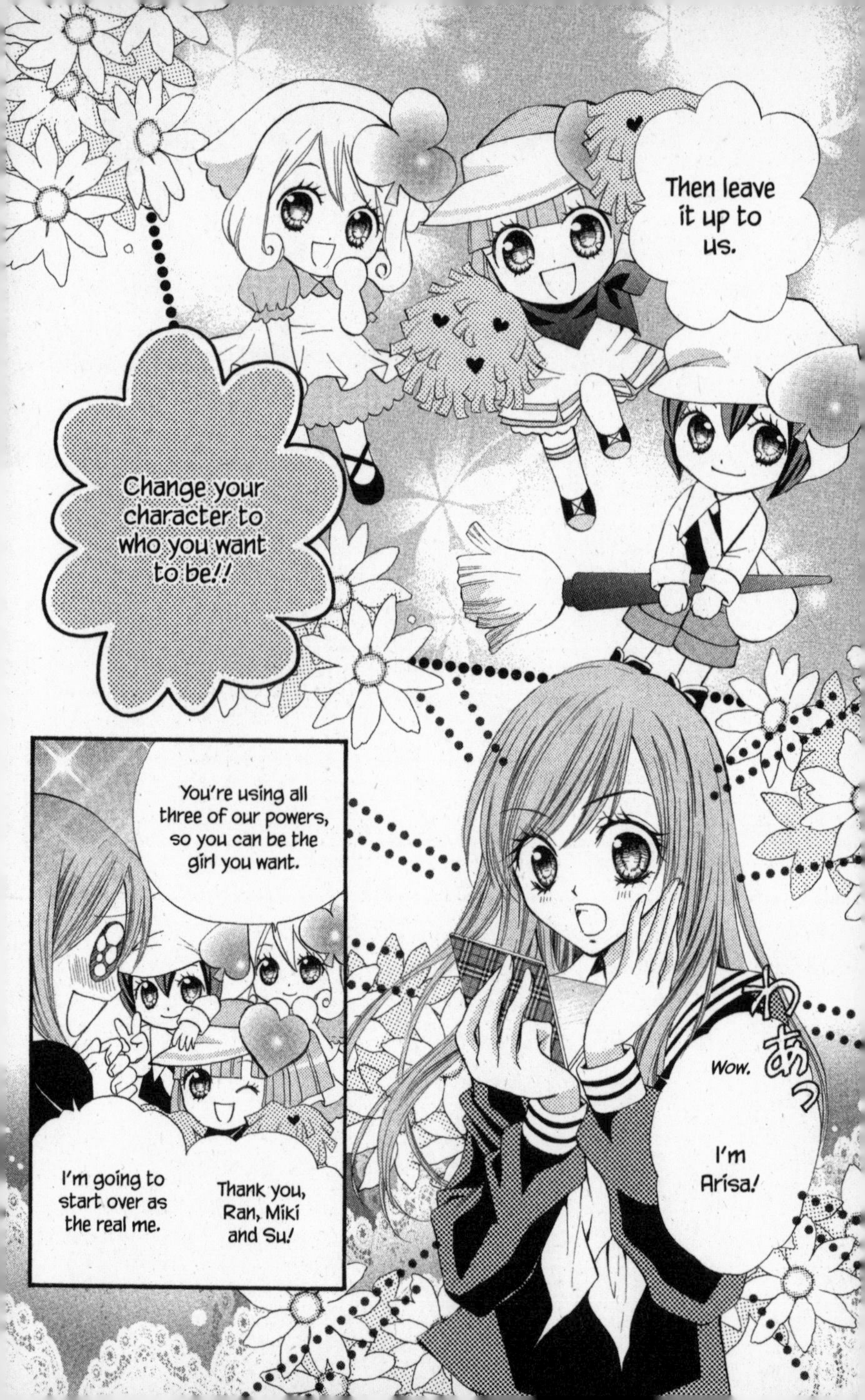
Then leave it up to us.
Change your character to who you want to be!!
わあっ
Wow.
I'm Arisa!
You're using all three of our powers, so you can be the girl you want.
Thank you, Ran, Miki and Su!
I'm going to start over as the real me.

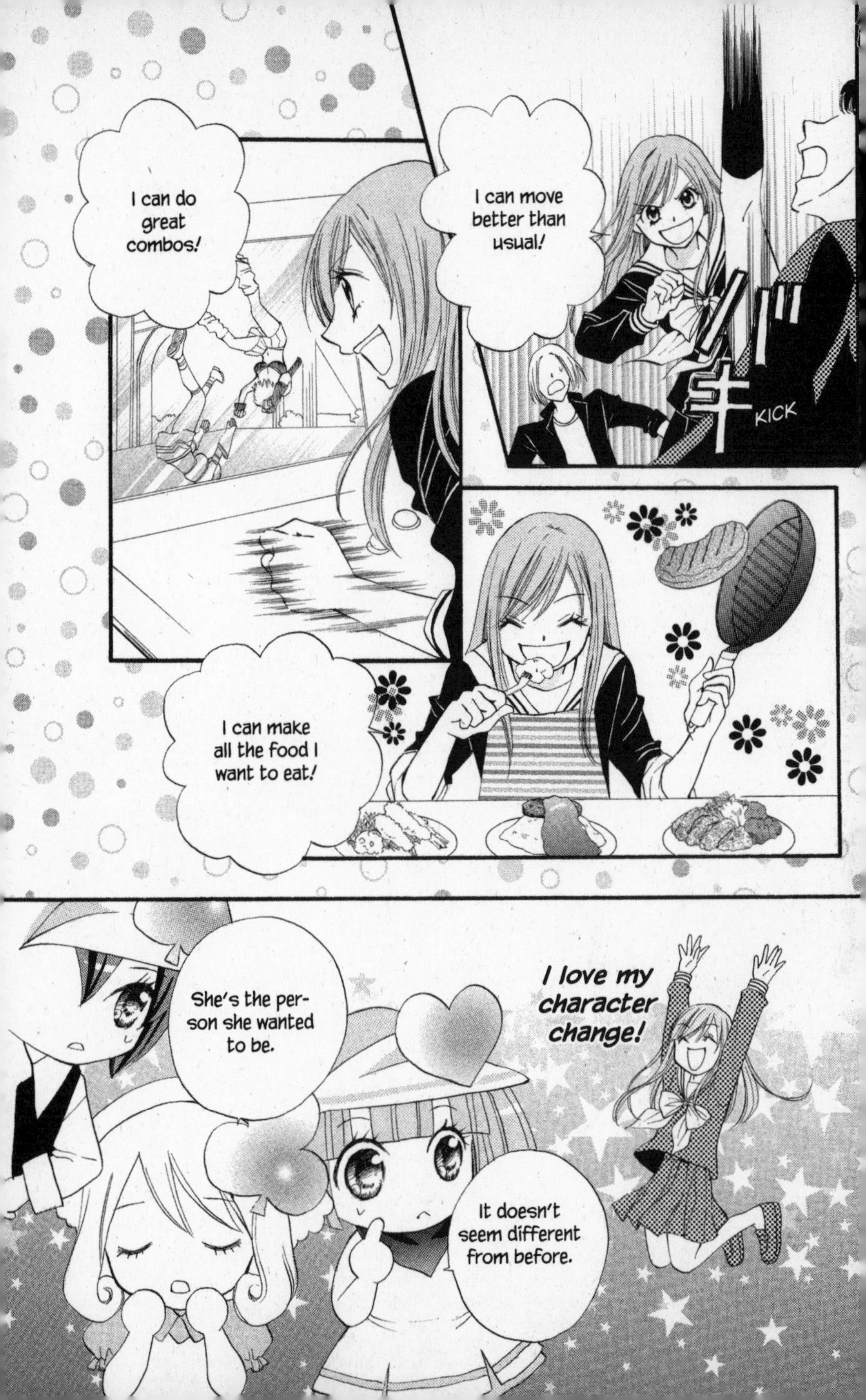
I can move better than usual!
KICK
I can make all the food I want to eat!
I can do great combos!
I love my character change!
She's the person she wanted to be.
It doesn't seem different from before.

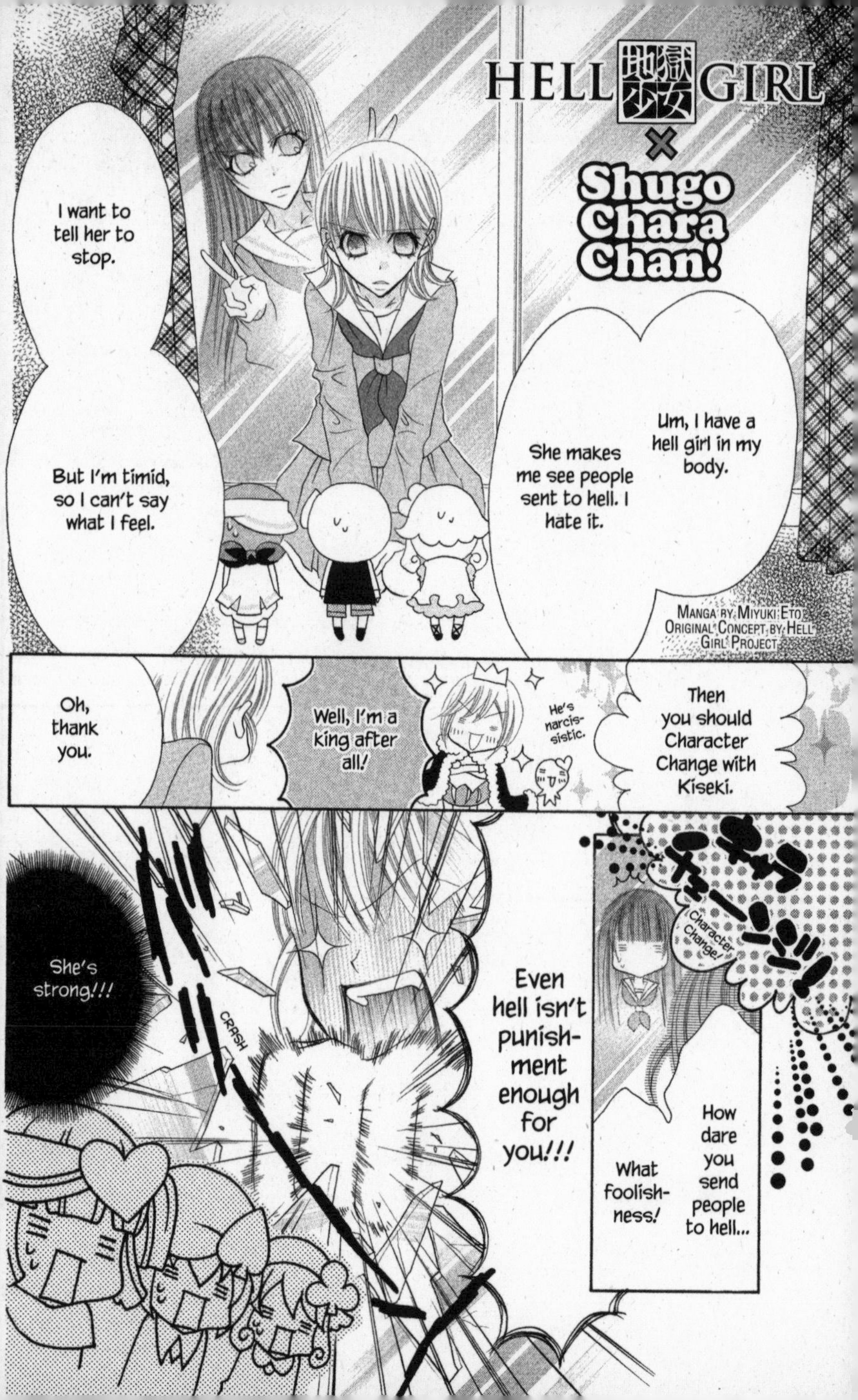
HELL 地獄少女 GIRL
×
Shugo Chara Chan!
Manga by Miyuki Eto
Original Concept by Hell Girl Project
Um, I have a hell girl in my body.
She makes me see people sent to hell. I hate it.
I want to tell her to stop.
But I'm timid, so I can't say what I feel.
Then you should Character Change with Kiseki.
He's narcissistic.
Well, I'm a king after all!
Oh, thank you.
Character Change!
How dare you send people to hell...
What foolishness!
Even hell isn't punishment enough for you!!!
CRASH
She's strong!!!

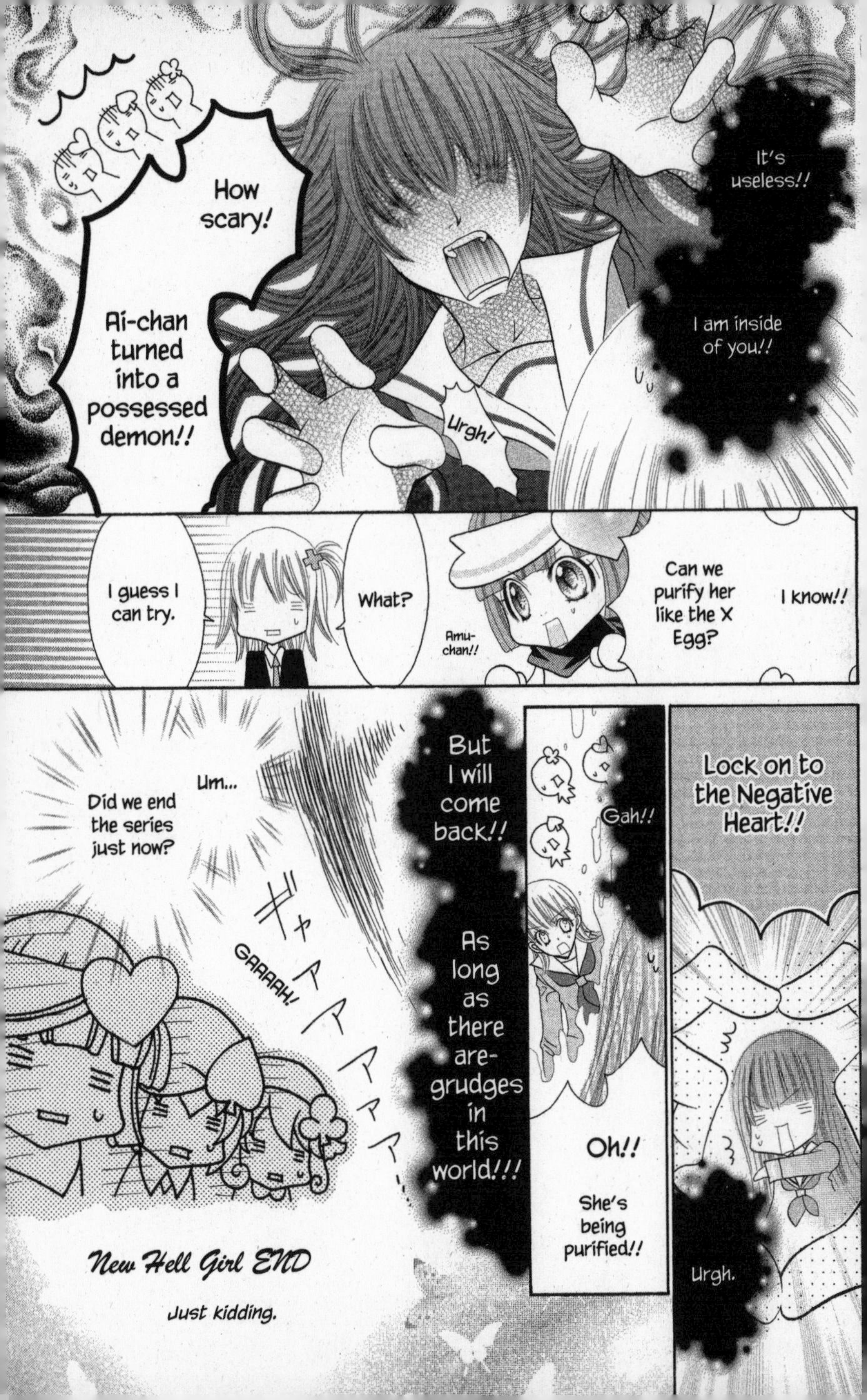
It's useless!!
I am inside of you!!
Urgh!
How scary!
Ai-chan turned into a possessed demon!!
I know!!
Can we purify her like the X Egg?
Amu-chan!!
What?
I guess I can try.
Lock on to the Negative Heart!!
Urgh.
Gah!!
Oh!!
She's being purified!!
But I will come back!!
As long as there are grudges in this world!!!
GAAAAH!
Um...
Did we end the series just now?
New Hell Girl END
Just kidding.

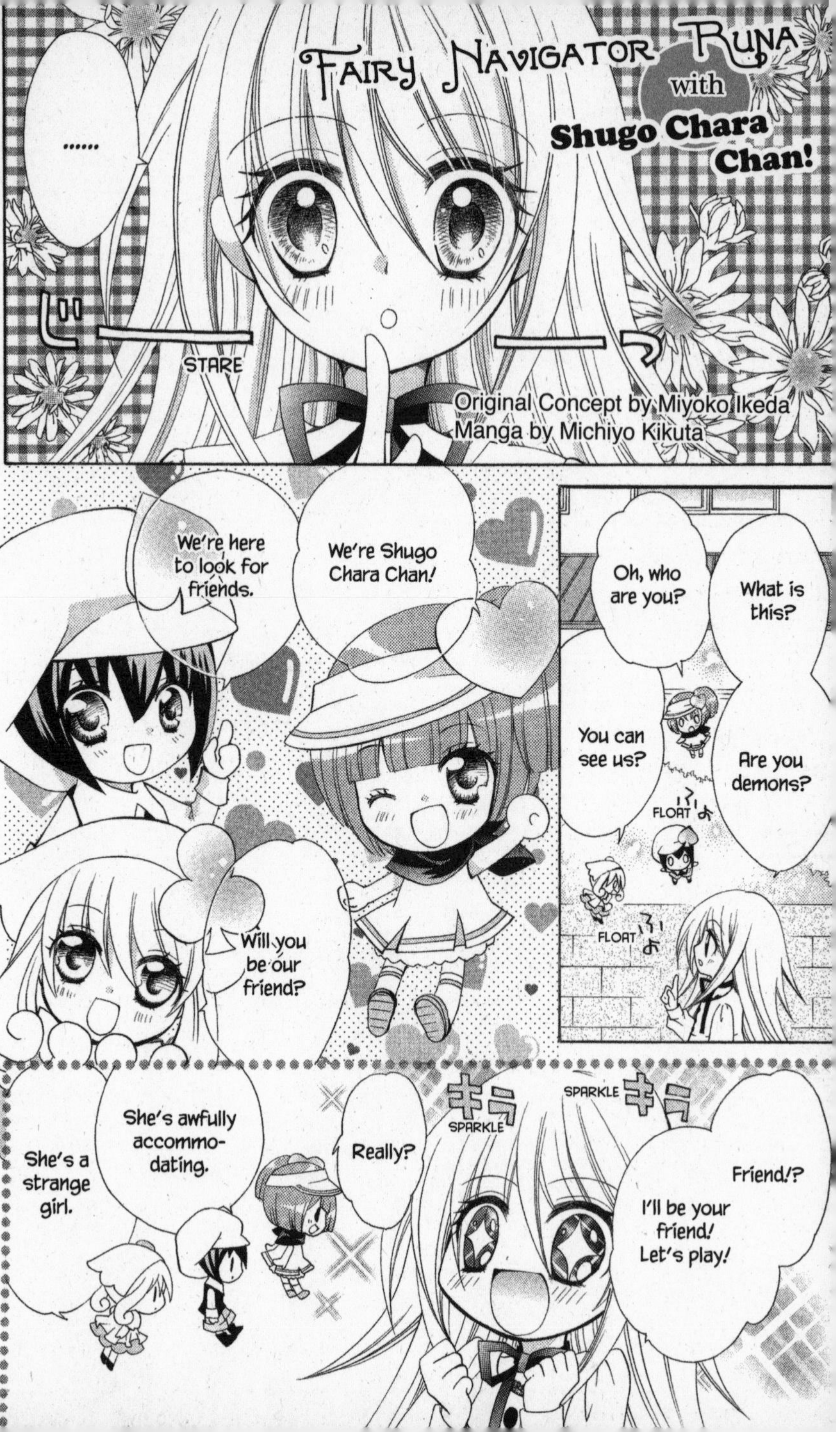
Fairy Navigator Runa
with
Shugo Chara Chan!
......
STARE
Original Concept by Miyoko Ikeda
Manga by Michiyo Kikuta
What is this?
Oh, who are you?
Are you demons?
You can see us?
FLOAT
FLOAT
We're Shugo Chara Chan!
We're here to look for friends.
Will you be our friend?
Friend!?
I'll be your friend! Let's play!
SPARKLE
SPARKLE
Really?
She's awfully accommo-dating.
She's a strange girl.

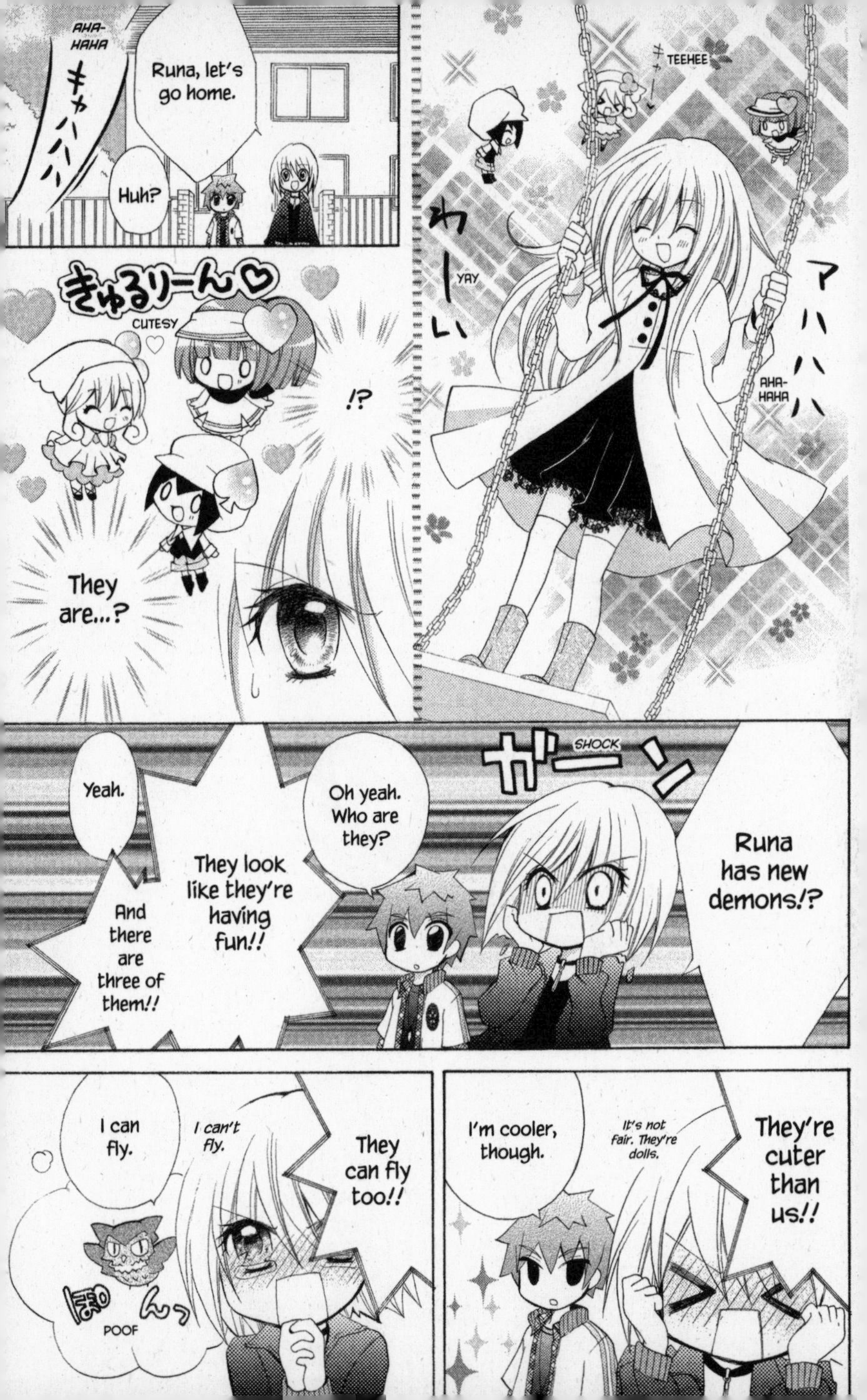

キャー
TEEHEE
アハハハ
AHA-HAHA
わーい
YAY
Runa, let's go home.
Huh?
キャハハハ
AHA-HAHA
!?
きゅるりーん♡
CUTESY
They are...?
Runa has new demons!?
ガーン
SHOCK
Oh yeah. Who are they?
They look like they're having fun!!
Yeah.
And there are three of them!!
They're cuter than us!!
It's not fair. They're dolls.
I'm cooler, though.
They can fly too!!
I can't fly.
I can fly.
ぽんっ
POOF

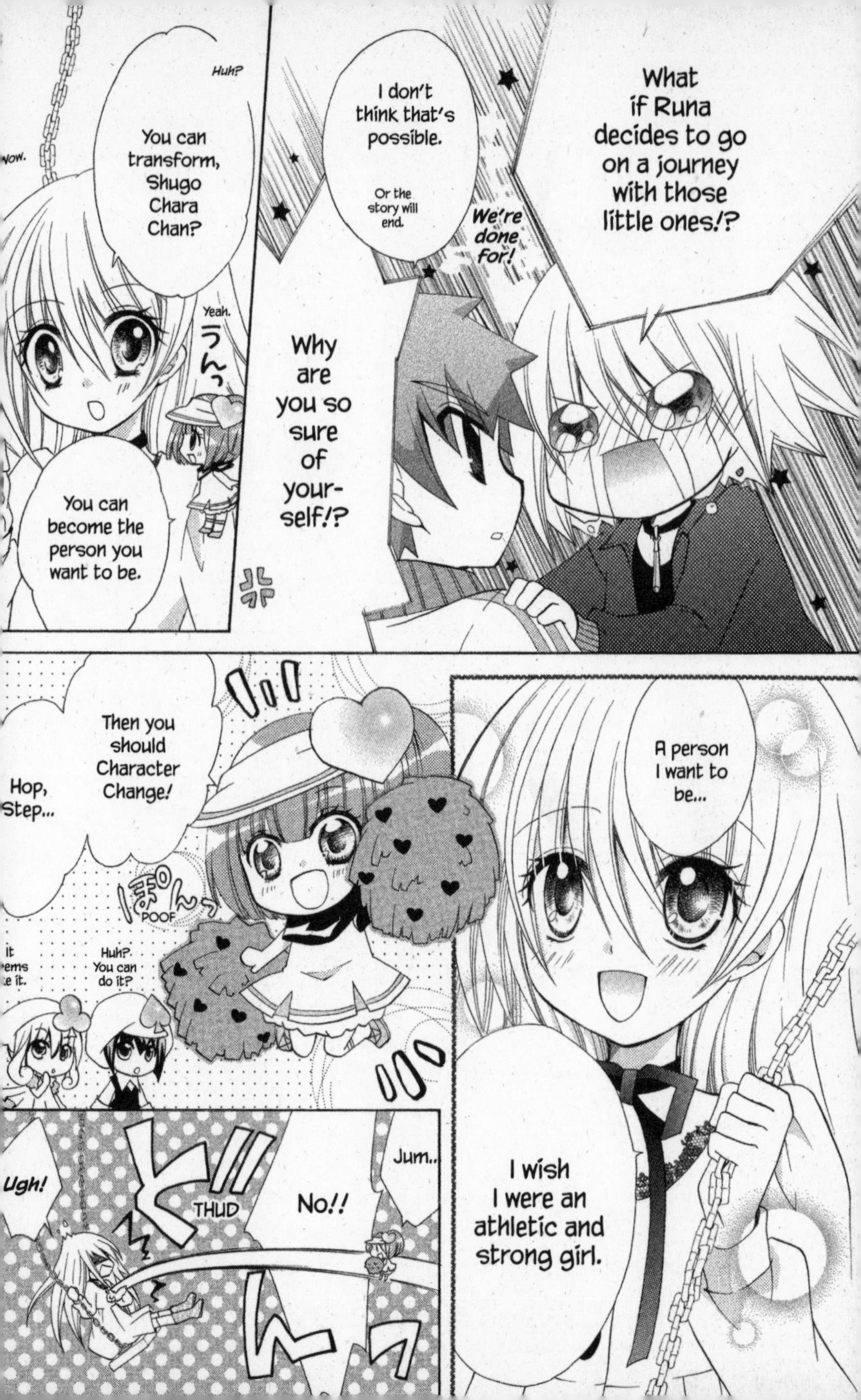
What if Runa decides to go on a journey with those little ones!?
We're done for!
I don't think that's possible.
Or the story will end.
Why are you so sure of yourself!?
Huh?
You can transform, Shugo Chara Chan?
Now.
Yeah.
うんっ
You can become the person you want to be.
A person I want to be...
I wish I were an athletic and strong girl.
Then you should Character Change!
Hop, Step...
POOF
Huh? You can do it?
Jum..
No!!
Ugh!
THUD

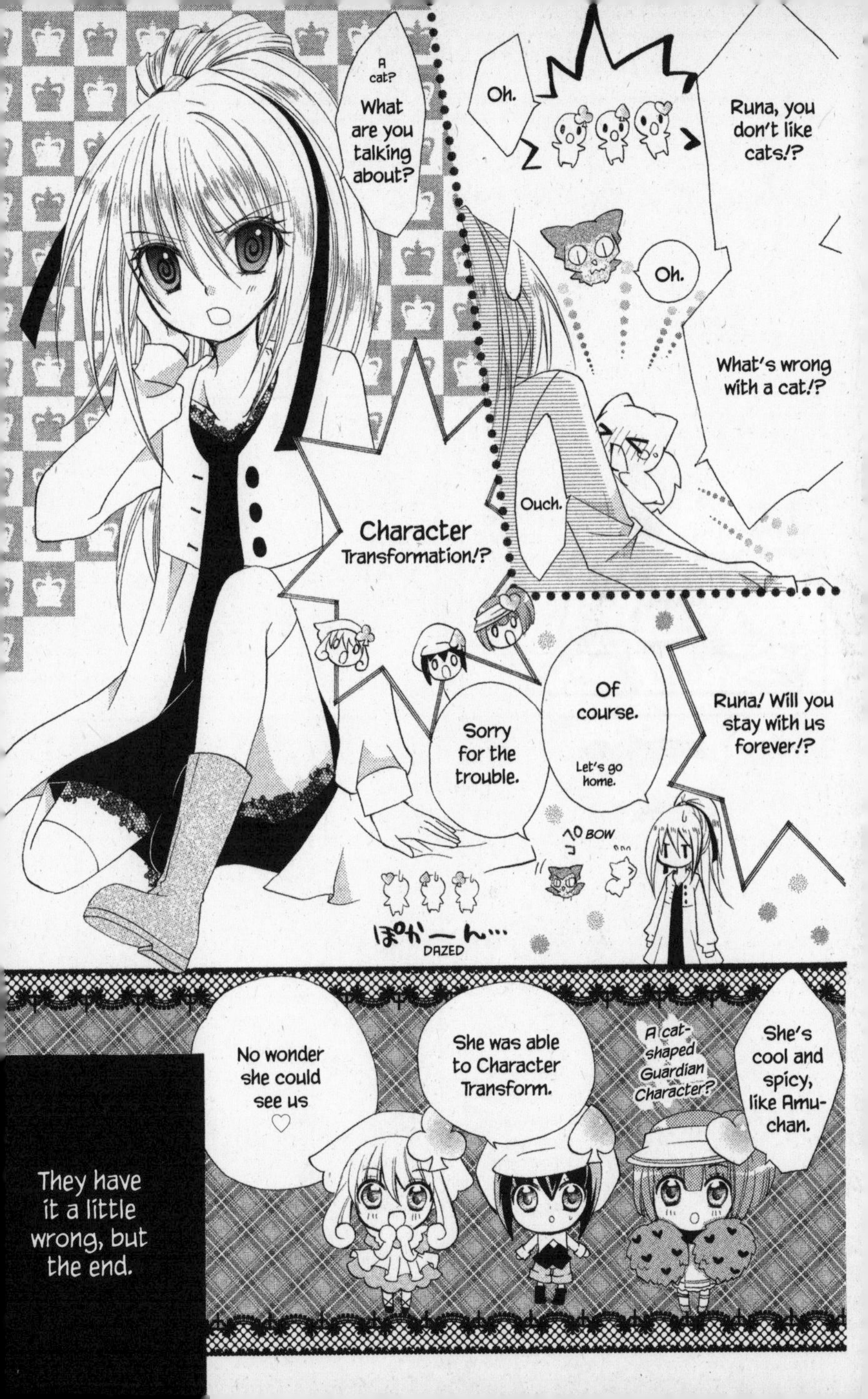
Runa, you don't like cats!?
Oh.
Oh.
What's wrong with a cat!?
Ouch.
Runa! Will you stay with us forever!?
Of course. Let's go home.
Sorry for the trouble.
BOW
ぽかーん… DAZED
A cat? What are you talking about?
Character Transformation!?
She's cool and spicy, like Amu-chan.
A cat-shaped Guardian Character?
She was able to Character Transform.
No wonder she could see us ♡
They have it a little wrong, but the end.

Don't Play With Your Food

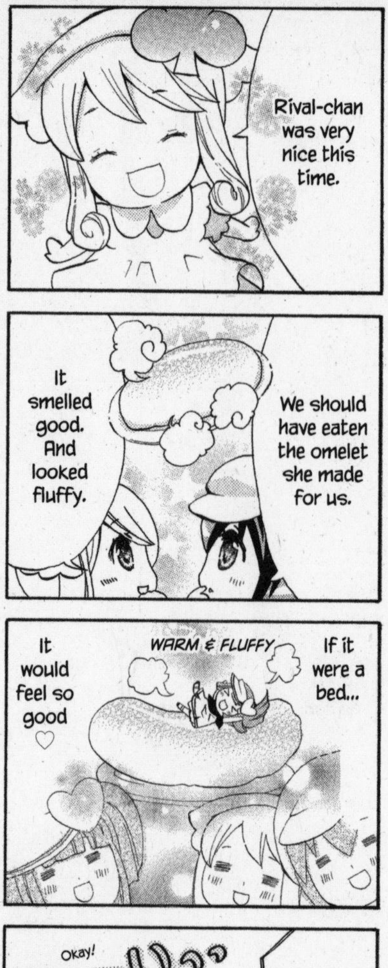

Rival-chan was very nice this time.
We should have eaten the omelet she made for us.
It smelled good. And looked fluffy.
If it were a bed...
WARM & FLUFFY
It would feel so good ♡
You have to eat food, alright!?
Okay!
はーいっっ

Perfect Me

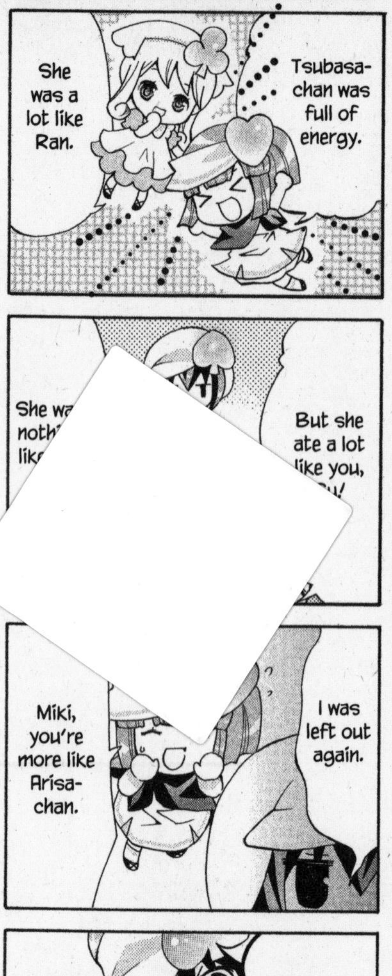

Tsubasa-chan was full of energy.
She was a lot like Ran.
But she ate a lot like you,
I was left out again.
Miki, you're more like Arisa-chan.
Athletic and smart, good manners and perfect girl. Not just similar... it is me!!
No, just a little bit like.
You're going over-board.

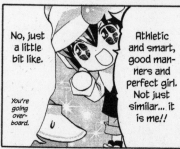

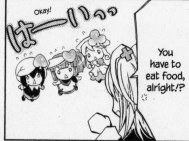

Published in "Nakayoshi" January 2009 - September 2009, "Nakayoshi February Special Edition Nakayoshi Lovely," "Nakayoshi May Special Edition Nakayoshi Lovely," "Nakayoshi July Special Edition Nakayoshi Lovely," "Nakayoshi September Special Edition Nakayoshi Lovely."

A Girls' Dream

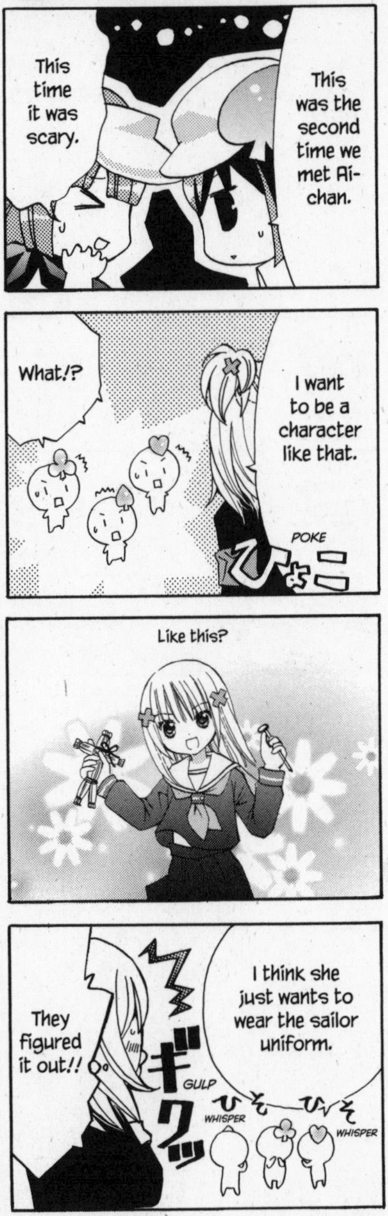
This was the second time we met Ai-chan.
This time it was scary.
I want to be a character like that.
What!?
POKE
Like this?
I think she just wants to wear the sailor uniform.
WHISPER
ひそ ひそ
WHISPER
They figured it out!!
GULP
ギクッ

Something Similar?

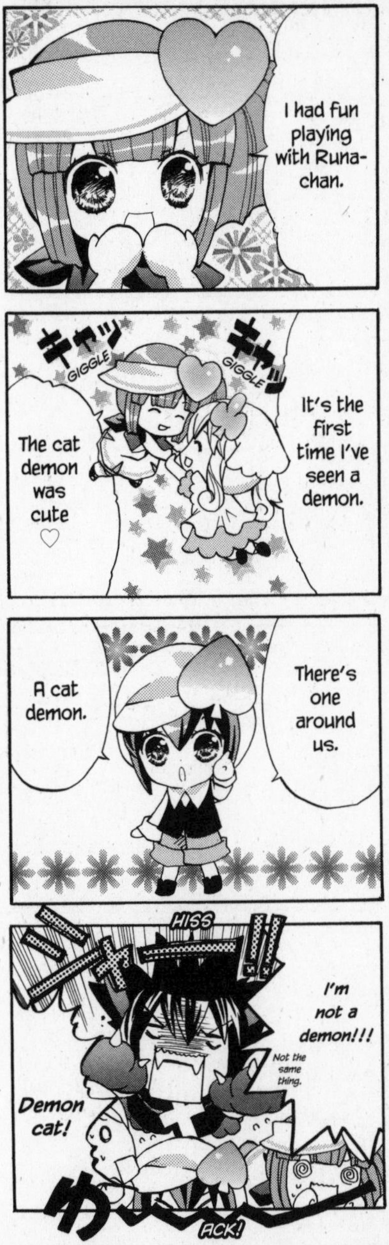
I had fun playing with Runa-chan.
キャッ
GIGGLE
It's the first time I've seen a demon.
キャッ
GIGGLE
The cat demon was cute ♡
There's one around us.
A cat demon.
HISS
I'm not a demon!!!
Not the same thing.
Demon cat!
ACK!

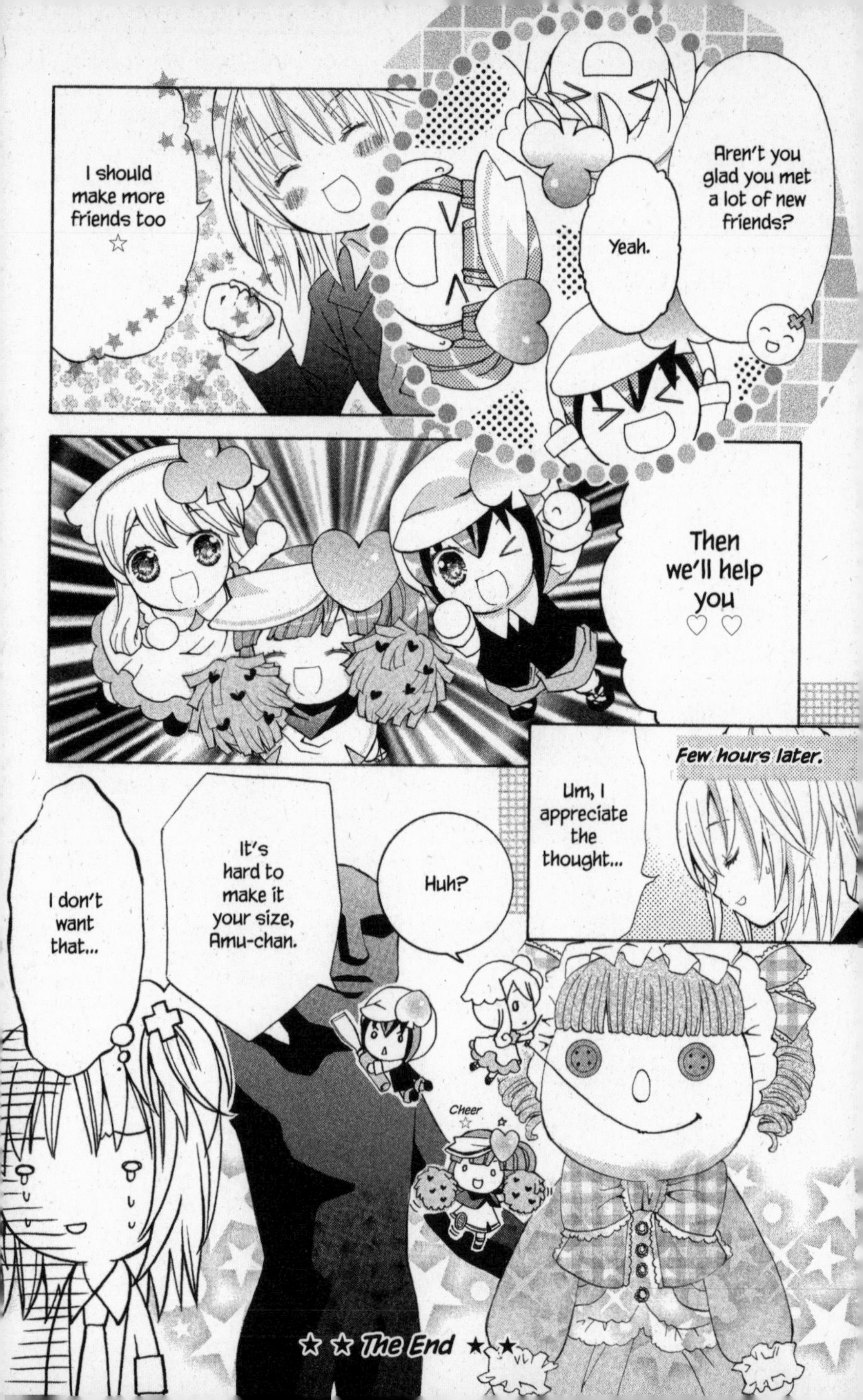
Aren't you glad you met a lot of new friends?
Yeah.
I should make more friends too ☆
Then we'll help you ♡ ♡
Few hours later.
Um, I appreciate the thought...
Huh?
It's hard to make it your size, Amu-chan.
I don't want that...
Cheer ☆
☆ ☆ The End ★ ★

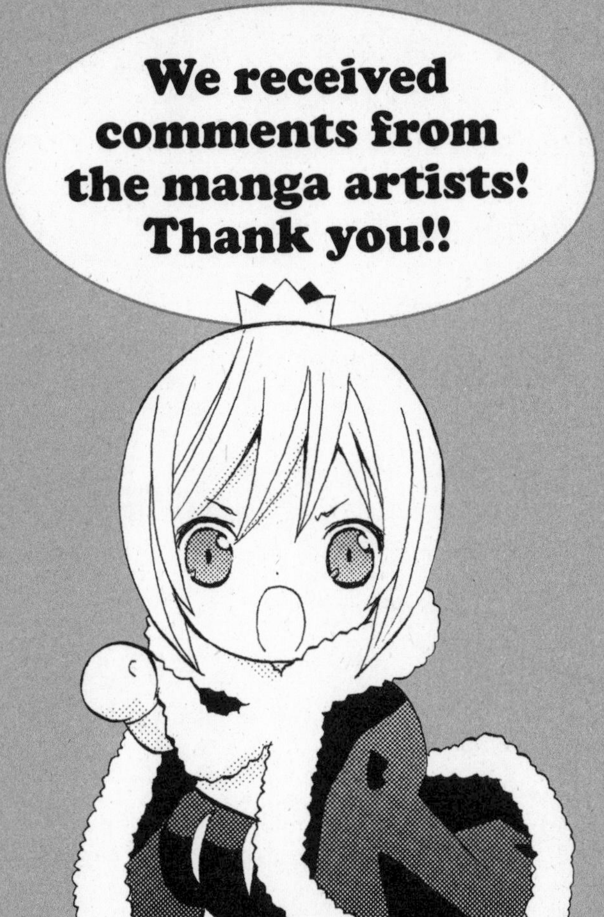
We received comments from the manga artists! Thank you!!

COMMENT

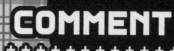

When
I drew "Shugo Chara
Chan!" I was imagining how the eggs
in my fridge turned into Guardian Eggs.

PS. Comment from Shime-chan:

"I'll go on a diet so you can carry me.
So take me to your home!"

Yuriko Abe

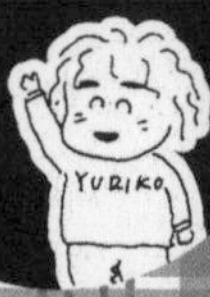
YURIKO

Thank you for letting me
participate in "Shugo Chara Chan!"
Since my series is dark, my heart got
lighter drawing "Shugo Chara Chan!" I had
fun drawing Su's girly poses ♡

Natsumi Ando

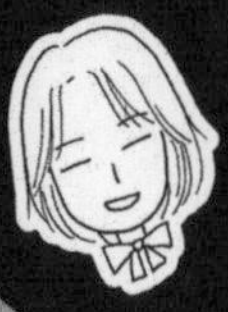

Thank you for letting me stop by again! The story of Hell Girl is dark and dreary, I had fun drawing a comedy. I don't have the artistic skill or calmness, so I want to Character Transform with Miki and become Amulet Spade.

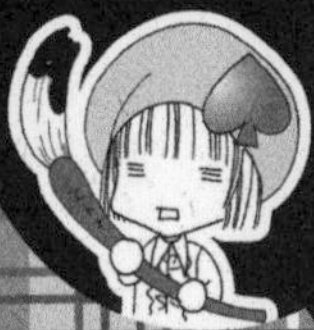

+ + + + + + + + + + + + + + + + +

Miyuki Eto

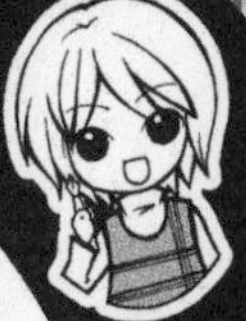

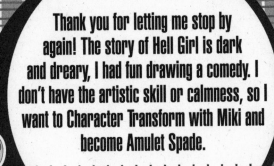

I was so excited to be able to draw my favorite "Shugo Chara Chan!" I had so much fun!! I'm so happy Runa and "Shugo Chara Chan!" got to be on the same page! I wish I got to draw Amu-chan too (lol). Thank you!!

+ + + + + + + + + + + + + + + + +

Michiyo Kikuta

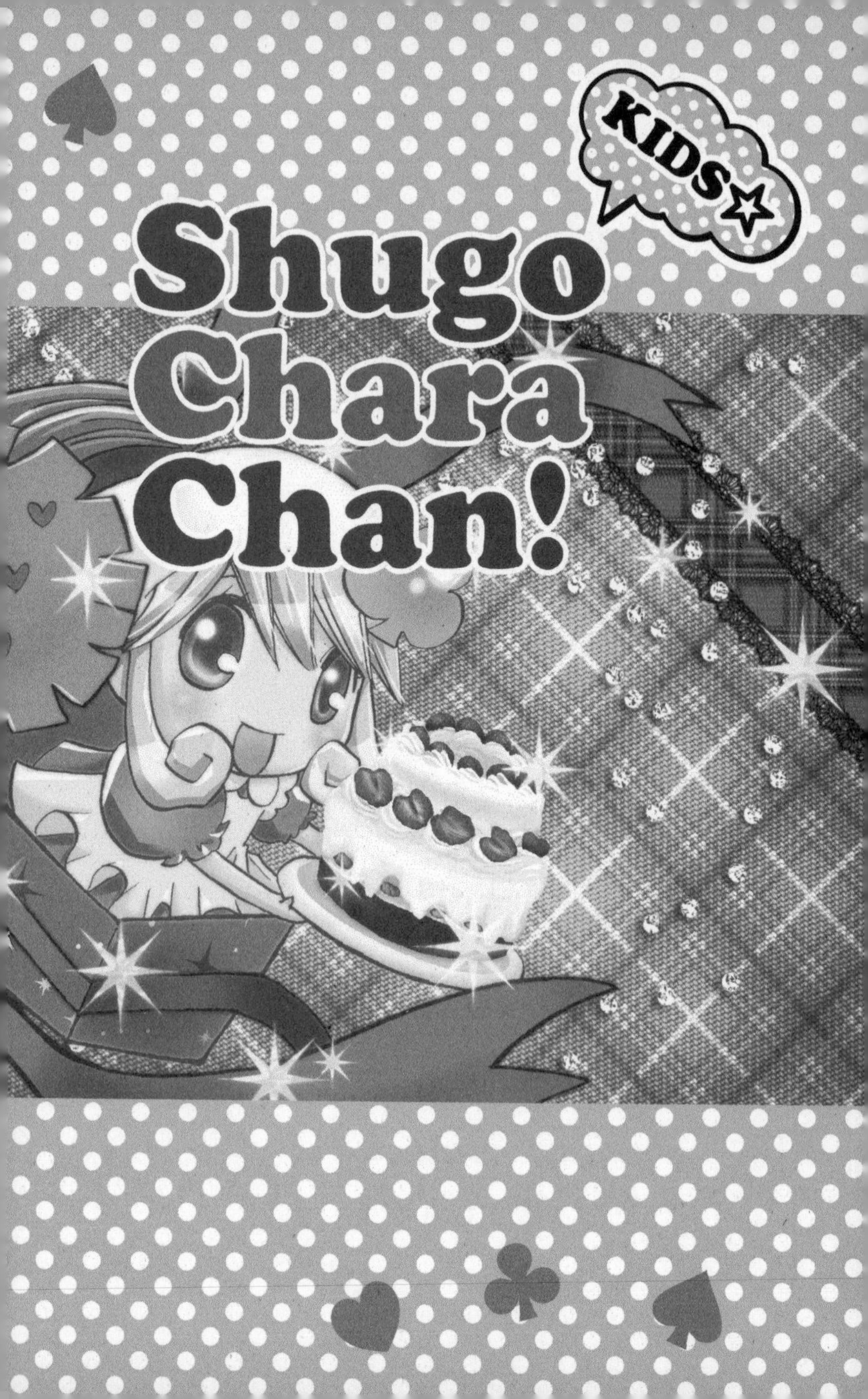
KIDS☆
Shugo Chara Chan!

Everybody
Loves
Christmas!
♥ Again

Christmas Cake Battle

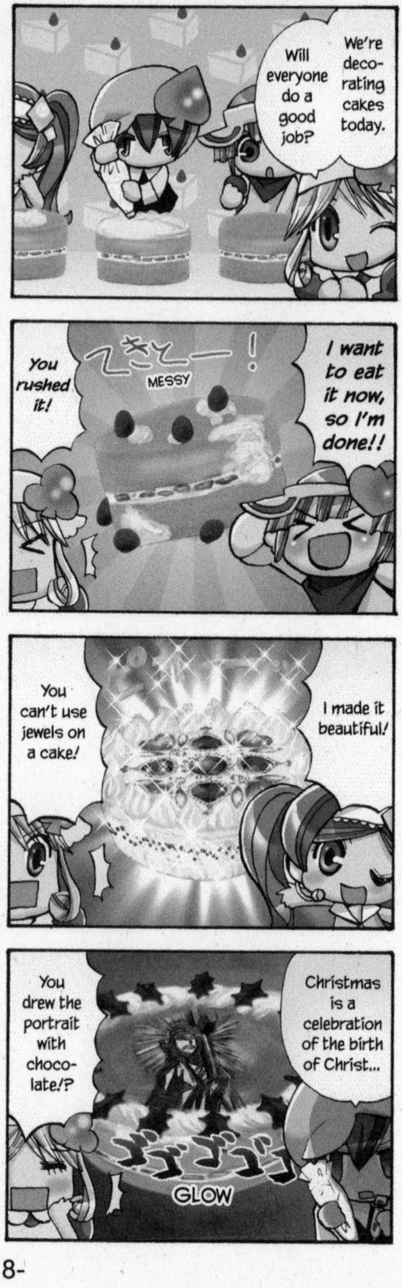
We're decorating cakes today.
Will everyone do a good job?
I want to eat it now, so I'm done!!
てきとー！
MESSY
You rushed it!
I made it beautiful!
You can't use jewels on a cake!
Christmas is a celebration of the birth of Christ...
You drew the portrait with chocolate!?
GLOW

Chimney

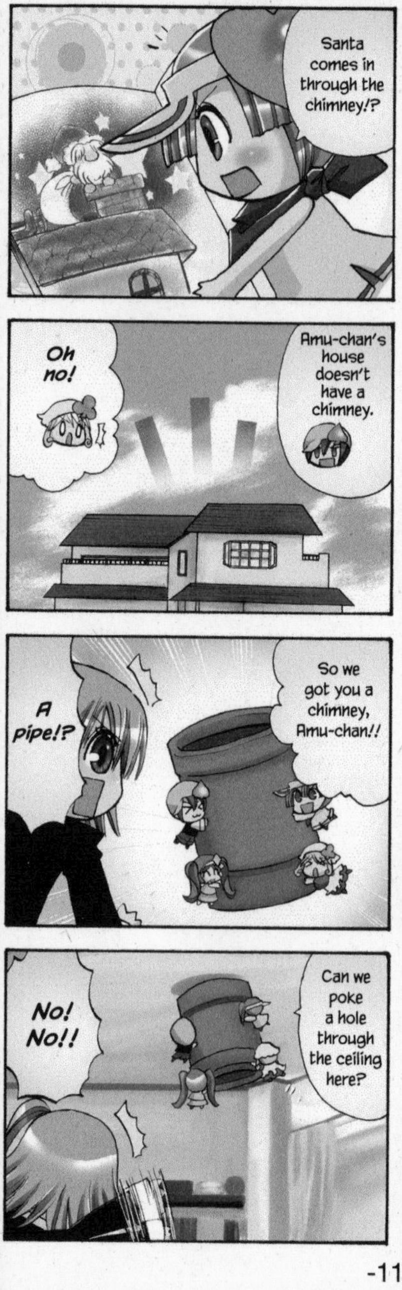
Santa comes in through the chimney!?
Amu-chan's house doesn't have a chimney.
Oh no!
So we got you a chimney, Amu-chan!!
A pipe!?
Can we poke a hole through the ceiling here?
No! No!!

Red Nose

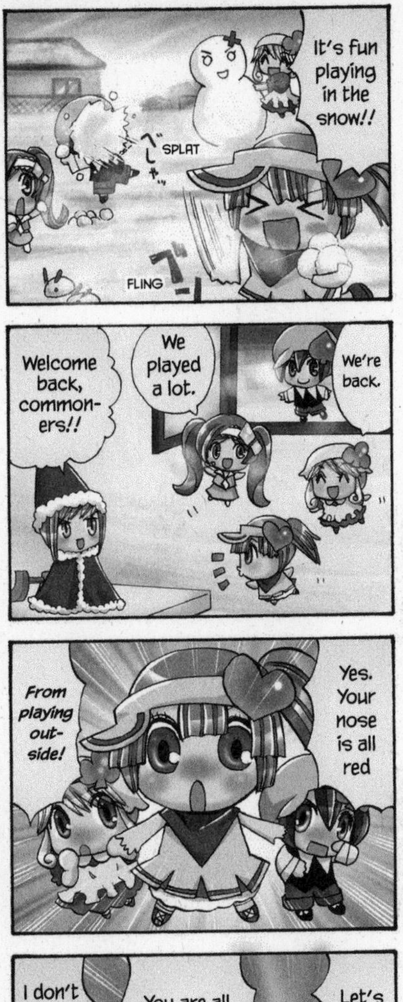
It's fun playing in the snow!!
SPLAT
FLING
We're back.
We played a lot.
Welcome back, commoners!!
Yes. Your nose is all red
From playing outside!
Let's play Santa!
You are all red-nosed reindeer!
I don't want to pull a sled!

Lots of Santa!

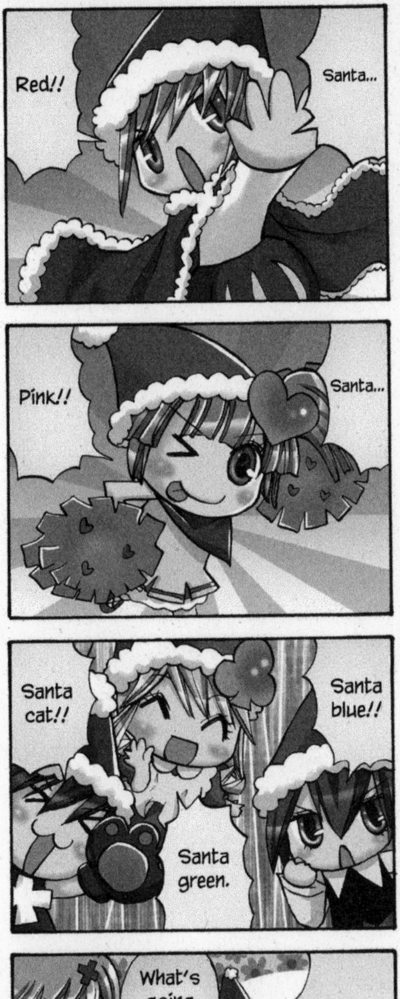
Santa...
Red!!
Santa...
Pink!!
Santa blue!!
Santa cat!!
Santa green.
No Santa cat!!
What's going on?
They all wanted to be Santa.

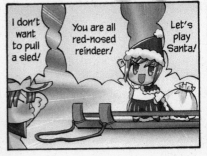

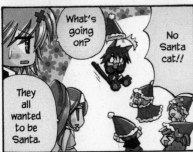

A Big Stocking

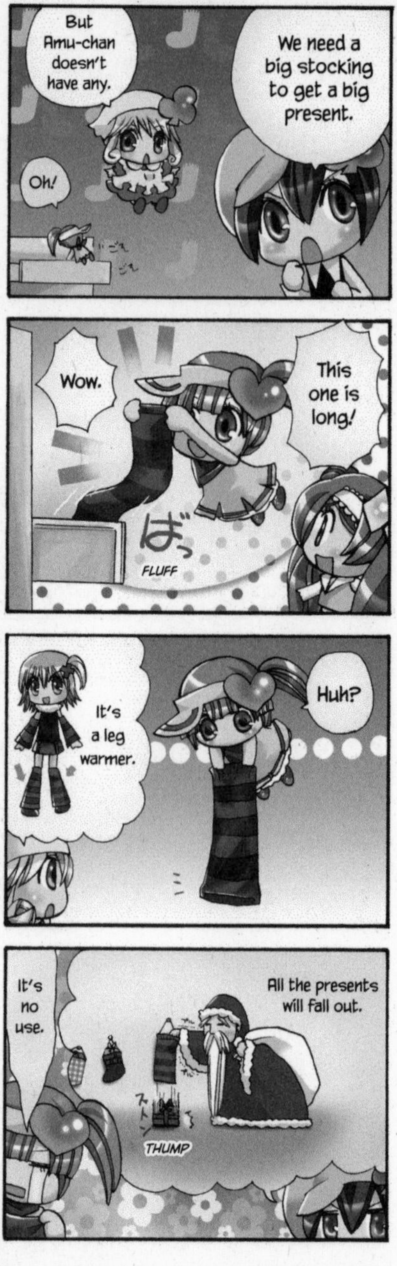
We need a big stocking to get a big present.
But Amu-chan doesn't have any.
Oh!
This one is long!
Wow.
ばっ
FLUFF
Huh?
It's a leg warmer.
All the presents will fall out.
It's no use.
THUMP

Tree is Lit

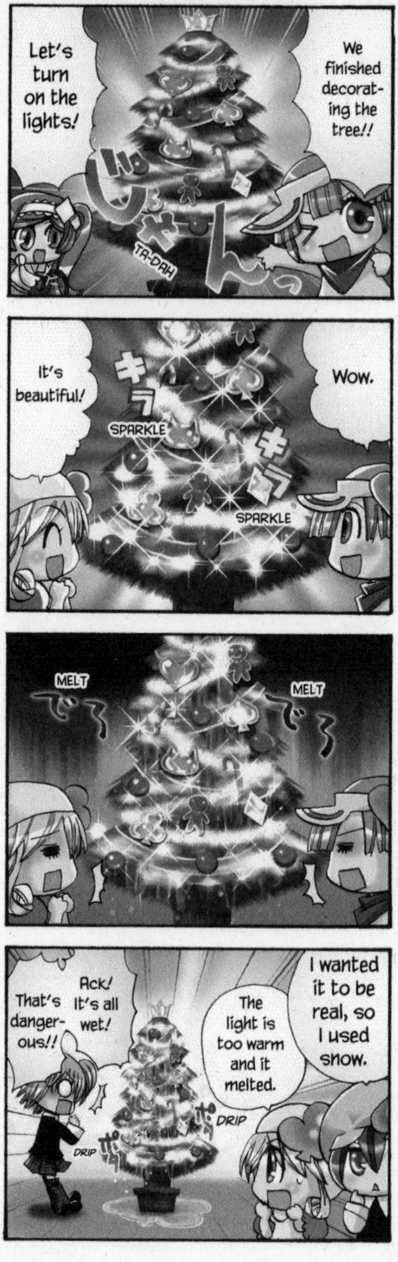
We finished decorating the tree!!
Let's turn on the lights!
TA-DAH
Wow.
It's beautiful!
SPARKLE
SPARKLE
MELT
MELT
I wanted it to be real, so I used snow.
The light is too warm and it melted.
Ack! It's all wet!
That's danger-ous!!
DRIP
DRIP

X Egg All Over?

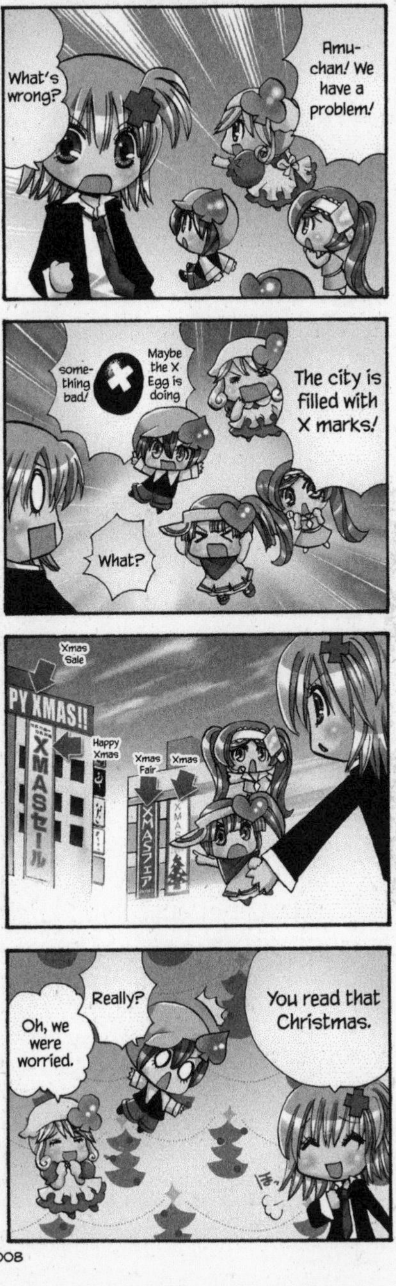
Amu-chan! We have a problem!
What's wrong?
The city is filled with X marks!
Maybe the X Egg is doing
something bad!
What?
Xmas Sale
PY XMAS!!
Happy Xmas
Xmas
Xmas Fair
You read that Christmas.
Really?
Oh, we were worried.

Part-Time Santa?

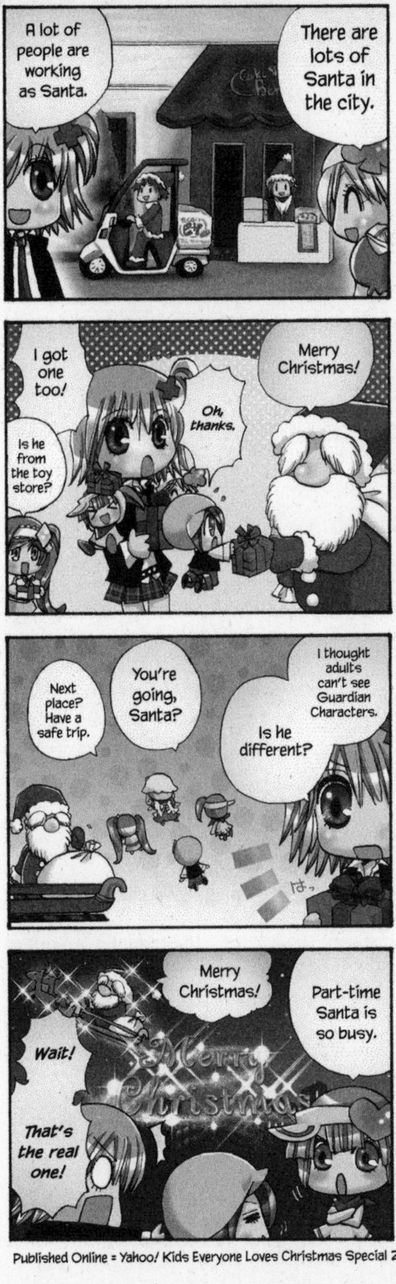
There are lots of Santa in the city.
A lot of people are working as Santa.
Merry Christmas!
Oh, thanks.
I got one too!
Is he from the toy store?
I thought adults can't see Guardian Characters.
Is he different?
You're going, Santa?
Next place? Have a safe trip.
Part-time Santa is so busy.
Merry Christmas!
Merry Christmas
Wait!
That's the real one!

Published Online = Yahoo! Kids Everyone Loves Christmas Special 2008

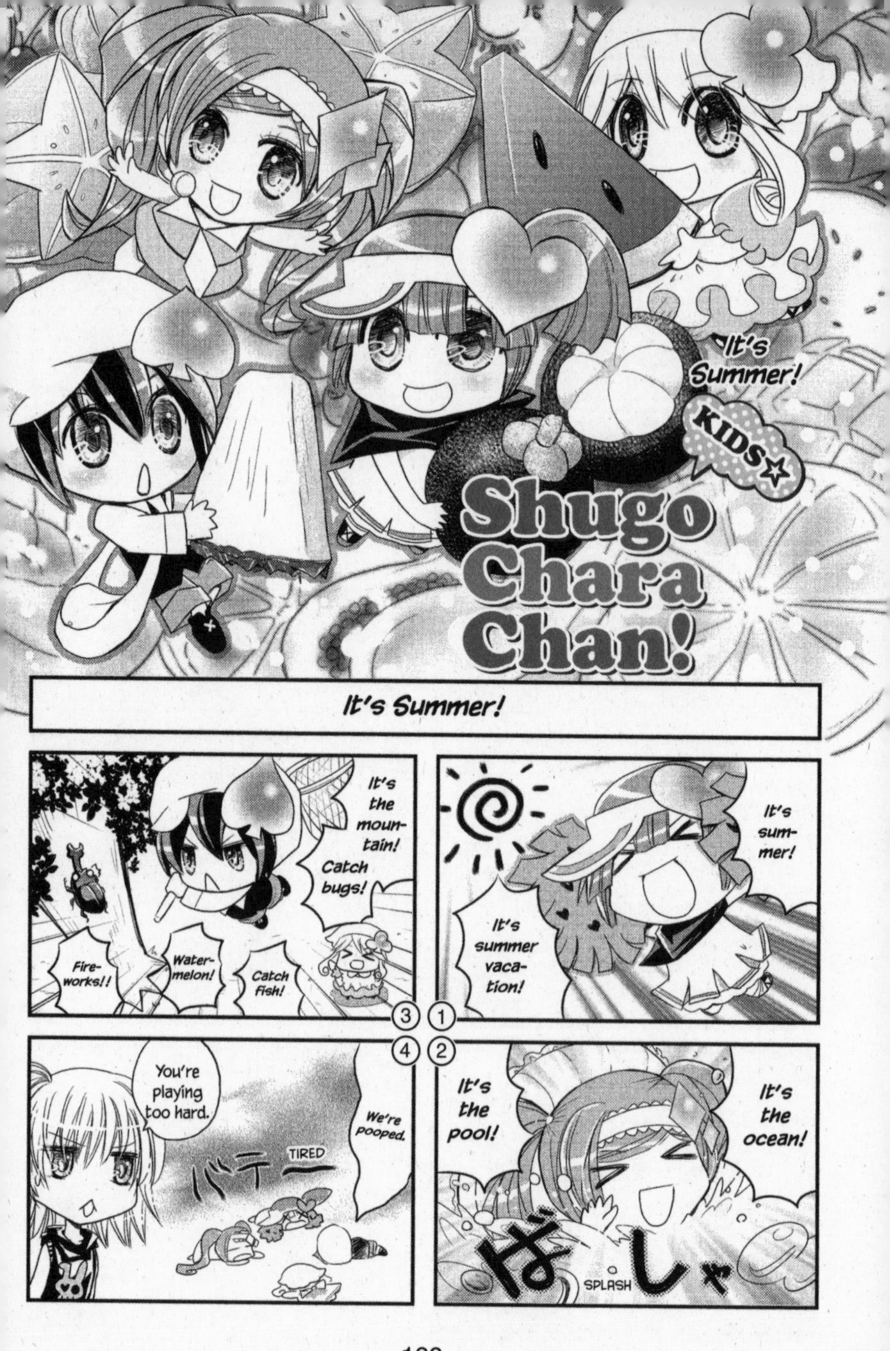
It's Summer!
KIDS☆
Shugo Chara Chan!
It's Summer!
It's summer!
It's summer vacation!
It's the ocean!
It's the pool!
ぱしゃ
SPLASH
It's the mountain!
Catch bugs!
Catch fish!
Watermelon!
Fireworks!!
We're pooped.
バテー
TIRED
You're playing too hard.

Cicada

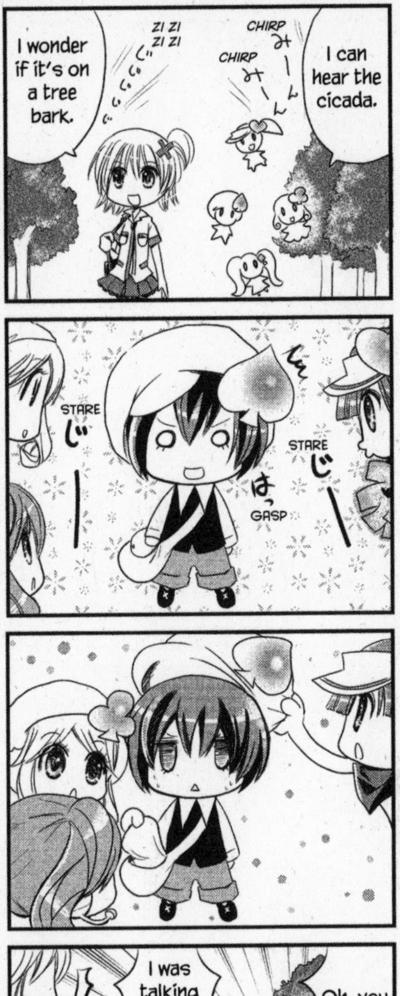
I can hear the cicada.
CHIRP
CHIRP
ZI ZI ZI ZI
I wonder if it's on a tree bark.
STARE じー
GASP は
STARE じー
Oh, you got it wrong.
I was talking about a tree bark.

Clouds

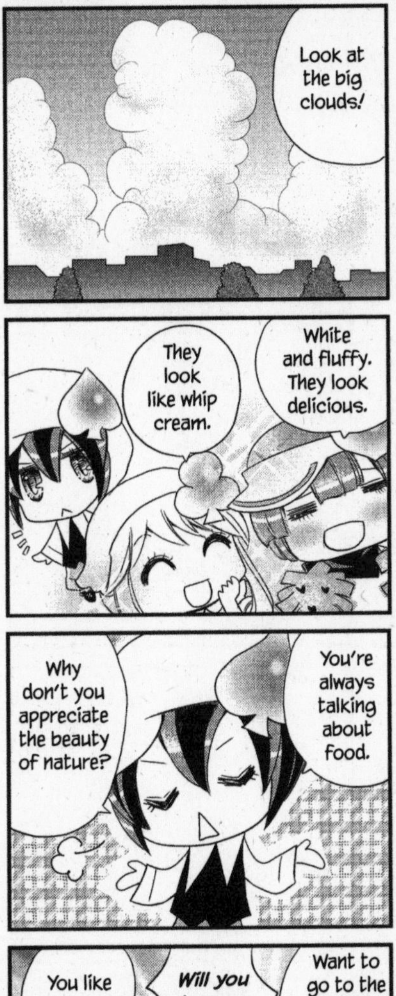
Look at the big clouds!
White and fluffy. They look delicious.
They look like whip cream.
You're always talking about food.
Why don't you appreciate the beauty of nature?
Want to go to the summer festival tonight?
Will you buy me cotton candy?
GLEAM
TURN ば
You like to eat too, Miki.

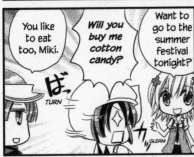

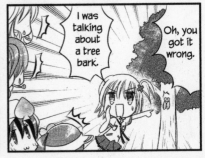

Bug Spray

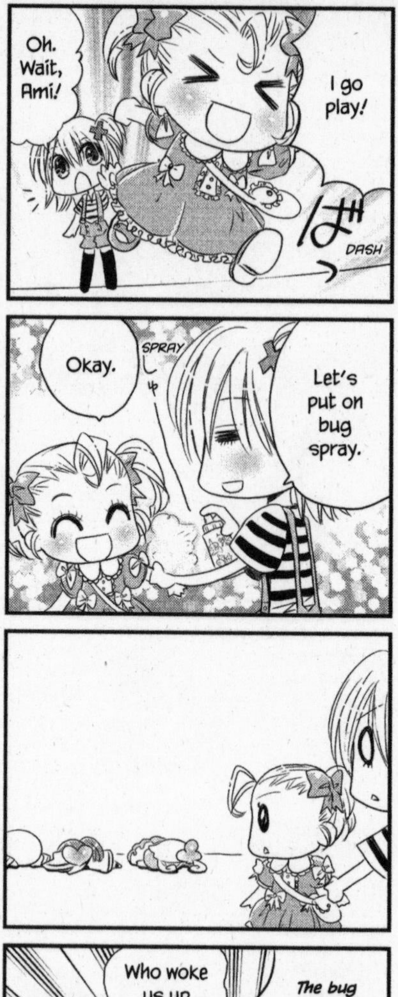
I go play!
Oh. Wait, Ami!
DASH
Let's put on bug spray.
SPRAY
Okay.
The bug spray hurt the Guardian Characters!!!
Who woke us up from our nap?
WAAAH!
YAWN

Sun Burn

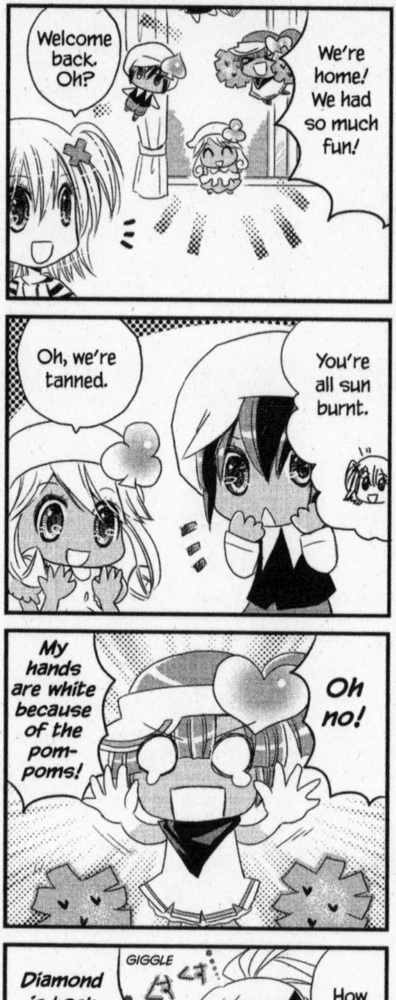
We're home! We had so much fun!
Welcome back. Oh?
You're all sun burnt.
Oh, we're tanned.
Oh no!
My hands are white because of the pom-poms!
How lame.
GIGGLE
Diamond is back to her X Character!

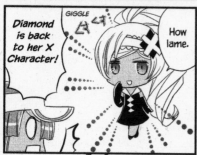

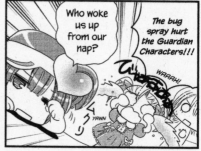

Noodles

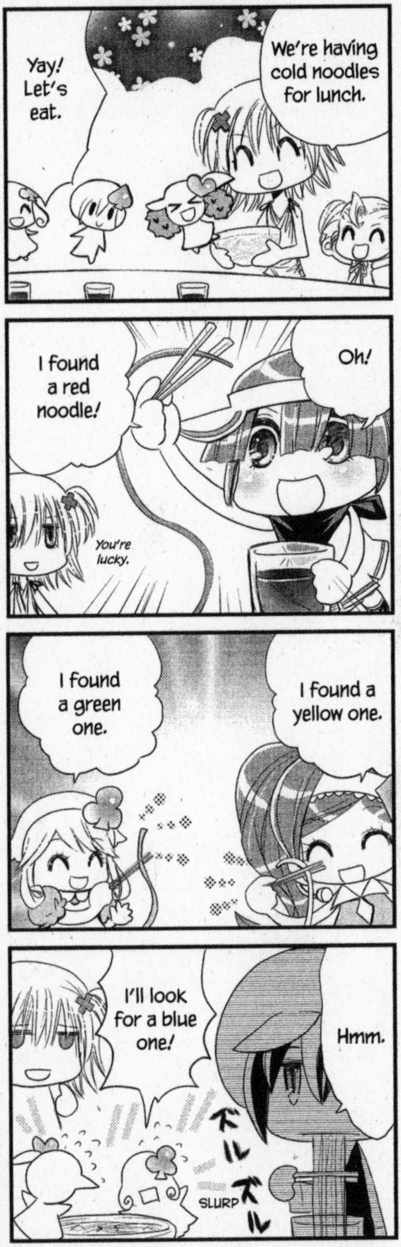
We're having cold noodles for lunch.
Yay! Let's eat.
Oh!
I found a red noodle!
You're lucky.
I found a yellow one.
I found a green one.
Hmm.
ズルズル
SLURP
I'll look for a blue one!

Snow Cone

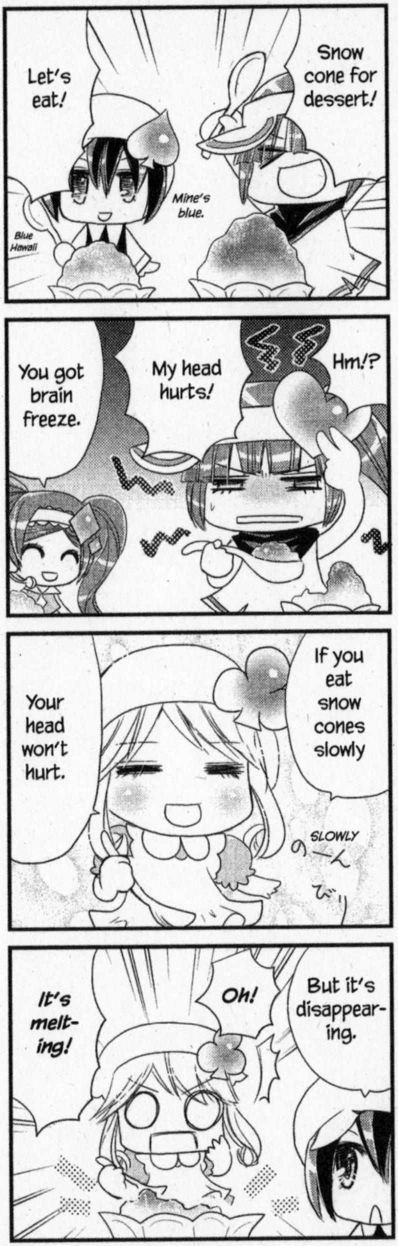
Snow cone for dessert!
Mine's blue.
Let's eat!
Blue Hawaii
Hm!?
My head hurts!
You got brain freeze.
If you eat snow cones slowly
Your head won't hurt.
SLOWLY
のーんびり
But it's disappearing.
Oh!
It's melting!

Fan

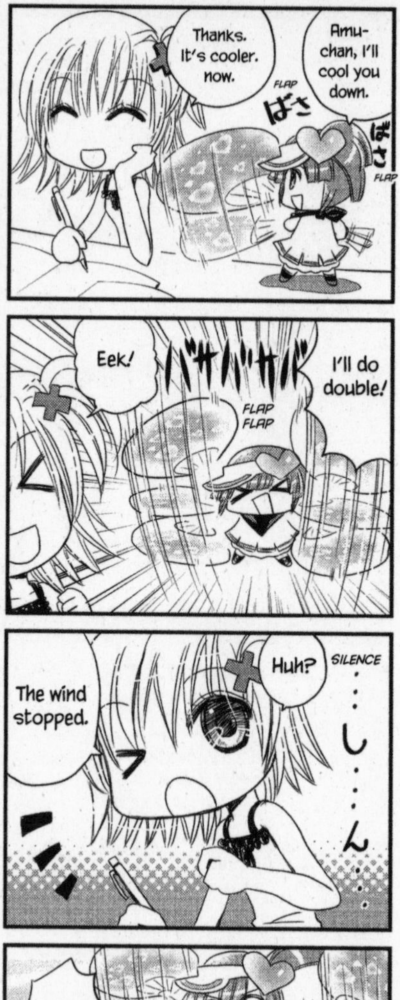
Amu-chan, I'll cool you down.
ばさ
FLAP
Thanks. It's cooler. now.
ばさ
FLAP
I'll do double!
バサバサ
FLAP FLAP
Eek!
SILENCE
し…ん…
Huh?
The wind stopped.
R- Ran!
FLAP FLAP FLAP

Video Games

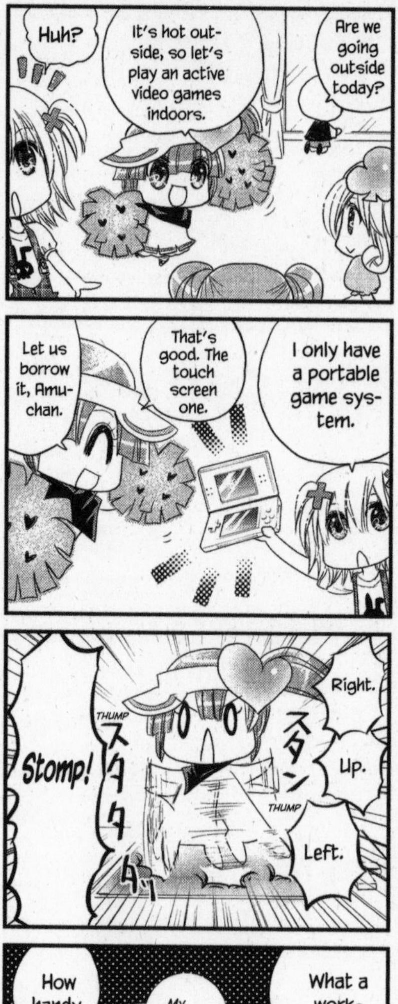
Are we going outside today?
It's hot outside, so let's play an active video games indoors.
Huh?
I only have a portable game system.
That's good. The touch screen one.
Let us borrow it, Amu-chan.
Right.
Up.
スタン
THUMP
Left.
スタタタッ
THUMP
Stomp!
What a workout!
WHEW
My turn.
How handy.
That's cool.

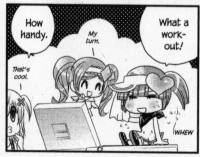

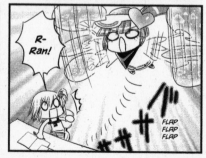

Sunflower

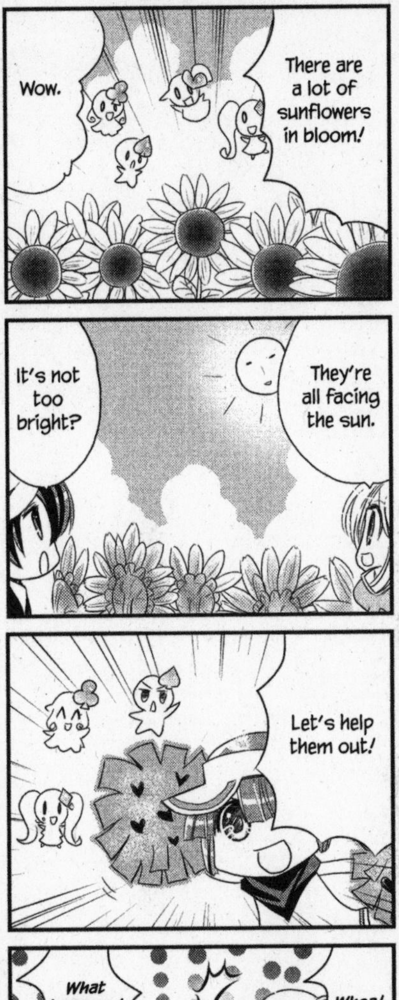

There are a lot of sunflowers in bloom!
Wow.
They're all facing the sun.
It's not too bright?
Let's help them out!
Whoa!
What happened to these sunflowers!?

Wind Chime

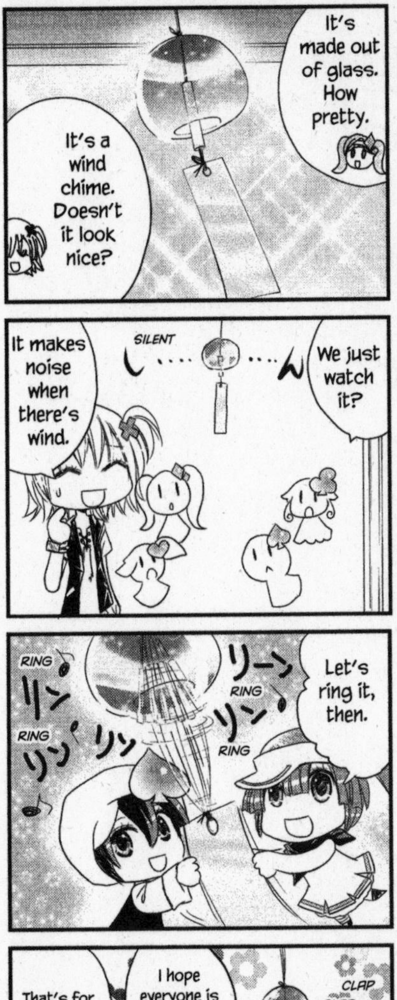

It's made out of glass. How pretty.
It's a wind chime. Doesn't it look nice?
We just watch it?
SILENT
し・・・・ ・・・・ん
It makes noise when there's wind.
Let's ring it, then.
リーン
RING
リン
RING
RING
リン
リッ
リッ
RING
CLAP
CLAP
I hope everyone is safe and at peace.
That's for New Year celebration.

Original manga

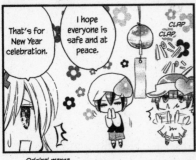

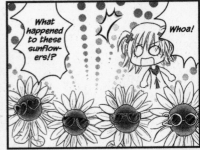

You can collaborate with Shugo Chara Chan! Coloring Page ☆

Make a copy and color the pages! Can you make them pretty?

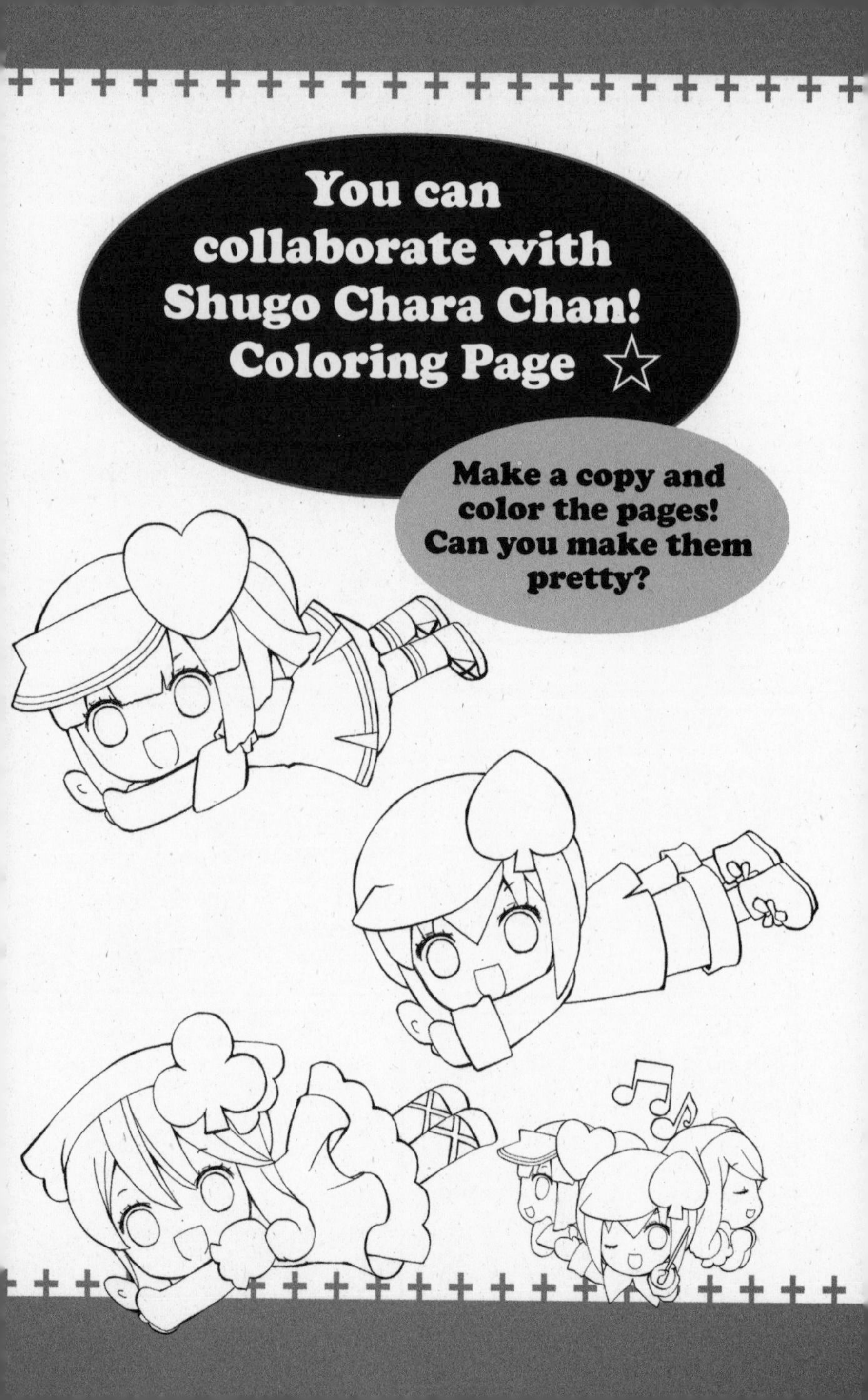

Afterword

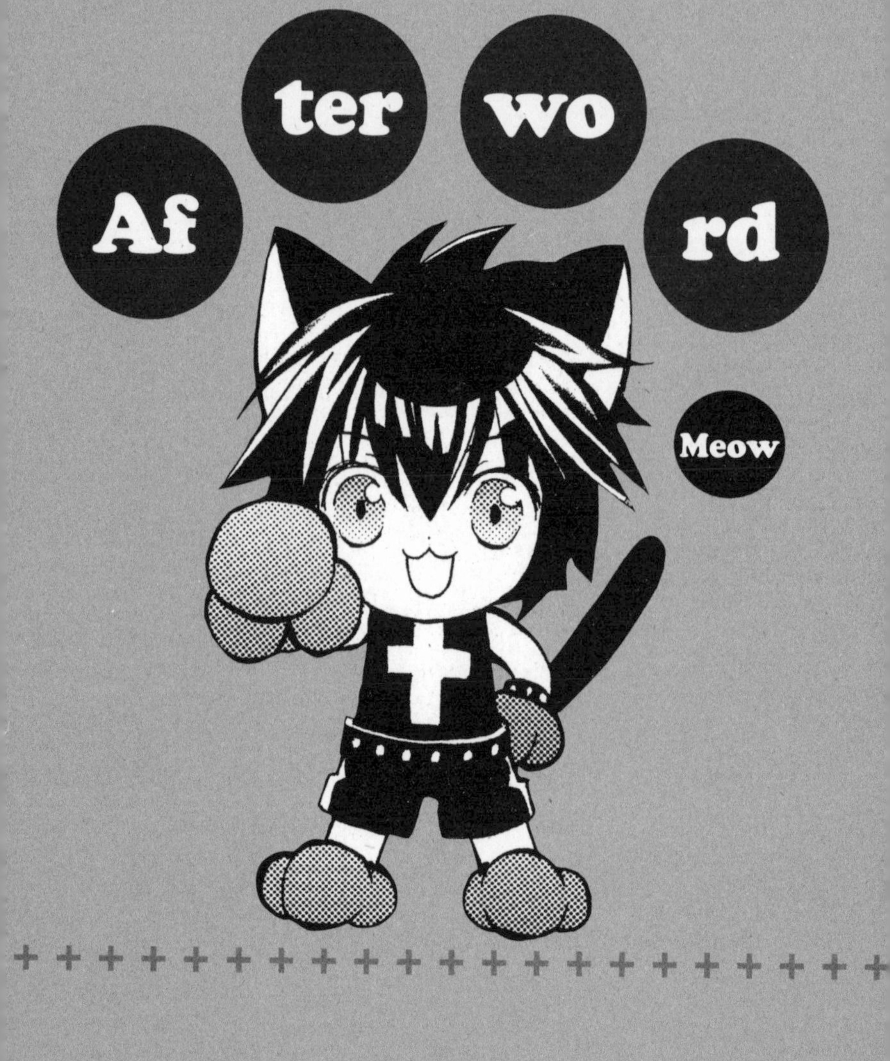
Meow

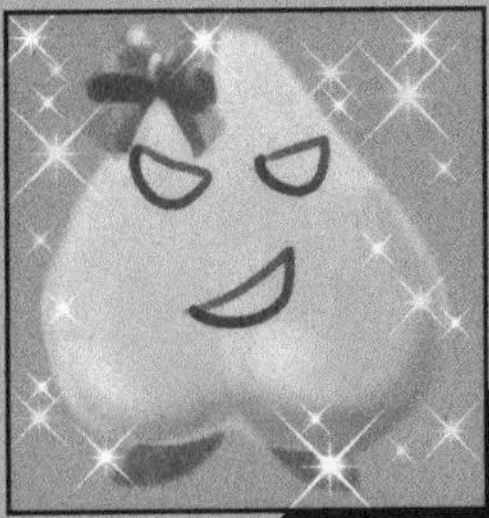

It's the second
volume of "Shugo Chara Chan!"
Clap clap! It's a wonderful spin-off
world created by Naphthalene Mizushima
sensei, Kinomin sensei and other
manga artists. We get to read a new
volume, which makes us, PEACH-PIT, and the
readers doubly happy! Read it
many times and smile lots ★

PEACH-PIT

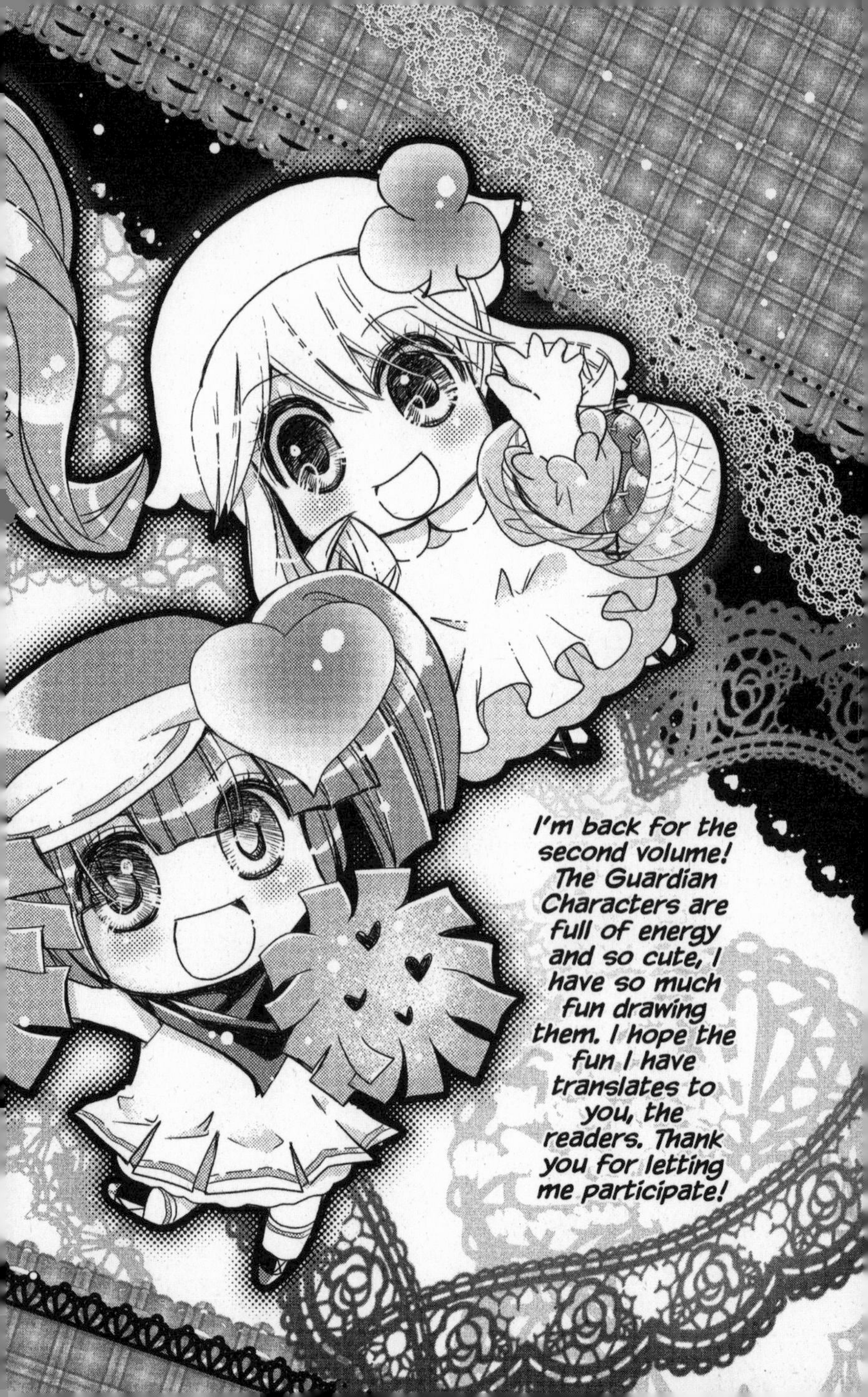
I'm back for the second volume! The Guardian Characters are full of energy and so cute, I have so much fun drawing them. I hope the fun I have translates to you, the readers. Thank you for letting me participate!

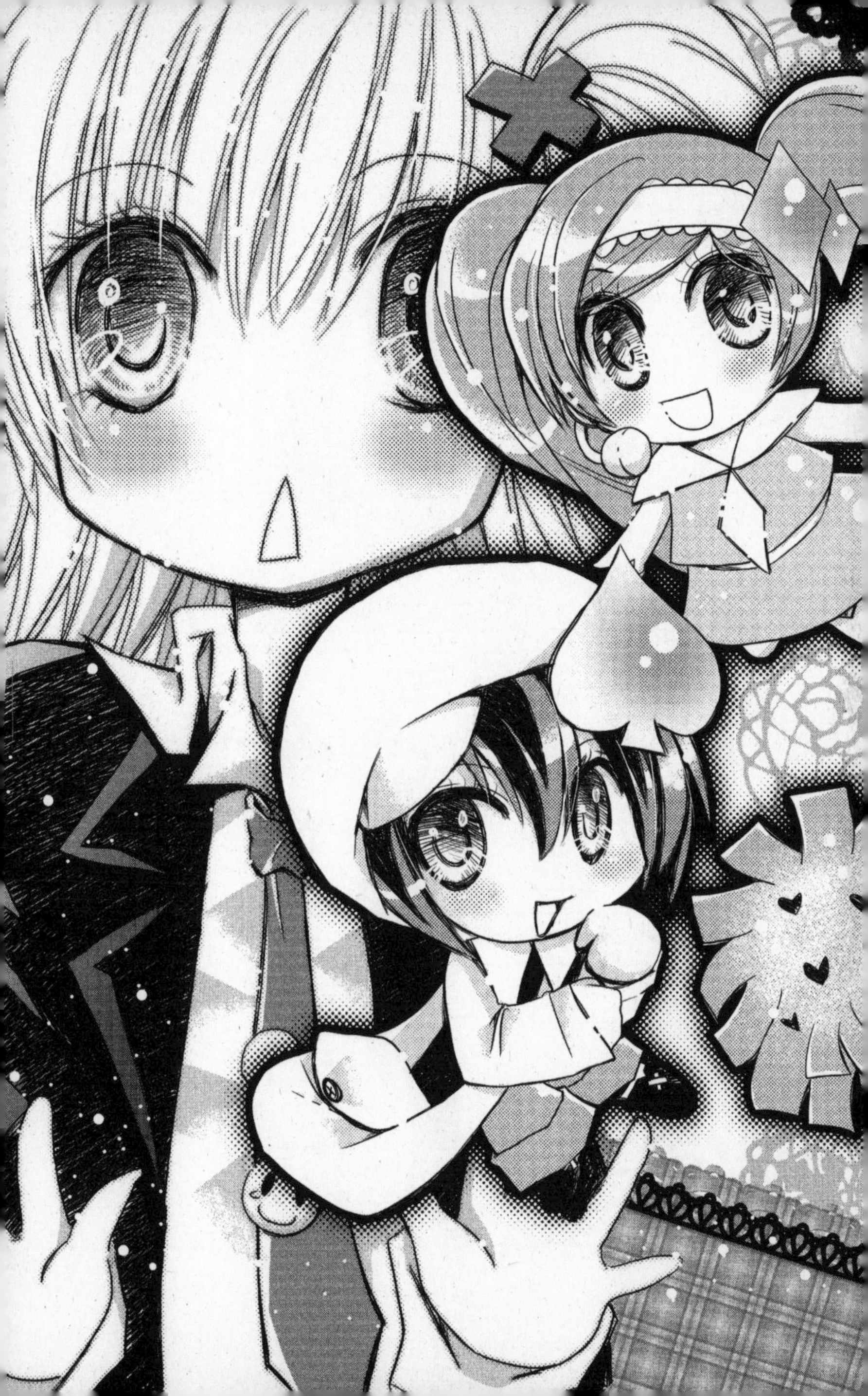

After Talk

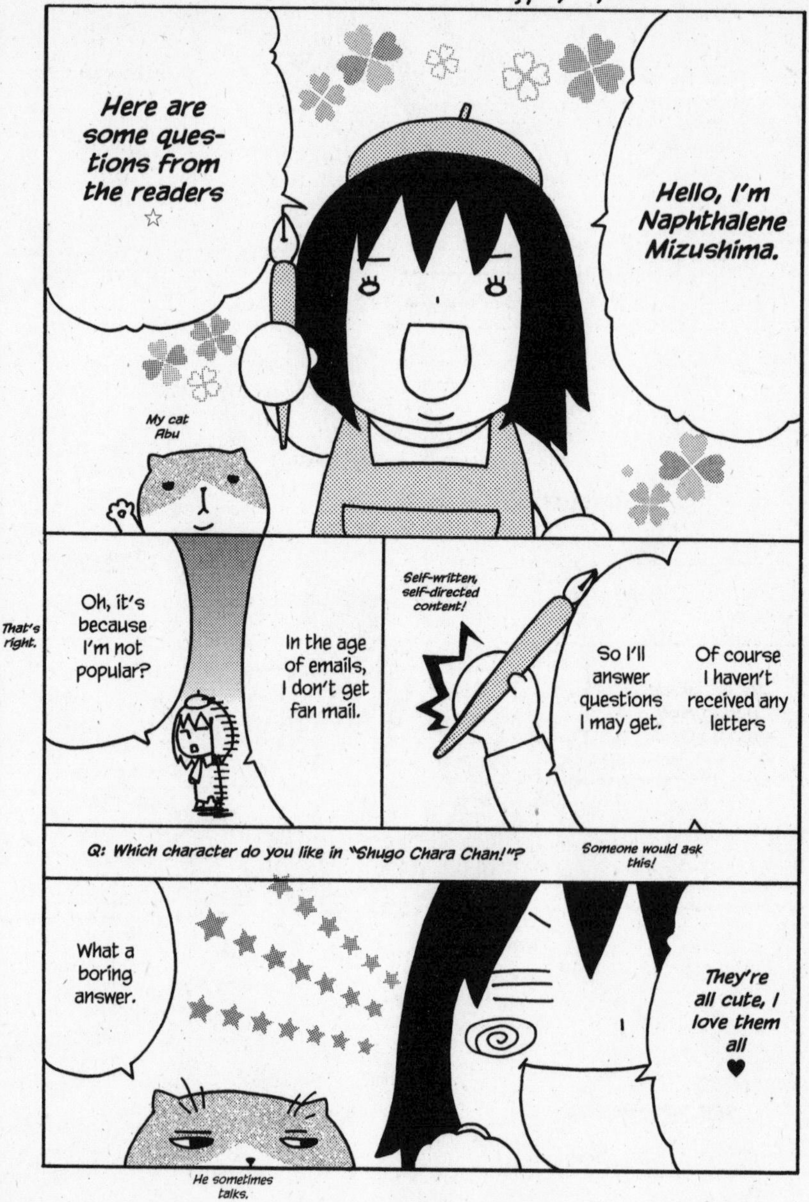
Hello, I'm Naphthalene Mizushima.
Here are some ques- tions from the readers ☆
My cat Abu
Of course I haven't received any letters
So I'll answer questions I may get.
Self-written, self-directed content!
In the age of emails, I don't get fan mail.
Oh, it's because I'm not popular?
That's right.
Q: Which character do you like in "Shugo Chara Chan!"?
Someone would ask this!
They're all cute, I love them all ♥
What a boring answer.
He sometimes talks.

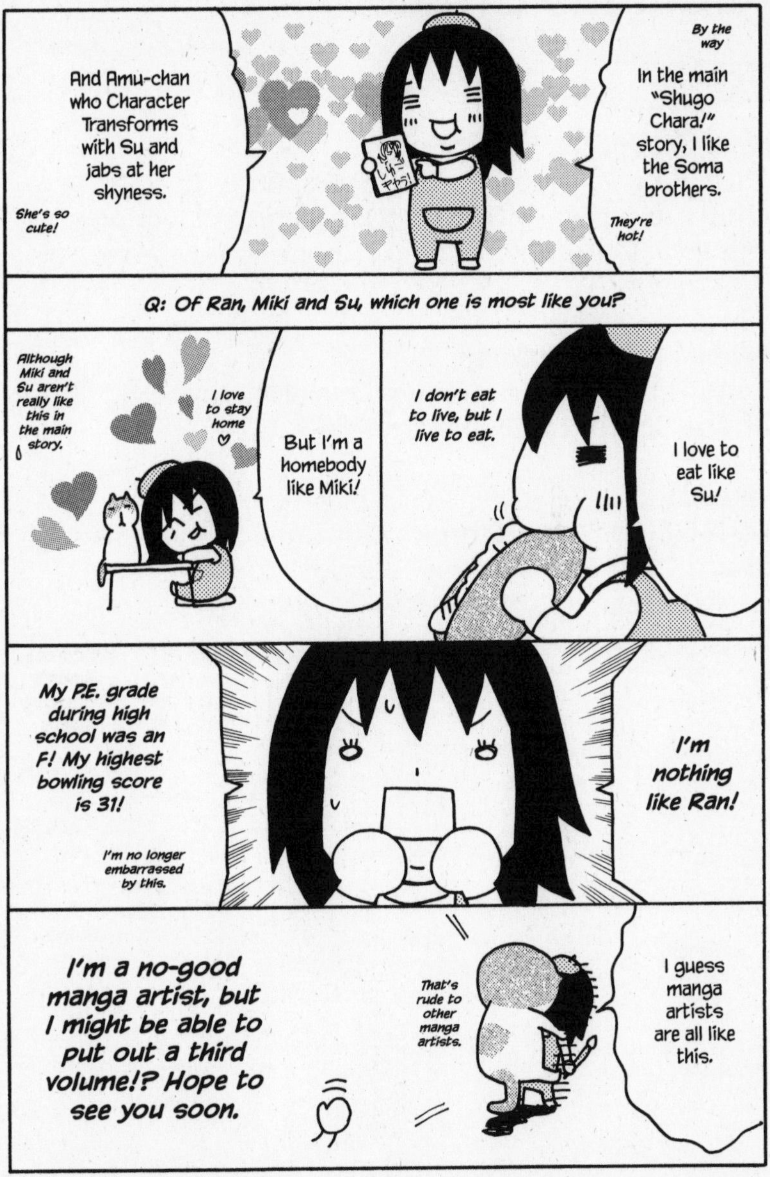
By the way
In the main "Shugo Chara!" story, I like the Soma brothers.
They're hot!
And Amu-chan who Character Transforms with Su and jabs at her shyness.
She's so cute!
Q: Of Ran, Miki and Su, which one is most like you?
I love to eat like Su!
I don't eat to live, but I live to eat.
But I'm a homebody like Miki!
I love to stay home ♡
Although Miki and Su aren't really like this in the main story.
I'm nothing like Ran!
My P.E. grade during high school was an F! My highest bowling score is 31!
I'm no longer embarrassed by this.
I guess manga artists are all like this.
That's rude to other manga artists.
I'm a no-good manga artist, but I might be able to put out a third volume!? Hope to see you soon.

About the Creators

PEACH-PIT:

Banri Sendo
Born June 7, Shibuko Ebara was born June 21. They are a pair of Gemini Manga artists working together. Currently running "Shugo Chara!" on "Nakayoshi."

Naphthalene Mizushima
Born February 2. Aquarius. Currently running "Shugo Chara Chan!" on "Nakayoshi."

Kinomin
Born October 26. Scorpio. Currently running "Shugo Chara Chan! Kids ★" on "Yahoo! Kids."

Translation Notes

Osechi, page 10
[10.2]
Traditional Japanese New Year celebration food served cold during the first three days of the new year.

Kazunoko, page 10
[10.2]
Herring roe. It is said that it symbolizes fertility and family prosperity.

First Dream, page 10
[10.7]
In Japan, they say that the contents of the first dream of the new year will reveal the luck of that year.

Mabo Eggplant, page 10
[10.8]
Mabo tofu is a Chinese cuisine made with tofu, ground meat and spicy sauce. Mabo eggplant is a variation that includes eggplants.

Kagami Mochi, page 11
[11.2]
Two oval-shaped rice cakes used for display during New Year's.

Kadomatsu, page 11
[11.8]
A traditional New Year's Day decoration made out of bamboo and other plants. It is placed in front of homes to welcome the toshigami, the god that comes to each household on New Year's Day.

Princess Kaguya, page 11
[11.10]
Kaguya Hime is an old tale about a mysterious girl who was discovered in a shining bamboo shoot as a baby. Although she has many suitors, she eventually goes back up to the moon where she is from.

Otoshidama, page 15
[15.7]
Otoshidama is New Year's money that children get. This is a custom that originated in China. The money comes in little paper pouches that are cutely decorated with characters.

Shishimai, page 17
[17.3]
On New Year's Day and other celebratory days, Japan has a custom of doing the shishimai, or lion dance. The lion dance is believed to ward off evil spirits.

Kinako, page 17
[17.8]
Kinako is soybean flour, sometimes used to cover mochi for flavoring.

Hanetsuki, page 18
[18.7]
A Japanese traditional game with 1300 years of history in which two players use wooden rectangular paddles to hit a shuttlecock.

Mamemaki, page 21
[21.2]
Mamemaki is part of a ritual performed during February, at the Setsubun. Setsubun means "seasonal division," but this term is usually used for the beginning of Spring. During a mamemaki, soybeans are thrown out the door or at a family member wearing a demon mask, while the people throwing the beans chant, "Demons stay out! Fortune stay in!" The beans are supposed to purify the house by driving away evil spirits.

Natto, page 21
[21.5]
Japanese fermented soy beans. Some people hate it for the smell and bitter taste.

Momo no Sekku, page 28
[28.2]
Beginning of Spring, when the peach blossoms bloom. Momo means peach.

Momo, page 28
[28.5]
Momo could also refer to futomomo, which means thighs.

Sakura Mochi, page 29
[29.2]
A Japanese rice cake wrapped in cherry blossom leaves.

Uguisu Mochi, page 29
[29.5]
A Japanese rice cake made into a round shape, then pulled at the edges to make it shaped like a mockingbird.

Sweet Sake, page 31
[31.9]
A traditional sweet Japanese drink with low alcohol content made from fermented rice. When made for children, there is no alcohol in it.

Kaki no Tane, page 34
[34.4]
Kaki no Tane is a Japanese snack of rice crackers and peanuts. The name means "persimmon seed," and comes from the shape of the crackers. They are thinly sliced in quarter moon shapes.

Sapphire, page 35
[35.10]
The main character of Osamu Tezuka's classic shoujo manga, "Princess Knight."

Issunboushi, page 35
[35.10]
A Japanese folklore about a young boy who was a size of a hand, who goes to fight an ogre using a needle as a sword.

Kashiwa Mochi, page 42
[42.2]
Japanese rice cake wrapped in an oak leaf. Usually eaten in May to wish for the family's prosperity.

Koinobori, page 42
[42.7]
Carp-shaped windsocks put up in Japan during Children's Day (or Boys' Day) in hopes that their sons will have success.

Kabuto, page 43
[43.2]
A Japanese helmet worn by samurai.

Chimaki, page 44
[44.9]
A traditional Chinese food made of sweet rice with fillings, wrapped in bamboo leaves.

Tanabata, page 63
[63.1]
Tanabata is a festival held annually on July 7. It is to celebrate the meeting of the stars Vega and Altair, who are separated by the Milky Way "river." They are allowed to meet once a year on July 7. It is custom to put slips of paper with wishes on bamboo leaves.

Orihime and Hikoboshi, page 63
[63.3]
The Japanese characterizations of the stars Vega and Altair in the tanabata story.

Konnyaku, page 81
[81.2]
Konnyaku is a type of food in Japan made out of yam. It is like gelatin, but much firmer and tastes very lightly like seaweed. Since it has no calories but is high in fiber, it is eaten as diet food. Many use it in dares because a chilled konnyaku in the dark feels slippery and pretty gross.

Disasters, page 86
[86.2]
In Japanese, disasters are known as "saigai." So everyone is making a joke about other "gai (guys)."

Momotaro, page 98
[98.1]
Momotaro is a hero from Japanese folklore. His name translates to Peach Boy, and in the popular version of the story he is born from a large peach. He eventually goes on a journey to defeat ogres that lived on an island. On the way, he befriends a dog, monkey, and a pheasant, who agree to help him if Momotaro gives them a snack he was carrying at his waist.

The Pretty Guardians
are back!

★

Kodansha Comics is proud to present
Sailor Moon with all new translations.

For more information, go to **www.kodanshacomics.com**

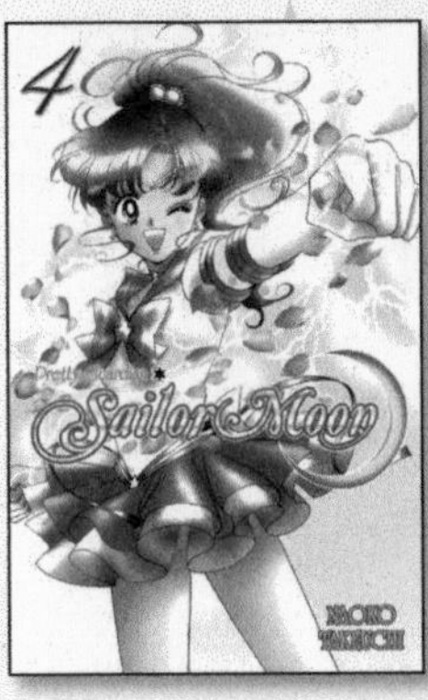
4
Pretty Guardian
Sailor Moon
NAOKO TAKEUCHI
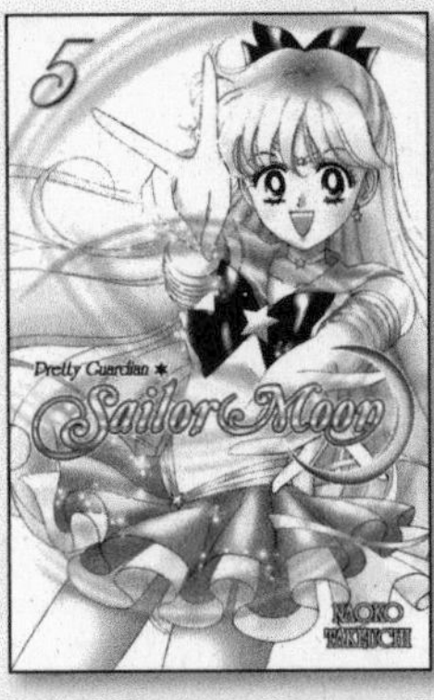
5
Pretty Guardian
Sailor Moon
NAOKO TAKEUCHI
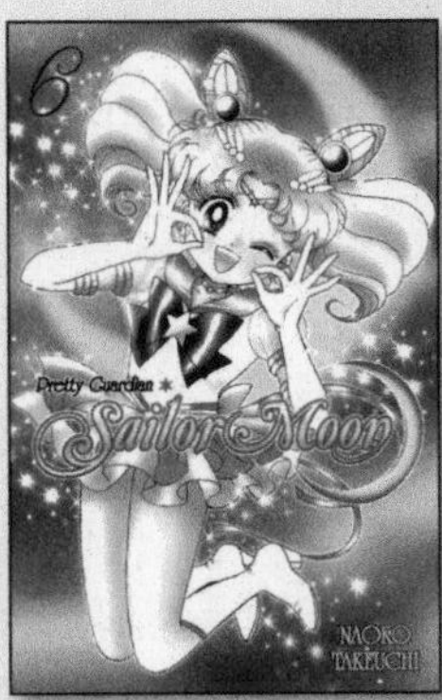
6
Pretty Guardian
Sailor Moon
NAOKO TAKEUCHI
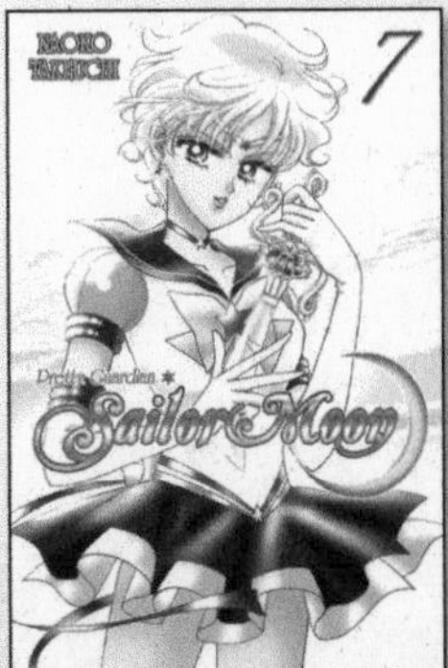
NAOKO TAKEUCHI
7
Pretty Guardian
Sailor Moon
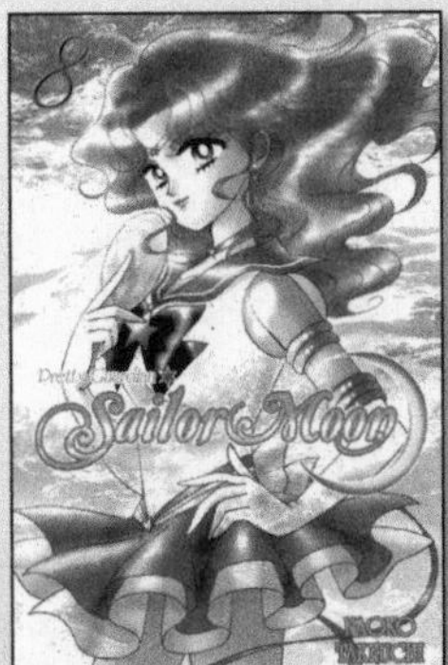
8
Sailor Moon
NAOKO TAKEUCHI
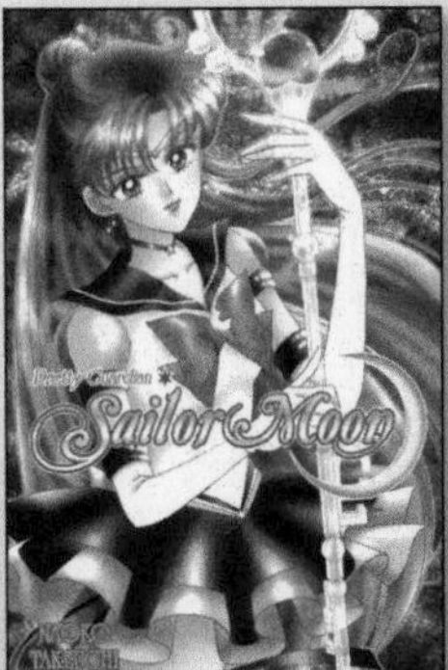
Pretty Guardian
Sailor Moon
NAOKO TAKEUCHI
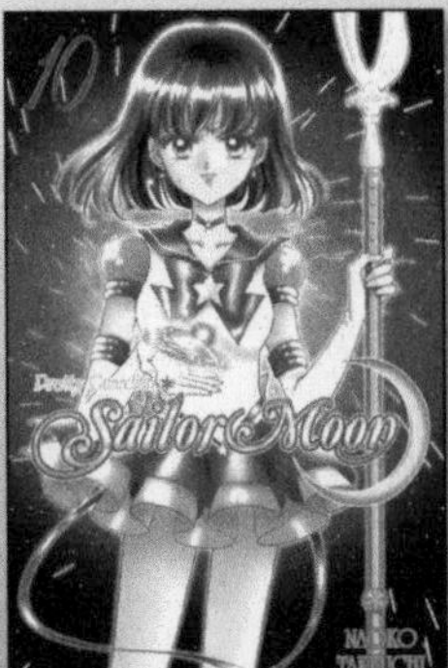
10
Sailor Moon
NAOKO TAKEUCHI
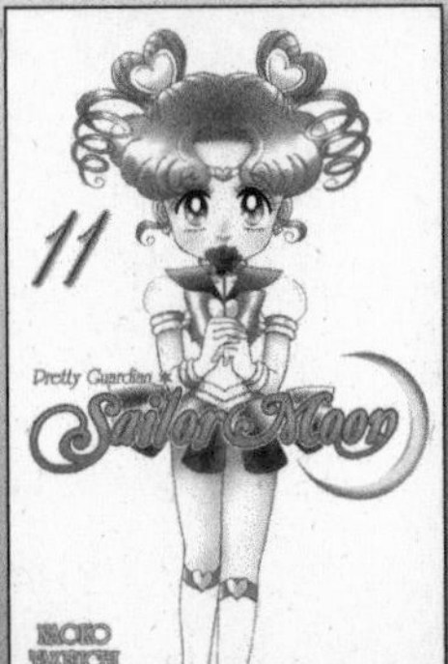
11
Pretty Guardian
Sailor Moon
NAOKO TAKEUCHI
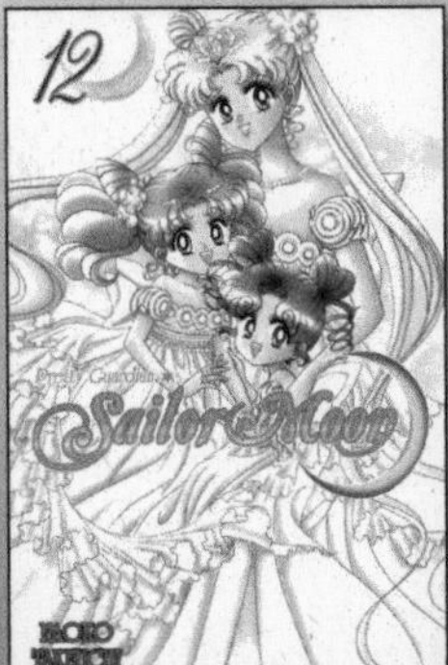
12
Pretty Guardian
Sailor Moon
NAOKO TAKEUCHI

KC
KODANSHA
COMICS

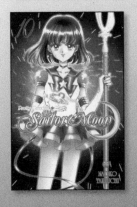

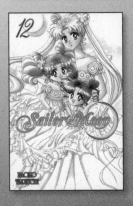

ANIMAL LAND

BY MAKOTO RAIKU

In a world of animals, where the strong eat the weak, Monoko the tanuki stumbles across a strange creature the likes of which has never been seen before–a human baby! While the newborn has no claws or teeth to protect itself, it does have the special ability to speak to and understand all different animals. Can the gift of speech between species change the balance of power in a land where the weak must always fear the strong?

ANIMAL LAND 1

MAKOTO RAIKU

Ages 13+

VISIT KODANSHACOMICS.COM TO:
- View release date calendars for upcoming volumes
- Find out the latest about upcoming Kodansha Comics series

Shugo Chara Chan! volume 2 is a work of fiction. Names, characters, places, and incidents are the products of the author's imagination or are used fictitiously. Any resemblance to actual events, locales, or persons, living or dead, is entirely coincidental.

A Kodansha Comics Trade Paperback Original

Published in the United States by Kodansha Comics, an imprint of Kodansha USA Publishing, LLC, New York.

Publication rights for this English edition arranged through Kodansha Ltd., Tokyo.

First published in Japan in 2009 by Kodansha Ltd., Tokyo.

ISBN 978-1-935429-97-5

Original cover design by Akiko Omo

Printed in the United States of America.

www.kodanshacomics.com

9 8 7 6 5 4 3 2 1

Translator: Satsuki Yamashita
Lettering: Rikki Simons

TOMARE!

[STOP!]

You are going the wrong way!

Manga is a completely different type of reading experience.

To start at the *beginning*, go to the *end*!

That's right! Authentic manga is read the traditional Japanese way—from right to left, exactly the opposite of how American books are read. It's easy to follow: Just go to the other end of the book, and read each page—and each panel—from the right side to the left side, starting at the top right. Now you're experiencing manga as it was meant to be.